Managing Children's Services
in the Public Library

Managing Children's Services in the Public Library

Second Edition

Adele M. Fasick

1998
Libraries Unlimited, Inc.
Englewood, Colorado

Libraries Unlimited, Inc.
P.O. Box 6633
Englewood, CO 80155-6633
1-800-237-6124
www.lu.com

Production Editor: Kay Mariea
Copy Editor: Louise Tonneson
Proofreader: Susie Sigman
Indexer: Christine Smith
Layout and Design: Pamela J. Getchell

Library of Congress Cataloging-in-Publication Data

Fasick, Adele M.
    Managing children's services in the public library / Adele M. Fasick. -- 2nd ed.
    xvii, 218 p. 19x26 cm.
    Includes bibliographical references and index.
    ISBN 1-56308-526-7
    1. Children's libraries--United States--Administration.   2. Public libraries--United States--Administration.   I. Title.
Z718.2.U6F37   1998
025.1'9762'5--dc21   97-41688
                                                              CIP

Contents

Preface

As the twentieth century draws to a close, change in libraries seems to be accelerating. In the six years since the first edition of this book was published, computers have been introduced into children's departments across North America and the Internet has become a major information resource. Yet funding for libraries has not increased to keep up with the growing demands. Providing adequate public library services for children has always been a challenge and never more than now. In a world full of competing media, youth services librarians must demonstrate that books can still charm and delight children and that library programs can be fun. This book does not deal directly with collections or programming; instead it examines the ways in which librarians can manage their services so collections and programs reach the intended audience.

This book focuses on the children's department of the library. Part I deals with organizing a program of services, planning and implementing policies, handling security and special events, recruiting staff, defending intellectual freedom, and managing work within the children's department. Part II emphasizes the department as part of the library system and includes chapters on working with administrators and other departments, preparing budgets and reports, planning facilities, and integrating children's services into the library system. Part III discusses developing a coordinated public relations program; fund-raising; and working with schools, homeschooling families, social agencies, individuals in the community, and other librarians and professional associations.

In preparing this book I have talked with many librarians; attended conferences and workshops around the world; and consulted articles, books, and websites. I want to thank all of the libraries that allowed me to use their materials and the colleagues who generously shared their ideas with me.

Introduction to the Second Edition

Making predictions about the coming century has become a popular game. Although many predictions never come true, they offer a glimpse of possible futures. In any agency that hopes to survive, decision-makers need to pay attention to predictions, analyze them, and decide which of them are likely to affect operations. The public library, like other social institutions, changes as social and economic conditions change, so appropriate library services can be planned only by taking account of likely future trends.

The predictions being made about the twenty-first century that affect library service to children include: a declining birthrate combined with longer life expectancy, resulting in an aging of the population; the privatization of many public services; a drop in literacy as visual media replace print media; the replacement of books as the prime medium for information storage and retrieval; and the possible disappearance of books, themselves, and with them traditional libraries.

Are any of these outcomes likely? It is impossible to know with any certainty, but the direction of some current trends may indicate the direction of future library services for children.

Changing Demographics

Children continue to be born, to grow up, and to require social services. Whether the birthrate goes up or down, the fluctuations are minor; a great many children will be born in North America; and, around the world, an increasing number of children will continue to be uprooted and moved to new places. The movement of refugees and other populations is likely to continue over the next 10 years, and this will affect public services in many jurisdictions.

While it is undoubtedly true that after the turn of the century a higher proportion of Americans than ever before will be more than 65 years of age, that does not mean the number of children and teenagers will decrease. While the proportions may change, the actual number of children will probably increase. The spotlight of attention during the next decade is likely to be on the elderly, so services to young people will be more threatened than they were during the years when the population bulge was in the lower age ranges. Although competition from the needs of older people with those of young people may make maintaining youth services in all areas more difficult, services to young people will still be vital to the continuance of any society. As the baby boomers who are now reaching the age of 50 and today's seniors age, they will be dependent on the generation following them for support services, the economic growth of the country, the discoveries and inventions that will change the world, and the political structure that will make it possible for the elderly to live well. A society cannot thrive if it neglects its most valuable asset—its young people.

Effect of Demographic Trends on Libraries

Demographic trends indicate that library services to children and young adults will continue to be important but can no longer be taken for granted. Competition for funding for youth services will increase as seniors struggle to maintain the services they feel they need. It will be the task of libraries, along with the schools and other social services, to educate the public about the importance of maintaining a high level of youth services.

In coming years, more young people are likely to come from immigrant families, many of them from countries without a tradition of library services. This will strongly affect library services to children. Library services will need to be enlarged and strengthened to meet the needs of diverse groups.

Changing Economics

Economic trends indicate a continuing decline in the manufacturing sector and a growth in service and knowledge industries, which increases the need for a highly educated population. The large number of children who, in the past, dropped out of high school in order to find unskilled jobs will have to be encouraged to remain in school to get an education that prepares them for working in this new society. Schools and other social agencies will be instrumental in this effort.

Another trend, partly economic and partly social, seems to be the reluctance of people to pay taxes to effect social change. This places all social agencies—schools, museums, libraries, and universities—under increasing pressure to cut costs, as they fight for a share of reduced tax dollars. Funding from nongovernmental sources will become more necessary to support existing services and add new services.

Effect of Economic Trends on Libraries

Public libraries can play a major role in fostering in children the desire for education and in helping them develop the skills for obtaining the kind of ever-changing knowledge necessary to survive and prosper in the new economy. This means that the children's library will need to be seen not just as a pleasant recreational facility, but as an important player in preparing young people for jobs in the global economy.

The reluctance of people to support public institutions means that libraries will continue to struggle with budgetary problems and seek out nonpublic funding. Youth librarians will have to become effective fund raisers, as well as service providers.

Changing Social Patterns

The number of single-parent families is not likely to decrease over the next several years. Divorce rates appear to have stabilized, but at a high level. Many children will continue to live in single-parent families, and a large number of these families are poor. The conservative governments of many jurisdictions are reluctant to support the social safety net that many Americans take for granted. With the aging of many voters, the reluctance to spend money on young families is likely to continue, at least, for the next few years. This may lead to a further polarization of the rich and poor, and information will be one area of such polarization.

Another social trend stemming from the demographics of a transient global population is that society is becoming more multicultural. Social agencies in large cities have become used to serving populations from many different language groups and cultures, but many smaller communities are still predominantly of European background. This is likely to change as immigrant groups move from the cities out to the suburbs and smaller communities.

Effect of Social Trends on Libraries

The probable continuation of single-parent families and poverty raise issues of access. The discrepancy between the lives of children from high-income families and those from low-income families is likely to increase. Public libraries were created to decrease social divisions and give children from working class families, many of whom are also racial or ethnic minorities, a chance to compete at the same level with other children. This role as a force for social justice may be increasingly important in the early years of the twenty-first century as a counterbalance to conservative political agendas.

Media and Technology Trends

Among the major changes that librarians have observed during the last 10 years have been changes in media and technology. Each new medium that has come along in the last century—movies, radio, television, and now computers—has been hailed as both a boon to education and a threat to libraries. None of them, so far, has displaced the book, but each of them has found a place in society and in libraries.

Some claim that books cannot compete with computer games, CD-ROMs, and the Internet. The death of the book has become a major topic in "doom-and-gloom" conversations, but it is important to remember that very few new technologies drive out old ones—they just fill a different niche. And it is not only librarians who believe that the book will survive. Nicholas Negroponte, one of the gurus of the digital world, in "The Future of the Book," pointed out that the consumption of coated and sheet paper in the United States has gone from 142 pounds per capita in 1980 to 214 pounds in 1993. Also, he claimed book publishing as an industry is larger than the U.S. television and motion picture industries, providing more than 50,000 new titles a year. Negroponte believes that the format of books will change dramatically and that many will be downloaded from computers onto some sort of electronic paper, but he agrees with most librarians that a need exists for content that can be tailored to small audiences. Books are likely to continue as a source of information into the foreseeable future (Negroponte 1996).

Effect of Media Trends on Libraries

Trends in media suggest ways in which libraries will change in the future. Some believe that in another few years, anyone will be able to use a computer to call up whatever information they require. According to these prophets, books and the libraries that house them will be obsolete.

Children need a variety of experiences, and books, videos, tapes, and personal computers all play a part. Alan Kay of the Advanced Technology Group of Apple Computers points out that

> Young children do much of their learning kinesthetically and it is almost certain that removing this will remove much of their foundation for assimilating new ideas. Current day computers do not provide force-feedback—sometimes called haptic interaction—(nor does television) and I believe young people need a lot of it (Kay 1994).

Despite the many changes in technology, children still need to experience the world through all of their senses. They should not only listen to nursery rhymes and fairy tales, they should mark the rhythm with their hands, walk through the journeys with their feet, act out the stories with their bodies, and create their reactions with crayon, paints, and music. Librarians should consider the value of varied experiences when others talk about computers satisfying all of children's information needs.

Another aspect of the new medias has been a blurring of the lines between age groups. For the past half century, books have been targeted at specific age groups and are the only major media so carefully divided by age. The newer media seldom target specific age groups. The vast majority of visual materials are offered as general market fare. Most school-age children watch more adult television shows than those for children. Television cartoons, although often thought to be children's media, are carefully designed to appeal to a wide age group.

Material found on the Internet blurs the age lines even further. In Internet exchanges people often do not know a provider's age. Some websites are designed for children, and a growing amount of material appropriate for children is available on the Internet. However, segregating this material in the same way as in libraries is impossible. Adults and children, alike, can surf the World Wide Web and visit sites designed with a variety of users in mind.

Another complication of computer use is that many of the people most comfortable with computers are children. The computer, like the VCR, has given a new status to children's knowledge. Older people are advised and encouraged to ask their children how to operate these strange new machines. While it is not true that all children are proficient computer users, probably even fewer adults are. This means that children will often be the leaders in using the new technology introduced by libraries, thus reversing some of our stereotypes about children being especially in need of librarians' help.

Changing Emphases in Managing Children's Services

All of the trends noted have had an effect on how children's departments are organized and how they work. Some of the guiding principles that will be emphasized throughout this book are the following:

- Traditional children's services in libraries are and will continue to be necessary but must be evaluated and defended in terms relevant to current social and media trends.

- Youth librarians must develop their skills as children's services advocates.

- Cooperation with groups outside the library, including the private sector, will become increasingly important.

- Librarians must embrace new technologies, with children's departments at the forefront of this movement.

- With new technologies, greater coordination between the children's department and the adult services departments, as well as between various types of libraries, will be necessary.

The chapters that follow spell out some ways that youth librarians can plan their services to ensure that libraries continue to offer valuable and relevant materials and services to their communities.

Planning a Program
of Services

Most public libraries offer a core of services for children. According to a series of studies conducted in the United States, these services have been described as the following:

> In most public libraries we would find at least a separate area of shelves and seating for children (if not a separate room), with a collection of varied materials, although books would constitute the most abundant format provided . . . . Reference, reader's advisory, preschool storyhours, and summer reading programs would be the services we would be most likely to find, along with programs for school-age children on a variety of topics (Willett 1995, 80).

Within these parameters, however, children's departments of public libraries differ in the mix of materials and services they provide and the ways in which they provide them. Effective public librarians tailor their services to the needs of the community, so the pattern of provision varies based on the characteristics of the population and the area. Consider some of the following typical libraries and the ways in which their services have been modified to meet specific needs.

Differing Patterns of Service

Library A is a large branch library in a prosperous suburban community with a high proportion of preschool-age children, many of them enrolled in day care programs. The children's collection includes about one-third picture books and easy-to-read books, one-third junior fiction, and the rest divided between nonfiction and other materials, including videos, compact discs, computer software, and cassettes. Six computers provide children access to computer programs and the Internet. In programming, the staff concentrates on providing service to groups of children from the day care centers. Because many of the centers have vans for transporting the children, programs are offered at the library. Multiple copies of popular picture books are purchased, because many groups want to borrow more than one copy. Preschool storyhours for families are given on Thursday evenings and on Sunday afternoons. Parents are encouraged to stay with their children, and librarians teach the parents songs and fingerplays to use at home, as well as provide books for borrowing.

Library B is located in a rural community, in which the population is spread over a large area, and where no public transportation is available. No specific age group predominates among the children. The library's collection consists of about 25 percent picture and easy-to-read books, 40 percent junior fiction, and 35 percent nonfiction, with a small collection of videos, compact discs, and cassettes. Because of the lack of local Internet service providers, none of the library's computers provide Internet access. A preschool program has been started on Friday mornings, when many parents come into town for shopping. Unlike Library A, librarians here encourage parents to leave the children on their own for the program. For many preschoolers, this is the only occasion they have to interact with children their age; and for many of the parents, it is a rare period of relief from child care. Most of the other library programming is aimed at school-age children, who are brought to the library for class visits. Each spring, the librarian visits every class in the local school and distributes summer reading program registration forms and book lists. Because most of these schoolchildren cannot get to the library by themselves, a homework hotline is in operation from 4:00 to 6:00 each afternoon, so that children can call the library for information they need for school projects. Several families in the area are homeschooling their children and rely on the library for supplementary materials. The librarian has established a file of homeschooling resources for these parents and attends meetings of the local homeschooling parents group that meets in the library.

Library C is a branch library in an inner-city neighborhood, where large numbers of new immigrant children from various ethnic groups are living in crowded apartments. About one-third of the library's children's collection is in Spanish and one-fifth in Vietnamese, with small collections in other languages. Thirty percent of the English-language books are picture and easy-to-read, 40 percent are junior fiction with emphasis on simple, straightforward realistic stories, and 30 percent are nonfiction and audiovisual materials. Videos and cassettes dealing with school project subjects are prominently displayed, and viewing and listening equipment is available for children to use in the library. One computer terminal is available to children for access to programs and to the Internet. Because of high demand, children must sign up for computer time. After-school use of the library is heavy, and many children remain for several hours before their parents pick them up on returning from work. Two priorities guide programming: active, fairly long-term projects to keep these "self-care" children occupied, and programs aimed at developing English language skills. Although picture books are often used in story programs, the age level is not limited to preschoolers; stories are chosen to appeal to a wide age range. Two Spanish and one Vietnamese storyhours are given by volunteers once a week, while once a month, an evening heritage program is held, during which English-language stories, as well as music and crafts from different cultures are featured. Parents are encouraged to attend these programs with their children. Between 4:00 and 6:00 every afternoon one librarian is assigned to the "Homework Help" desk, where, in addition to information, pencils and paper are provided for children working on school projects.

These scenarios demonstrate some of the differences in children's services at various libraries. While general principles guide the provision of materials and services for children, each library is unique in its mix of population served, available budget, and service priorities.

No matter what pattern the overall services of the children's department eventually takes, it should be based on two fundamental considerations: the mandate of the library and the needs of the community.

Mission Statements

The basic mandate of a public library is usually articulated in the library's mission statement. Examples of mission statements include:

> The mission of the Cleveland Public Library is to be the best urban library system in the country by providing access to the worldwide information that people and organizations need in a timely, convenient, and equitable manner (Cleveland Public Library 1997).

> The mission of the Flint Public Library is to support the development of an informed citizenry by collecting, transmitting and ensuring open access to the world's ideas and information, and by providing programs and services that enhance accessibility to these ideas and information (Flint Public Library 1997).

> We welcome and support
> all people in their
> enjoyment of reading
> and pursuit of
> lifelong learning.
>
> Working together,
> we strive to provide equal access
> to information,
> ideas and
> knowledge
> through books, programs
> and other resources.

> We believe in the freedom
> to read,
> to learn,
> to discover.
> (Chicago Public Library 1997)

Suggestions for developing a mission statement are discussed in the Public Library Development Project's manual *Planning and Role Setting for Public Libraries* (McClure et al. 1987). The manual suggests that a mission statement should be a carefully worded statement that gives fairly precise indications of the major concerns of the library. Not all of these concerns are related to the children's department, and those that are relevant are guidelines, rather than specifics about providing youth services. Many libraries have generalized mission statements, which may be interpreted in different ways. Nonetheless, the mandate is the statement that justifies expenditures on children's services and serves as the basic support for a librarian's program of services. It is usually wise to incorporate reference to the mission statement in program-planning documents.

Aspects of Services

The second cornerstone of the program of services is the requirements of the particular community in which the library is located. The mandate indicates the overall purpose of the library, but its purpose can only be fulfilled in terms of particular situations. Different library services are needed in different communities, even when the mandate of the library is stated in the same terms.

In order to make a program of services operational, the librarian should consider the types of services that might be provided by the library and the groups of patrons to be served.

Building a Collection

Providing a collection of materials is usually considered the basic task of a library. Certainly the physical aspect of a children's department is a collection of books and other materials. Current developments in information technology have made the idea of a "collection" more flexible. Access to electronically stored information can be as important as the provision of physical packages of information (books, magazines, and recordings). At the present state of technology, a children's department will typically try to combine the provision of on-site materials with access to off-site information. No matter how the collection is defined, the program of services within the department serves several purposes: to make the collection accessible, to provide recreational and educational opportunities for children of the community, and to enhance the image of the library.

Services to Make the Collection Accessible

A collection of materials is of little value unless it is made accessible to users. The services for making resources accessible include: cataloging and classification of materials to ensure that items can be located, reference services to help individuals or groups find specific information for school or personal needs, and readers' advisory services to help individuals or groups find recreational or educational materials. Access to information about the location and format of materials makes it possible to use interlibrary loan, download Internet materials, and have access to other services.

Services to Provide Educational and Recreational Programs

The familiar storyhours for toddlers, preschoolers, and older children are designed to develop literacy and encourage reading. Film showings, summer reading clubs, arts and crafts programs, and the like are designed to give children cultural and recreational experiences that might otherwise be unavailable to them.

Some library-sponsored programs are not directly linked to library goals. These might include craft programs, dancing, creative dramatics, computer clubs, and language classes. Often, these classes draw on the expertise of outside personnel as leaders, while the planning, registration, and publicity may be handled by the library. If this is so, these classes must be considered part of the overall plan of service of the children's department.

Services to Enhance the Image of the Library

An increasing number of libraries are providing websites on the Internet. These serve several purposes: attracting attention to library services, increasing the availability of materials and services, and enhancing a library's image. Because many young people have access to the Internet at home and school, children's departments can broaden their appeal by being highly visible on the Internet. Figure 1.1 illustrates the content of these websites. Further information about developing a website can be found in Chapter 13.

Many one-of-a-kind programs by professional musicians, theater and dance groups, or individual performers are designed to provide favorable publicity for the library and, thereby, increase awareness of the materials and services available.

Welcome to the West Islip Public Library

We're located on the south shore of Long Island, NY,on the beautiful Great South Bay. We're the
first public library in Suffolk County to have a home page
on the Web and we offer free Internet accounts for West Islip's library patrons
through the SuffolkWeb system.

Click <u>here</u> to search the Web

Try our <u>Help Page</u> if you need help setting up Windows 95 for graphic access.
Visit another version of our website <u>here.</u>

Browse the Library Catalog
(Log in as "wislip")

Search our Videocassette Collection
<u>A - E</u>   <u>F - J</u>   <u>K - O</u>   <u>P - T</u>   <u>U - Z</u>

Library Information

<u>Library Hours...</u>
Meet the staff..., <u>send us e-mail</u>
UPDATED! <u>Autumn '97 User Group Meeting Schedules</u> UPDATED!
Calendar of Events

Specialized Collections of Links

<u>Sites for Teens</u>   <u>Sites for Kids and Families</u>

<u>Job Information Listings</u>   <u>Librarian's Resources</u>

<u>Long Island Information</u>   <u>Guides for Using the Internet</u>

Long Island Web Sites

Fig. 1.1. Example of a Public Library Website. Reprinted with permission of the West
Islip Public Library.

Perspectives on Client Groups

Age Differences

While age is only one of the characteristics that differentiate various client groups, it is an important one in most children's departments because of its strong impact on client's needs. Figure 1.2 depicts how the age of client groups varies in different children's departments. Programs of service at the public library's children's department should target the major age groups in the community.

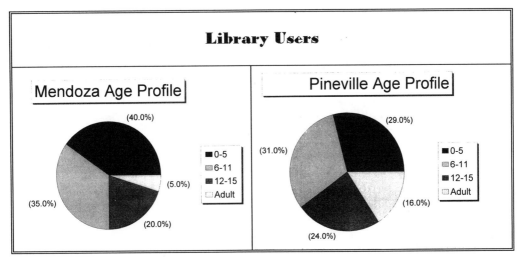

Fig. 1.2. Age Breakdown of Library Users.

Preschool Children

Children under one year of age are frequently brought by parents to the children's department. Some libraries provide playpens where the children may be left for short periods of time. Books of nursery games and rhymes serve these youngest clients, and some libraries hold brief storyhours for babies. When children reach the toddler stage, the range of materials and services provided for them greatl increases. Toddlers require special materials—sturdy board books and appealing toys If programs are offered for children under three, provision must be made for a hig] ratio of adults to children in such a setting. To control the activities of toddlers direct supervision of each child must be available at all times.

By the time children reach the age of about three, their needs and behavio differ from those of toddlers. Children of this age can handle standard pictur(books, and a wide range of materials should be available to meet their varied an(growing interests. Three- and four-year-old children do not require as much adul·

supervision as toddlers, so their programs can be held in larger groups with fewer personnel. Many of the programs and services provided by traditional children's departments are aimed at the needs of preschool children. Providing library furniture in a size and design suitable for these children is important, and separate story or program rooms for them are often also necessary.

School-age Children

In most communities school-age children have the opportunity to use both their school library and the resources of the public library. For this reason, programming and special services aimed at this group are often more limited than those for preschool children. Nonetheless, in most communities there is heavy use of the library by schoolchildren both for recreational and school-related materials. A large proportion of the materials and most of the reference service in a typical children's department are slanted toward school-age children. Because schoolchildren can use the library, for the most part, only during the late afternoon, evening, weekend, and holiday periods, they tend to make heavy demands during these times.

Transitional Users

Most children's departments are designed to serve children under the age of 12 or 13. Many children move quickly into the adult department, but others find it difficult to make this adjustment. Children whose reading skills are limited or whose native language is not English are more likely than others to have difficulty making this transition. Some libraries do not provide trained young adult librarians who can help children make this transition. In a 1988 study 45 percent of the libraries surveyed had neither a young adult librarian nor a young adult coordinator on staff (Services and Resources 1988). The current percentage of libraries without young adult personnel is likely to be even higher. Public libraries that lack specialized young adult staff have a responsibility to provide materials and services that will help transitional users bridge the way to adult services. A selection of teenage books, magazines, and other media are often necessary in a children's department.

Adults

Although adults are not the primary target audience for a children's department's services, many services are, in fact, designed for adults. Parents require assistance in selecting books for children; students of children's literature need access to materials in the department's collection; teachers use public library collections as a supplement to school resources; homeschooling parents rely on public libraries for many resources; and day care and youth workers draw upon library resources to meet the needs of their programs. Adults form a significant portion of the children's department clientele. However, the proportion of adults using the children's department will vary depending on the community—a downtown city library is likely to serve adults more often than a small community branch. The needs of adults are often different from those of the children. Literature students often ask for historical children's books that are not usually kept in children's collections; youth workers may want materials that are specifically aimed at their programs; and parents sometimes request the inclusion or exclusion of materials expressing particular points of view. Extensive use of the children's department by adults may necessitate the provision of adult-sized furniture or study carrels, and their presence sometimes affects the overall noise and activity level considered acceptable. Occasionally, adults in the children's department may pose a threat to children. Security aspects of adults using the children's department are covered in Chapter 6.

Differences Unrelated to Age

Individual and Group Services

In addition to age differences, other groupings affect the services required in the children's department. One of the primary differentiations made is between individual and group services. Many services for children, such as readers' advisory and reference services are designed primarily for individuals who want to find materials or information. Individual service today needs to be provided not only to these children, but also to the growing number of children who spend time at the library between the end of the school day and the parents' arrival home from work. These children, sometimes referred to as latchkey children or "self-care" children, often are not primarily interested in the library's collection but in having something to do. The number and needs of these children varies from one community to another, and some of the challenges associated with their use of the library are discussed in Chapter 6.

Because social changes have led to many children spending much of their time in groups—day care, day camps, school, and play groups—many libraries are focusing more on group, rather than individual services. Storyhour programs, for instance, can be designed for groups, as well as for individual children brought to the library by a parent or caregiver. Different scheduling and publicity methods are needed by the library, depending upon whether the aim is to attract individuals or to provide a service for an identified group.

For many libraries, school visits take up a major portion of daytime service hours. In a study of Indiana public library services, Fitzgibbons and Pungitore (1989) estimated that 8,120 classes visited public libraries in 1987. An earlier study in New Jersey (Razzano, 1986a) found that 95 percent of the libraries hosted class visits for children. Arranging these visits requires contact with school teachers, careful scheduling, and sufficient preparation time to tailor visits to the needs of specific classes. Some teachers want the public library staff to provide an introduction to reference sources, both print and online, or to library catalogs, while others prefer emphasis on recreational reading. Librarians must decide how much time to spend on class visits and what kind of service is reasonable. Decisions are based on the community's situation, such as the strength of the school libraries and the number of schools requiring service.

Parent groups have a significant need for children's library services. Some libraries offer these groups a place to meet and hold discussions or to listen to speakers, while others provide them with collections of specifically chosen parenting materials. These services are an outgrowth of the services provided for individual parents. The formation of formal groups of parents, however, makes this service more visible and provides greater public relations opportunities.

Ethnic Diversity

Some library patrons may need materials in their native languages. Selecting and acquiring foreign language materials for children can be difficult and time consuming. If several groups require materials in different languages, the librarian may need to ask neighborhood groups for assistance. Providing services, such as storyhours for different language groups is an even more complex task and usually requires outside assistance, unless staff members possess the necessary language skills.

For ethnic groups whose principal language is English, librarians may want to collect materials that reflect their background and heritage. Folktales and legends from particular cultures may be added to the collection in an effort to increase children's sense of their heritage. Storyhours featuring English translations of stories from another cultural group may be a regular part of the program. As with different language groups, the library may draw on the resources of community members with strong roots in a culture.

Special Needs

Most librarians recognize that the needs of disabled children dictate the selection of certain materials and services. Specifically, the needs of children with disabilities affect collection development, department layout plans, and programming and must be considered when designing the overall children's department program.

Other groups that may need to be considered when planning a children's department are transient children—those whose parents are migratory workers, on temporary assignments or doing contract work; those who are homeless living in shelters or elsewhere; and those who are hospitalized and institutionalized, depending on the facilities available in their institutions. These groups will vary from one community to another, but librarians should assess the needs of all groups in the community when planning a program of services.

As homeschooling becomes more widespread, services for these children must be considered. Several active associations of homeschooling parents work with libraries to suggest relevant materials and services.

Planning Process

Planning a departmental program to serve a variety of groups and individuals is a difficult administrative task. Three major components comprise the process: studying the community; assessing current services; and setting goals and objectives.

Studying the Community

Librarians need to know the makeup of their community, in terms of education, income, language background, and age. A community with a high proportion of school-age children and few preschoolers will require different library services than one in which those proportions are reversed. Obtaining community statistics from other agencies is generally more efficient than a library conducting its own survey. For example, the basic information about any community can be found in census reports. Census figures are never completely up-to-date, but they give a baseline against which changes in the community can be measured. Community planning offices and school districts frequently have more recent figures than are available from the census bureau. (For other suggestions about community factors that affect library services, see Van Orden 1988, 63–67.)

Library statistics on registration, circulation, and program attendance give additional information about the community, or at least about the portion of it that uses library services. In designing a departmental program, it is useful to break down library statistics by age level. If this is not routinely done a sampling system can be used to obtain an approximation (for specific details, see Walter 1992).

Armed with statistical knowledge about the community, a librarian can make direct observations. Most librarians live in the same jurisdiction as the library where they work, but often they do not live in the same neighborhood. The weekly neighborhood newspaper is an important source of local information. Telephone books and community directories give valuable information about the number and type of schools, churches, recreational facilities, and community groups. A few hours spent driving and walking around the community and visiting local shopping outlets can provide a great deal of information about the type of housing that is prevalent in various areas and the range and price levels of goods in stores. The ages and activities of children in the community provide information about their interests and needs. Systematic observation can be a valuable tool for acquiring the basic information necessary for planning library activities.

Assessing Current Services

To plan for the future, librarians must know the current strengths and weaknesses of their department. Almost all libraries collect statistics as an aid in evaluating services. The problem is that the rise and fall of circulation or program attendance may not be a good measure of the value of library services. Statistics should be the beginning and not the end of the evaluation process. Certainly a large drop in circulation or in program attendance is cause for concern, but the reasons for changes, rather than the changes themselves, need to be studied.

The children's department will require circulation statistics to assess how they are affected by programs. Do children check out books and other materials when they come to programs, or do they just attend programs? Are preschool children being stimulated to take a greater interest in books and reading by attending the storyhour programs, or is it just a way of passing time? Does the large number of circulating nonfiction books reflect an interest in the collection or a weakness in school libraries? Is a heavy use of computers the result of wide interest, or is the use dominated by a small number of avid users? Which of the computer resources available are being used and are they used for recreation or for school projects? Is a narrow representation of children taking out the majority of books or is circulation spread fairly evenly across all registered youth library borrowers? Are booktalks and programs broadening children's reading interests, or are many children checking out only one type of book? Answers to these questions will help in evaluating a library's services.

Most of these questions cannot be answered merely by keeping statistics of services. What is needed is an ongoing collection of qualitative data that provides background for the statistics. Some ways of collecting these data include:

- analysis of circulation during the hours that precede and follow programs, which can be used to discover the effect of the program on children's use of materials;

- an evaluative questionnaire for parents and caregivers who bring preschool children to programs, that gives evidence of how these programs are affecting children;

- taking a few minutes to talk to children about the books that they choose or reject, which helps to give parents or caregivers insight into their reasons. Although not a formal or scientific study, these conversations can help to evaluate programs.

These exercises need not take inordinate amounts of time as long as they are systematically accomplished. By enabling better evaluation of library services, they will pay dividends in setting goals and objectives, planning future programs, and justifying budget requests.

The next step in the overall planning process of a children's department is to set goals and objectives. This will be the topic for the following chapter.

Developing Tools to Meet Program Goals

After a department establishes the general outlines of its service program, steps should be taken to implement it in the most effective way. Among the tools that managers find useful in monitoring its progress is setting goals and objectives for specific aspects of the plan. Having a defined set of goals and objectives demonstrates to administrators and to the public that a department has a clear sense of purpose and that it can measure the extent to which the aims of the program are met. It will also make a department more effective in serving its public. In addition, objectives help librarians to demonstrate, in quantitative terms, the action being taken and its purpose. These quantitative measures are increasingly necessary to justify budget requests and continued support.

The goals of a library and of a department grow out of the mission statement of the parent institution. A mission statement sets forth, in general terms, the purpose of the institution. Several examples of library mission statements were given in the previous chapter. Examining the library's mission statement and developing related departmental goals is a wise first step in planning. Goals and objectives are designed to make concrete the aspirations expressed in the mission statement.

Definitions

GOALS are long-range, broad, general statements describing a desired condition or future toward which the library will work during a three- to five-year period.

OBJECTIVES are short-range statements that describe the results to be achieved in a specific time period. More specific than a goal, they are measurable, achievable, time-limited, and begin with an action verb (McClure et al. 1987, 46).

PRIORITIES are often established among association goals and objectives in order to rank their importance or urgency and to provide guidance when limited resources necessitate dropping some activities.

The process of establishing, attaining, and evaluating goals and objectives is continuous. Goals are set for longer terms than are objectives, but even goals must be examined periodically to check whether they are still appropriate. Goals grow out of the mandate of the library and in many libraries are intended to remain unchanged for five to ten years, although the ideal is a shorter time frame. Objectives are set for shorter periods of time—usually one or two years; at the end of that time, the success or failure in meeting the objective can be measured. Objectives, which relate to a specific goal, should grow naturally from the goals of an organization. It should also be possible to see how the objectives work to carry out the direction of the goals. Figure 2.1 depicts this relationship.

Because of the difference in their levels of specificity, goals may be established either on a library-wide basis, or by individual departments. Objectives are almost always set at the departmental level.

The cost of activities, which stem from a department's objectives, becomes easier to justify because the activities are rooted in overall departmental goals. In the example in figure 2.1, it is clear that sending a staff member to a preconference session is a necessary activity to achieve a planned objective.

Stating Goals and Objectives

Goals

Goals are usually stated in general terms, so that they will remain valid for several years and cover a variety of circumstances. For this reason, the goals of many public library children's departments sound similar. The following goals are adapted from the UNESCO Manifesto on Public Libraries (1994):

- To create and strengthen reading habits in children from an early age;
- to support both individual and self conducted education as well as formal education at all levels;
- to provide opportunities for personal creative development;
- to stimulate the imagination and creativity of children and young people;
- to promote awareness of cultural heritage, appreciation of the arts, scientific achievements and innovations.

Goals are overall aims of a department. They set the general direction in which service is heading and are a starting point for designing programs of service. Sometimes they have to be broken down into subgoals before setting objectives. An overall goal of a children's department might be stated thus: "To select a variety of media to satisfy the informational, recreational, and intellectual needs of a diverse community of children."

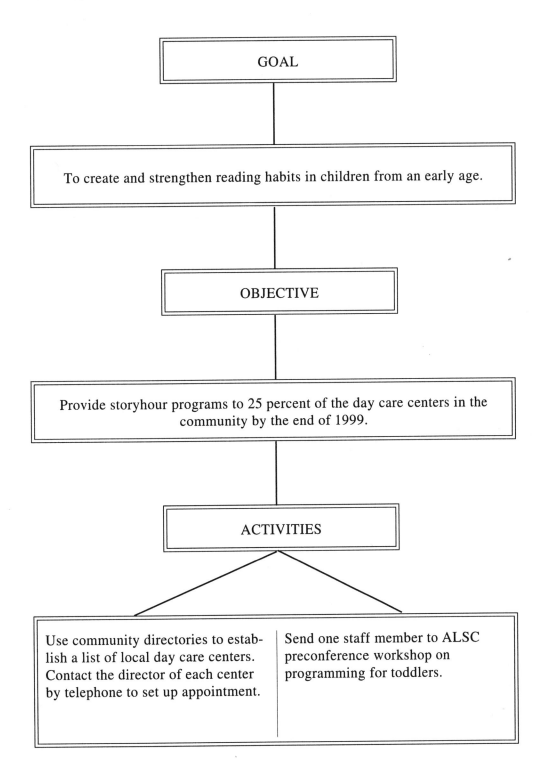

Fig. 2.1. Goals and Objectives for Service.

Goal statements are almost always general statements with which no one would disagree. The advantage of writing out goals is that the process makes librarians think about what they are or should be doing. Goals, in themselves, are not powerful management tools. "To provide equal access to library service for all children" sounds fine, but it does not indicate what specific actions should be taken, aside from opening the library doors in the morning. Objectives state what goals mean in terms of operation.

Objectives

Objectives are courses of action developed to meet goals. They give specific, measurable, and time-oriented indications of how well a department is moving toward the attainment of goals. It is the specificity of objectives and the fact that they are measurable that make them useful. Goals can be nonspecific because their purpose is only to point in the direction in which the library should move. Many goals will never be completely achieved. Objectives, on the other hand, spell out what the department intends to do, how they expect to do it, and how they will know if they have achieved their aims. At the end of the time period, it is apparent whether or not the objectives have been met.

An objective should describe an intended outcome rather than a procedure. It is not as important what the department is doing (the input) as why it is being done—what the output will be. The objective "to provide sufficient personnel so that a librarian is at the reference desk after school hours" is not as useful as "to answer 80 percent of children's reference questions." The first objective states what the librarian is going to do but does not necessarily indicate an outcome. Having an unapproachable librarian at the reference desk would technically meet the objective but would not greatly improve reference service. Some objectives, however, only indicate the procedure because the intended outcome is obvious. When writing these types of objectives, the intended outcome should be obvious to other people, not just to its creator.

An objective describes both a specific activity and what will be measured to demonstrate that the objective has been achieved. Rather than "Increase service to new immigrants in the community" an objective might read "Provide a collection of 300 Chinese language books and offer a weekly preschool storyhour in Chinese." In other words, a performance measure should be included in each objective. This is one of the most crucial and difficult parts of setting objectives.

Objectives should include a time frame. They should indicate what is expected to be accomplished by a certain date, so a check may be made on the objective's progress. For example, an objective might be "To provide Internet access in each library branch by the end of 1998." Sometimes objectives are broken down into stages: "To provide a collection of 200 Hindi books by the end of 1998, and a collection of 500 by the end of 1999."

Most departmental objectives are designed for periods of from one to five years. Very few challenging objectives can be met in less than one year, and very few plans can be made for more than five years. Short-term objectives for specific programs or projects may be used in addition to overall departmental objectives.

Setting Departmental Objectives

To devise realistic objectives, encourage input from all levels of staff in the department. The first action is usually to call a staff meeting to discuss the project. The department head reminds the staff of the departmental goals and talks about the reasons for setting objectives. Everyone is encouraged to suggest ideas about the areas in which objectives might be set and the types of activities that should be considered. The next step is often the formation of a committee to prepare written objectives. If the staff is small, the department head may work alone to draw up a draft of the objectives. The following guidelines may be useful to the group or individual writing the objectives.

Guidelines for Objectives

- Objectives should flow from the mission statement of the institution and the goals of the department.
- Objectives should be clear, specific, and realistic.
- Objectives should be measurable and quantified whenever possible. This guideline often causes trouble because some librarians feel that some aspects of service cannot be quantified. The objective should, in this case, indicate how aspects, such as enthusiasm at storyhours or greater response from teachers, are to be judged.
- Objectives should be attainable, but challenging. They must strike a balance between an overenthusiastic "Consult with all teachers about their assignments" and statements that require no change of service—"Answer reference questions." The purpose of setting objectives is to move the department toward meeting its goals. Setting objectives is pointless unless something is achieved by meeting them.

The staff members who will be responsible for meeting the objectives need to accept them as reasonable. Objectives cannot be seen as plans sent down by administrators who do not understand the day-to-day operations of the department. For this reason, even though an individual or a small committee may have been responsible for drafting the objectives, they should be discussed and revised by all members of the department both professional and nonprofessional.

If staff members have never worked with objective-setting, they may perceive the process as a threat. It may be wise for the department head to encourage the staff initially to set limited and easily met objectives. When employees recognize that objectives can benefit them by providing a means of documenting their achievements, they may be ready to set more challenging objectives on the next round.

First-time users of objectives may go to the other extreme and set unrealistically ambitious objectives. One way to avoid this is to measure on a short-term, usually monthly, basis how well the objectives are being met. If objectives are too ambitious, this will become apparent in one or two months. The objectives can then be reasonably modified in time for the formal year-end assessment.

Working with Objectives

Objectives can enhance the effectiveness of a department only if the staff remains aware of them. Some departments use visual reminders, such as notices on the staff bulletin board, to remind people about departmental objectives. These can take various forms:

> Our objective is to develop a list of suitable science websites. How many have you discovered this month?
>
> Our objective is to have five class visits per week. So far this month, we have had only four.

As with all notices placed on bulletin boards, these must be changed frequently or people will cease to notice them, much less read them. It also helps if bright colors and interesting graphics are used to draw attention to the message.

Department heads may mention objectives at staff meetings or in informal conversations. This should never be done in a threatening way, of course, but simply as a good-natured means of reminding everyone of the department's objectives.

Although objectives are formal statements designed to be formally evaluated, there must be some flexibility in their use. Occasionally, an unexpected disaster, such as a fire, will cancel out all of the previously planned objectives. Even lesser events, such as a succession of staff illnesses, resignations, and changes in the library administration, or community problems caused by a plant closure or agricultural crisis, may require modification of a department's objectives.

When it becomes clear that some objectives are unreachable, a staff meeting and discussion can lead to modifications that make the objective realistic. Naturally, these changes should not be made every year, or else the setting of objectives will come to seem meaningless. Like all management tools, however, objectives must be modifiable in the light of unforeseeable events.

The department head should assess objectives throughout the year. If it is clear that they are not being met, it is better to make early adjustments rather than to announce at the end of the year that the objectives have been a disastrous failure. At other times, it may be best to forget about a particular objective and to work on the underlying problems that the failure to meet it may reveal. If objectives are being met, it is useful to let the staff know they are doing well. The bulletin board and staff meetings may be used to announce the successes in meeting objectives on a monthly or quarterly basis.

Evaluating Achievement

Assessment that objectives are being met is usually done on a yearly basis, although its time frame may be longer than that. As mentioned earlier, most objectives are set for a period of two to five years. But, at the least, an annual assessment is needed to ensure that the department stays on track in meeting its planned goals. The annual assessment is a formal one, with the results given to all staff members, so that they can see how the department is doing.

The method of evaluation should be set at the same time that the objective is adopted. Some evaluation measurements are obvious: for collection development, the number of books purchased in a particular area; for programming, the number of programs or the attendance; for staff development, the courses or workshops attended. Other objectives, such as those concerned with the number of reference questions successfully answered or the amount of reading guidance given, may need special sampling and counting techniques.

Output Measures

If special, nonroutine measurements are needed, provision should be made for these at the time the objectives are set. A good guide to ways of measuring services is the American Library Association's *Output Measures for Public Library Service to Children: A Manual of Standardized Procedures* (Walter 1992). If specific periods are set aside during the year for measuring of services, the task need not be onerous, according to Walter. The output measures that are described in this manual fall into the six areas discussed on pages 20-21.

Library Use Measures

Children's Library Visits Per Child is the average number of visits to the library by those age 14 and younger, per child (14 and younger) in the community served.

Building Use by Children indicates the average number of children, age 14 and under, who are in the library at any particular time.

Furniture/Equipment Use by Children measures the proportion of time, on average, that a particular type of furniture or equipment is in use by children, age 14 and under.

Materials Use Measures

Circulation of Children's Materials Per Child measures the use of children's library materials loaned for use outside the library, relative to the number of children, age 14 and under, in the service area.

In-Library Use of Children's Materials Per Child indicates the use of children's library materials within the library, relative to the number of children, age 14 and under, in the community served.

Turnover Rate of Children's Materials relates the circulation of children's materials to the size of the children's department collection.

Materials Availability Measures

Children's Fill Rate is the percentage of successful searches for library materials by users age 14 and under.

Homework Fill Rate is the proportion of successful searches for information or library materials for homework use by library users, age 14 and under.

Picture Book Fill Rate is the percentage of successful searches for picture books.

Information Services Measures

Children's Information Transactions Per Child is the number of information transactions per child, age 14 and under, in the community served made by library users, age 14 and under, and adults acting on behalf of children.

Children's Information Transaction Completion Rate is the percentage of successful information transactions by children, age 14 and under.

Programming Measures

Children's Program Attendance Per Child measures annual attendance at children's library programs per child, age 14 and under, in the community served.

Community Relations

Class Visit Rate measures visits from school classes to the library relative to the total number of school classes in the community.

Child Care Center Contact Rate is the number of contacts between the library and child care centers relative to the number of child care centers in the community.

Annual Number of Community Contacts is the total number of community contacts made by library staff responsible for services to children during the year (Walter 1992).

Using some or all of these measures can help the library to decide whether objectives are being met. The decision as to which measures to use in evaluating whether objectives are met is made at the time the objectives are set.

Total Quality Management

While many libraries have found the use of output measures valuable for evaluating programs, others use a different system called Total Quality Management (TQM). Like many management tools, this was first developed for profit-making organizations. The original idea, developed by W. Edwards Deming in the 1930s, was based on continuous monitoring and improvement of an organization to increase customer satisfaction. The method involved the formation of circles of workers that would identify problems, analyze procedures, and monitor the processes for which they were responsible. More recently, TQM has been broadened to develop an organizational culture that invites participation from all workers and aims to constantly improve the quality of products and services.

Several municipal governments and nonprofit organizations have adopted a policy of TQM. A library's evaluation system may also be structured in this format. It would mean soliciting comments and evaluations of programs from patrons, as well as from staff members. In a children's department, the patrons would include parents of young children, the children themselves, and other adults who use the services. Focus groups are often used to obtain reactions to individual programs, materials, or services. Less formal methods of soliciting feedback, such as through comment sheets and conversations, can also be used.

Using the Results of Evaluation

Whatever method is used to evaluate a department's success in meeting its objectives, remember that it should be chosen when the objectives are first set. If not, the department may find itself unable to decide whether its objectives are met.

When objectives are successfully met, staff members congratulate themselves and are frequently eager to move on to setting new objectives for another year. Dealing with the failure to meet objectives is much more difficult. If a department has set the objective of contacting 50 percent of the teachers in their jurisdiction but manages to reach only 25 percent, the staff may feel discouraged. In this situation, the department head needs to help the staff analyze the reason for failure and finds ways either to move toward reaching the objective or to set one that is more realistic.

After determining the success of a department's objectives, a staff meeting should be called. The degree to which each objective is met should be announced, and the reasons for success or failure discussed. Some of the causes of failure in certain situations include the following:

- Objectives are unrealistic when compared with the practice of most public libraries. An example would be an objective of having 90 percent of the children in a community borrow at least one book.

- Objectives are unrealistic in terms of the personnel available. For example, to have at least 10 class visits per week in a library with only two staff members.

- The objectives are made unreachable through a change of conditions. For example, the assistant librarian has left and not been replaced, forcing the head of the children's department to carry out two library jobs for six months.

- Budget is not sufficient to meet the objectives. For example, the cost of 500 Chinese language books has been higher than expected, resulting in the purchase of only 400 books.

- Personnel is not able to manage change resulting from an attempt to meet objectives. For example, an attempt to train a staff member to sign storyhours has failed because he or she was unable to learn to sign within the time allocated.

Frequently the cause of the failure to meet an objective indicates the steps that need to be taken to ensure success next time. Occasionally the department head may feel that failure is due to the inadequacy or lack of interest of a particular staff member. In that case, the staff evaluation interview ought to focus on the objective involved. Setting and measuring objectives can, in fact, become a useful staff evaluation tool. Failure should not lead to discouragement, but to a renewed commitment to setting better objectives that can and will be met by the department.

3

Developing Policies and Procedures

Listservs, electronic mailing lists that enable participants to discuss common interests, have become a valuable means of exchanging professional information. Any librarian who reads the listservs focused on public library services comes to realize that developing appropriate policies is a challenge in many libraries. Queries, such as these, are frequent:

"Does anyone know of a successful policy on how to deal with unattended children in the library? We ask the children to leave for the day if they become noisy or disruptive, but are concerned that denying them the use of the library will discourage the kids from coming back. We want to encourage library use, not discourage it. What do other people do?"

"We have a policy of allowing children 30 minutes on our public access computers, but we find that some children hang around waiting for another terminal to open up. What should we do when one child is using a computer for the third or fourth time in an afternoon and another child wants to use it? Does anyone have a successful policy dealing with this?"

"My library will provide Internet access starting next month. The library has earned good publicity from this but already I've had three parents tell me they are worried about their kids finding porn online. Does anyone know of a successful Internet policy to ease these fears and not deny children the use of the Net?"

The policies that are most difficult to develop and implement are those covering rapidly changing situations, such as the introduction of Internet access or the increase in unattended children in a library. Basic policies, however, such as those concerning materials selection, are equally important in a well-organized library. Having well-defined policies that are officially approved by the library's governing body acts as a first line of defense against charges of providing inappropriate materials or services. Policies are not only a protection for the library, however. Institutions also develop policies to ensure that individuals are treated equitably and that standards of service are maintained. Patrons want to be sure that they and their children have the same access to materials and services as others do, and that the rules governing library rules seem reasonable. As one writer notes:

> "Policies should help library users feel comfortable, not guilty or incompetent. They can broadly express a library's philosophy of service and protect both staff and patrons through equitable guidelines and accompanying procedures. They can also set the tone for how staff interacts with library users" (Wagner and Wronka 1995, 42).

Types of Policies

Two broad categories of policies are present in most libraries: service policies that deal with such areas as the use of the library, selection of materials, programming, and service provision; and staff policies covering personnel and contingency planning. In special circumstances, particular libraries may develop other types of policy statements.

Service Policies

Library Use Policies

Policies governing the way library cards are obtained and how they are to be used are helpful when questions arise about responsibility for materials. A recent thread on a children's services listserv elicited different opinions about checkout procedures when children forget to bring their library cards. Some libraries permit the child to borrow materials if they have any type of identification—something that many children do not have. Other librarians suggest that the circulation clerk could check the child's name in the registration database and allow materials to be borrowed on the basis of this identification. The underlying problem, of course, is the financial responsibility for lost or overdue items. One participant in the listserv mentioned a parent's complaint that another child had borrowed a book by giving the name of her son and that the son should not be responsible for the resulting overdue fine.

These comments illustrate the complexity of trying to devise a policy that is sensible enough to protect the library yet flexible enough to allow for a child's forgetfulness. Policies should focus on providing service, rather than on rigid adherence to rules. No perfect system can be recommended for all children's departments. Each library must base its policy on the nature of the community and the expectations of parents, administrators, and the library board.

Policies about behavior in the library can also be difficult to develop. One of the issues of greatest concern in recent years has concerned unattended children. As recently as five or ten years ago, when a child was left in the library at closing time, many librarians would accompany the child home. Now, many library policies forbid librarians to take a child anywhere outside of the library without specific parental approval. Also, requiring a disruptive unaccompanied child to leave the library could cause concern among parents, especially when a neighborhood is considered unsafe. Because of these concerns, having a well-publicized policy on unattended children makes a great deal of sense. One example of such a policy is shown in figure 3.1.

Cedar Rapids Public Library

Unattended Children

Children under the age of nine who are left unattended or appear to be in the facilities without adult supervision can be a cause of concern to the library. Issues of safety, liability, and responsibility motivate the library to address this potentially serious problem. It is the policy of the board of trustees to require that parents not leave children under the age of nine unattended in the library.

The following procedure will be used if it is determined that a child is lost or left unattended for more than one half hour:

1. A staff person will notify the supervisor of the day and the security guard that we have a lost or unattended child in the building.
2. The supervisor or the security guard will attempt to locate the child's parents in the building through a page on the intercom.
3. If the parent or responsible adult cannot be found in the building, a staff member will stay with the child while the supervisor of the day or the security guard continues to attempt to locate the parents.
4. If the parents have not been located within an hour, or if the library is closing, a staff member will be directed to notify the police.
5. Under no circumstances shall a staff member take the child out of the building.

Adopted 1/25/90.

For more information, contact: Roger Rayborn
raybornr@crpl.cedar-rapids.lib.ia.us

Fig. 3.1. Cedar Rapids Public Library's Policy Concerning Unattended Children. Reprinted with permission of the Cedar Rapids Public Library, Iowa.

Selection Policies

Selection policies are among the most traditional types of policies for libraries. The American Library Association, as well as most state and provincial professional associations recommend a well-written selection policy as a bulwark against attempts of private citizens to demand removal of certain materials from libraries. Potential censorship is not the only reason for having a selection policy. It can also be important in demonstrating the need for funding to maintain collections and services.

Policies for the selection, acquisition, and withdrawal of print and nonprint materials may be combined into one or separated into several documents. The policies for the children's department may be a subsection of the overall library selection policy or may stand alone. In either case, departmental policies are covered by the philosophy of the general library policy, which includes statements about intellectual freedom and the library's goals and objectives.

Selection policies often include procedures used in selecting, acquiring, and weeding materials, as well as selection principles. Because the library board should approve the basic selection policy, it is usually wise to keep the procedures in a separate statement for staff use. In this way, the entire document does not have to be brought to the board each time a change in procedures is made.

Whether contained in one or in several documents, selection policies and procedures for materials should cover such areas as:

- Goals (meeting recreation and information needs)
- Intellectual freedom statement
- Balance of collection
- Age of potential clientele
- Type of service to adults
- Relationship to school media center collections
- Provision for needs of special groups (e.g., disabled, immigrants)
- Materials excluded (by format and content)
- Gifts
- Collection levels for various content areas
- Method of selection

    Selection tools used

    Basis for evaluation (e.g., reviews, personal inspection)

    Individuals involved in selection

    Obtaining input from community

    Special methods for specific materials (e.g., non-English language)

    Special procedures for particular formats (e.g., CD-ROMs, software)

- Method of acquisition

    Dealers and other suppliers

    Procedures (usually systemwide)

- Weeding

    Appropriate copyright date to discard (obsolete materials)

    Appropriate length of time since last circulation to discard

    Decision on mending materials

    Procedure for systematic weeding

The first part of a selection policy describes the overall philosophy of the department. It sets the stage for the specific procedures by stating the audience for whom the collection is designed and the professional commitment to intellectual freedom and a balanced collection that guide the selection process. It is this part of the policy that can be used as a defense against censorship attempts. If the library is officially committed to providing a balanced collection of information for all of the children in the community, the librarian is in a better position to defend the purchase of materials with subjects such as homosexuality, creationism, and witches.

General statements about the relationship of the public library to schools also makes it possible to justify not buying materials that are adequately supplied by the schools. Although some overlap is always expected among collections, the differences in the aims of the two collections should be clearly stated in the policy.

The gift policy is important as an explanation to would-be donors of unsuitable material. This section should state that any material accepted as gifts should meet collection standards.

The development of standard collection levels for different content areas is a useful way to ensure that a balanced collection is acquired. The levels chosen should reflect:

- the composition of the community, for example, the predominant age level of the children, or the presence of specific language groups;

- the adequacy of the provision of school media resources;

- the strength or weakness of local interest in certain topics.

Methods for Implementing Selection Policies

As mentioned above, methods of selection, acquisition, and weeding are not always included as part of the selection policy because such methods tend to change more frequently than basic philosophical principles. A statement of the method of selection can be an appendix to the basic policy. This statement would specify the journals and other selection aids to be scanned on a regular basis; the method of evaluation, whether by reviews, individual judgment, or selection committee; the method of obtaining input from patrons and other community members; and the method of dealing with particular bodies of material by format, language, or other characteristics.

In most large library systems, the children's department inputs materials order lists in a general acquisitions department database. The decision about which dealers and other suppliers are to be used is made at the library system level. Some libraries have a portion of their budgets allocated on a departmental level for the immediate purchase of quickly needed materials. This type of budget enables the librarian to buy items at a local outlet. Although many children's librarians have little contact with suppliers, it is always a good idea to know where library materials are purchased and to be alert for information about improved services.

The procedures for weeding are an important part of collection management. The selection policy should indicate the earliest copyright date acceptable for keeping materials in various content areas, including reference books. Criteria for deciding when a book is in sufficiently poor condition to be discarded should also be established. The final step is to have a plan for systematically weeding each section of the collection. Having clear criteria enables much of the weeding task to be done by nonprofessional employees such as pages or shelvers who are usually inexperienced high school students. They should check each item for its condition and its date of publication. Candidates for discard should be placed in a work area where the librarian can make a final decision as to which materials should be replaced. Before discarding the final copy of a book in the system, the librarian should check whether it should be preserved in storage or a special location.

Internet Use Policies

Internet access has been one of the most popular resources offered in public library children's departments in recent years. Its introduction has led to concerns about children using the Internet inappropriately by accessing adult materials, downloading and using copyrighted materials, and monopolizing the use of computer terminals. Developing policies about the appropriate use of the Internet is a concern of many children's departments. Figure 3.2 gives an example of one public library's Internet use policy.

The Michigan Library Association is one of several professional associations that have prepared documents to guide librarians in their provision of Internet services. Among their suggestions for libraries are these:

1. Using a document such as this one, create your own library policy on patron access before offering such access.

2. Make available a statement relating the provision of electronic resources directly to the library's mission statement.

3. Alert parents to the possibility of access to material that is inappropriate for children.

4. Have available a statement on online safety for children, such as the pamphlet entitled "Child Safety on the Information Highway," which is available from the National Center for Missing and Exploited Children.

Homer Public Library

Internet Use Policy

The Homer Public Library provides public access to the Internet in keeping with its role as a source of information, intellectual development, and enrichment for the community.

The Homer Public Library has no control over the information accessed and cannot be held responsible for the content or quality of the information retrieved.

As is the case with all other library materials, any restriction of a child's access to the Internet is the responsibility of the child's parent or legal guardian.

Due to our limited resources, this Internet access is primarily for research and information sources only. Individual sessions should be limited to 1/2 hour.

It is prohibited to use this access for any illegal or criminal purpose.

Fig. 3.2. Homer Public Library's Internet Use Policy. Reprinted by permission of the Homer Public Library, Homer, Alaska.

5. Have available a statement relating to online manners and ethics as related to the *Library Bill of Rights*.

6. Post time limits for Internet use.

7. Combine all of the above into a manual for online use specific to your library (Michigan Library Association 1995).

Many Internet policy statements devised by public, school, and academic libraries are available on the Internet. Another good source for information about Internet policies is the American Library Association.

Programming Policies

Programming policies identify the target groups for programs: infants, toddlers, preschoolers, school-age children, or adults. Every department will have more than one target group, but unless resources are ample, most libraries will not attempt to attract all possible groups. In communities with strong school media center programs, the public library's focus may be on children who are not in school. Adults may be a primary target in communities where most children are in day care facilities from an early age. At other libraries many school-age children may be spending after-school hours at the public library, so librarians may choose to provide programming for them.

Spelling out policies for target groups enables the library to allot resources realistically for various groups. Recognizing priorities enables the librarian to defend judgments about where library staff and resources are most needed and to resist pressure from vocal members of the community who demand specific programs.

Programming policies should specify the scope of programming that the library supports. Some libraries insist that all programming be aimed at increasing use of the collection. Others believe programs that bring people into the building to see a film or participate in a game night serve a legitimate purpose in publicizing the library. The overall policies provide guidelines for staff members who want to introduce new types of programs. They also give the librarian a way of making decisions as to whether staff members should organize a craft club or devote their time to running an additional preschool storyhour.

Libraries have varying policies on the level of personnel who should participate in programming. Some librarians believe that all levels of personnel, including clerks and pages, should be allowed to present storyhours or other programs for children. In other libraries only professional librarians or experienced clerical staff are allowed to give storyhour presentations. Some departments find it useful to have librarians select the books and plan programs but allow other personnel or volunteers to present the program. With the increasing importance of administrative work in children's departments, some librarians believe that professionals should plan and supervise the overall schedule of programs but should not spend time in the day-to-day operation of them. To make this possible, these departments may emphasize training day care workers, teachers, and other adults to present programs. Other libraries depend chiefly on paid professional entertainers to provide most library programs.

Whatever the decisions made by the library, it is helpful to have them spelled out in a programming policy. Many library workers enjoy presenting programs to children and may be reluctant to forfeit this pleasure unless a firm policy concerning the type of work that is appropriate to their position is in place.

Staff Policies

Service policies are public documents that are of interest to patrons. Most libraries publicize them widely through newsletters, websites, and in the media. Other policies deal with staff and are chiefly of interest within the library.

Contingency Policies

Problems and emergencies of many kinds can occur in libraries, as in other institutions. Plans should be made so that each staff member knows how to handle specific events. One of the basic principles of management is that someone is always in charge of a department. Ordinarily, the department head is the responsible individual. When that individual is away from the department, someone else must take over the responsibility. The ladder of responsibility generally moves down through the professional staff to the clerical staff in order of seniority. If, on occasion, no professional or clerical staff is present in the department, the most senior page would be expected to stay in touch with a designated individual in another department.

The handling of emergencies in the library will be discussed more fully in Chapter 6. The important point for administrators to remember is that policies should be drawn up for steps to be taken in the event of emergencies, and these policies should be made known to all staff members.

Personnel Policies

Personnel policies are developed on a systemwide basis in most libraries. The staff of the children's department work within the parameters of these policies and apply them to situations within the department. Although a degree of flexibility must be allowed to deal with unique situations, most employees like to know that policies are in place that govern the way in which they are hired, evaluated, and promoted.

Professional Staff

The first encounter that potential employees have with the institution is during the hiring process. The hiring of professional staff in large library systems is often handled by the personnel department. Potential librarians are screened through their written applications, and promising candidates are interviewed by personnel officers. When the field has been narrowed to two or three possible choices, the chief librarian, branch head, and head of the children's department may interview these individuals. The final hiring decision for the probationary period is generally made by this committee.

During the interview of a potential children's librarian, the head of children's services is usually assigned the task of asking questions about the candidate's qualifications as a children's specialist. Questions designed to elicit the candidate's knowledge about materials and programming for children are appropriate. The interviewer may also try to discover the attitude the candidate takes toward children as library patrons. In order to carry out the goals of the department, the candidate should be in general agreement with the accepted philosophy of service. On the other hand, a candidate who has fresh new ideas to contribute can often be more valuable to the department than one who is content to follow the established pattern. Questions that allow candidates to express their ideas and opinions are often more useful than those requiring specific answers.

Interviewers should avoid asking questions that might be construed as indicating sexual, racial, or ageist bias or that probe inappropriately into a candidate's personal life. While candidates, during the interview, may give information about child care arrangements, marital plans, or family commitments, this should be left to the discretion of the candidate.

Clerical Staff

In many libraries, members of the clerical staff are not hired for work in a specific department. They may be allocated to children's, adult, or technical services departments depending on need. If staff members from the children's department have an opportunity to choose, it is obviously better if clerical staff in the children's department enjoy working with children and are not irritated by the noise and confusion that children sometimes create. Most libraries have an informal system of assigning clerical staff to the department they prefer, even though it is not specified in the job classification.

It is helpful to have a realistic and fairly detailed job description prepared for clerical staff. In many libraries little distinction is made between the work of clericals and professionals in programming and giving reading guidance. Book selection and reference services are more frequently allocated specifically to professional staff. All staff members should understand those tasks they are not expected to perform, in addition to those that are considered part of their job. More about task allocation will be covered in this chapter.

Pages or Shelvers

The children's department in most libraries is responsible for choosing and supervising any pages who work in the department, although the actual hiring procedure is carried out by the personnel department. Because the jobs performed by pages are usually routine in nature and do not require specific training, most libraries hire high school students for this position. Some libraries have hired older workers, sometimes retired people, and occasionally volunteers are used. Because high school students are most commonly hired as pages, the following comments are focused on this group. No matter what individual is hired, the recruitment and interviewing procedures are similar.

Most pages are part-time employees who work after school or during the summer. Because these employees are not expected to bring any specific skills to the job, their selection depends chiefly on their attitude, dependability, and willingness to learn. In interviewing candidates, the librarian will want to ask about previous work experience, although this is likely to be limited. Volunteer work and participation in school activities are often considered indications of lively and interested students, although heavy commitment to other activities could result in absenteeism from the library job. Many libraries also require that the student have reasonably good grades in school, because students who are in danger of failing courses may take time off or quit at exam time, which is a particularly busy time for libraries. In some libraries the pages already on staff are the chief source of new applications. This often works well, because students who have a friend working at the library usually have a realistic idea of what the job entails. The librarian must be sure, however, that this system does not lead to the exclusion of some students from the possibility of working in the library. As in all kinds of hiring, the employer should try to encourage applications from the entire pool of potential employees.

Task Allocation in Children's Department

Librarians, especially those who work in small libraries, often do not make clear distinctions between various types of tasks. Allocating tasks incorrectly can lead to two types of problems. First, professional librarians may spend their time on such nonprofessional tasks as inputting user information into a database, checking out books, or shelving. A management analyst observing this would suggest that the library is wasting money by paying a professional salary to someone doing nonprofessional work. The second type of problem is that the nonprofessional staff may perform such tasks as reference service or selecting materials for the collection. Staff members without professional training are unlikely to offer the same level of service as professional librarians. Even though some basic reference questions can be answered by experienced nonprofessionals, a distinction should be made between basic questions and those that should be referred to the librarian. In addition to the issue of providing the best possible service, a clear inequity also arises in paying clerical employees less than the professional librarians and expecting them to perform the same tasks.

For these reasons, the library should identify all of the tasks that are performed in a children's department and decide to which level of personnel they would most appropriately be assigned. One way of doing this is to divide the tasks into categories, such as administrative, collection development and maintenance, programming, and services to individuals. An example of such a division is given in figure 3.3.

Once these tasks have been identified, the librarian can consider what level of personnel is needed to handle them adequately. Some of the tasks need to be broken down into smaller components, as has been done for "reference questions" in figure 3.3. Most librarians would encourage a page to tell a child where the CD-ROMs are located but would expect to have a reference question referred to another staff member. An experienced clerical staff member may easily help a child find a picture of a dinosaur in an encyclopedia but should know to refer a more complicated reference question to a librarian. In the same way, the task of handling publicity, for example, should be organized so that setting the aim of the publicity is the task of a professional librarian, planning the actual layout of a poster or flyer might be accomplished by a specialized graphics person, and the production and distribution is handled by clerical staff.

One way the task allocation could be made is depicted in figure 3.4. In this library a clear distinction is made between the work of professionals and that of the clerical staff. Many libraries are unable to make such a distinction because staffing problems make it necessary to have the library open at times when no professional is on duty. Even though in situations in which task allocation must be flexible, some thought should still be given to the level of personnel most appropriate for various library tasks.

Tasks Performed in Children's Department

Administrative
Hiring
Evaluating staff
Scheduling
Communicating with library
    administration
Serving on library committees
Setting goals and objectives
Setting programming policies
Training staff
Planning staff training
Giving staff workshops
Consulting on design of facilities
Selecting decoration for children's
    department
Planning renovations
Choosing computer systems
Training staff in use of computers

Collection Development
Setting collection policies
Selecting materials
Ordering materials
Processing materials
Circulating materials
Developing circulation policy
Shelving
Mending
Handling complaints
Weeding
Selecting equipment for access to
    electronic media
Training patrons in use of computer
    systems

Programming
Setting policy for target groups
Scheduling classes
Contacting schools
Publicity
    Designing
    Producing
    Contacting groups
    Distributing information
Planning program series, including
    summer reading programs
Planning individual programs
Presenting programs to children
Training adults to give programs
Making support materials (puppets,
    name tags, craft projects)

Service to Individuals
Reference questions
    Directional questions
    Brief facts questions
    Detailed reference questions
Reading guidance
Registration of borrowers
    Setting policy
    Preparing cards
Handling overdues
Dealing with difficult patrons
Planning library instruction
Giving library instruction
Giving instruction on computer
    systems

Fig. 3.3. Tasks Performed in Children's Department.

The plan for task allocation allows for the preparation of job descriptions for each position in the department. When the department head presents to each staff member a clear picture of how the positions in the department are designed to complement one another, staff members are more likely to understand administrative decisions. Task allocation can then be used to develop procedures for routines within a department, such as work schedules.

Task Allocation in Children's Department

Administrative

PROFESSIONAL
Hiring
Evaluating staff
Communicating with library administration
Serving on library committees
Setting goals and objectives
Setting programming policies
Training staff
Planning staff training
Giving staff workshops
Giving input on facilities design
Selecting decoration for children's department
Planning renovations
Giving input on computer systems
Planning staff and patron training on computers

CLERICAL
Scheduling
Training staff (other clericals and pages)
Assisting patrons with computers

Collection Development

PROFESSIONAL
Setting collection policies
Selecting materials
Developing circulation policy
Weeding—setting policy
Handling complaints

CLERICAL
Ordering materials
Processing materials
Circulating materials

PAGES
Shelving
Mending
Weeding

Programming

PROFESSIONAL
Setting policy for target groups
Contacting schools
Designing publicity
Planning program series, including summer reading programs
Training adults to give programs

CLERICAL
Scheduling classes
Distributing information
Planning individual programs
Presenting the program to children
Making support materials (puppets, name tags, craft projects)

PAGES OR OTHERS
Producing publicity materials
Presenting individual programs
Making support materials (see above)

Service to Individuals

PROFESSIONAL
Reference service
    Directional questions
    Brief facts questions
    Detailed reference questions
Reading guidance
Registration of borrowers—setting policy
Dealing with difficult patrons
Planning library instruction
Giving library instruction
Assisting patrons with computer use

CLERICAL
Preparing borrowers' cards
Handling overdues
Giving library instruction
Reference services
    Directional questions
    Brief facts questions
Assisting patrons with computer use

PAGES
Answering directional questions
Assisting patrons with computer use when appropriate

Fig. 3.4. Task Allocation in Children's Department.

Scheduling

Many of the day-to-day disagreements in a children's department stem from the scheduling of work assignments. The administrative goal is to have the library appropriately staffed at all times and to divide the work fairly among employees. Most children's departments are open during evenings and weekends—times that are considered undesirable by some employees. Usually these hours are rotated among staff members in a regular pattern, although some departments are fortunate enough to have some staff members who prefer evening and weekend hours. In some library systems overtime is paid for Sunday work, which encourages staff members to volunteer to work on that day.

Because these hours are often the busiest times, most systems insist that professional personnel staff the department at those times. In a few libraries the weekend staff, or the Sunday staff, are all nonprofessional, which is likely to result in a decreased level of service.

To avoid unfairness and bad morale, it is important to have an overall policy in place for scheduling. The policy should specify the hours during which the children's department will be staffed, the level of staffing required, and the rationale for rotating staff hours. This policy should also spell out the circumstances under which changes in scheduling can be made—for staff members who are taking library school courses, personal and family emergencies, and so forth.

After the policies have been established, a senior clerical assistant usually does the scheduling. That individual will usually be responsible for collecting information about vacation preferences and will, after discussion with the department head, draw up the vacation schedules.

Writing and Publicizing Policies

New policy statements often grow out of specific problems noticed by librarians. The introduction of Internet access or an increase in the number of unattended children may suggest that a policy covering the new issues would be useful. All levels of staff should be involved in developing service policies. Much of the front line contact with patrons is handled by support staff, and if they have difficulty in following rules set by librarians, they could become resentful and undermine them. Gathering input from all staff is likely to result in the fair implementation of realistic policies.

Policies of all kinds require frequent updating. They should be reviewed by the department heads at least once a year. It is important to retain earlier versions of policies in one location for reference. This is especially important for personnel policies, because individuals may have grievances based on the regulations in force when they were hired. Other policies should also be kept, so that the library has a historical record of changes. One person in the library should be responsible for maintaining these archives.

Staff members need convenient access to both service and personnel policies. Because of the changing nature of policies, they are frequently kept in loose-leaf binders so that pages may be easily replaced. Presenting the policies on different colored papers will make them easier to access. A complete set of library policies should be available in each department, as well as in staff lounges or other meeting places.

Because many people do not read policy statements, they should be periodically discussed at staff meetings. A wide range of staff members should be involved in making substantial revisions to policies. When staff members feel that their suggestions have been welcomed and considered, they are more likely to accept responsibility for carrying out the policies.

Some library policies, such as those for children's programming, are not of major concern to all library staff members. Nonetheless, all staff members should be aware of them and their philosophies. Within a community, all members of a library staff are seen as representatives of the institution and may be questioned about library matters. The library's credibility is enhanced when all staff members know about all library policies instead of only those affecting their own department.

In addition to the library staff, the community should be informed about library policies. This knowledge begins with members of the library board who can become spokespersons for library policies in the community. Many people have little contact with members of the library board, however, making it necessary to communicate with the general public. The policies that concern most members of the public are those dealing with programming and the selection of materials. Information about these policies should be available both inside and outside of the library.

Many libraries mount their policy statements on their websites to make them accessible to their community and the world. Policies concerning patron behavior may also be posted in the library. Complete files of policies should be available in the library for examination.

Publicity within the library may include flyers outlining the selection and programming policies of the children's department. Parents concerned with materials in the library or about their availability may be given these flyers. Adults wanting particular types of programs in the library may understand the reasons they are unavailable if provided with access to information about the programming policy. Information about how individuals can suggest changes in policies should be included.

For the benefit of community members who do not visit the library frequently, information about library policies should be available through the media, as well as on the website. When a new policy is approved by the library board, copies should be sent to local media for publication and comment. While a formal policy statement may not be published, a well-written information release can give the public most of the details. Occasionally, librarians worry that publicizing their policies will bring objections to decisions made in the library. However, many libraries have found that informing the public about their policies has the opposite effect—it tends to defuse objections because the public realizes that an effort is being made to present a balanced collection and appropriate programs.

In addition to using formal media channels, librarians can publicize their policies through personal appearances at parent associations and other community groups. Many parents are concerned about their children's reading activity, and librarians often find themselves welcome at these groups. In addition to talking about specific reading activities, these appearances are an opportunity to explain how the library operates and the reasons behind its policies. If a talk on a specific topic does not allow time for much discussion of general policy, at least some publicity material about policies may be distributed.

Evaluating Implementation

Policies that are not maintained weaken, rather than strengthen, a department. When reviewing the policies for updating, the department head should informally poll staff members to determine whether policies are being followed. These informal responses should be followed by a more formal assessment of how the record of programs presented, for example, agrees with the policy statements. If programming for school-age children is a policy priority, the record of programs should not show an emphasis on toddler programs. When a noticeable discrepancy between policy and practice is present, the policy must be reviewed. Perhaps the staff no longer believes that the policy is workable and it should be changed. Or, perhaps the practice has slipped into an undesirable pattern and should be altered.

If policies are regularly evaluated and updated, they are useful tools for planning and monitoring department activities. Within the department, policies are a reminder of priorities. In communicating with library administration and the public, they are the reference points by which decisions and activities can be justified.

Creating a Productive Work Environment

No matter how realistic and well-articulated the goals and objectives of a department are, they will not be met unless the department head, by being a good manager, creates an environment in which staff members can turn them into reality. To some children's librarians management may not seem to be as important a skill as storytelling or puppetry, but effective children's librarians must have skills beyond those needed to work with patrons. Management is essentially the process of getting things done. Because most libraries today are trying to achieve their goals with fewer resources and less personnel than were available in past years, using those resources effectively is important. A successful manager inspires people to work toward library goals and monitors the progress, so that these goals can be achieved. Unless a department is well-managed, its personnel and other resources will not be effectively used to deliver the best possible library service.

A library department head is a first-line supervisor, that is, someone who transmits policy on a day-to-day basis to all employees. "Whether the organization is small and has only a few levels, or very large with multiple levels of hierarchy, the supervisor always occupies a position somewhere in the middle of the organizational chart and must communicate effectively in several directions to function optimally in the organization" (Kratz and Flannery 1997, 43). Communication skills enable a supervisor to understand the needs of the organization and to transmit them in a way that will enable other levels of workers to carry out necessary tasks. Another major set of skills that a supervisor needs is decision making skills. Effective decision-making turns policy into practice and programs.

Department Heads as Supervisors

Many—but not all—of the techniques for supervision in libraries are similar to those in other management situations. Most children's departments are small units, by business standards. A department head typically supervises fewer than a dozen people, often only two or three persons. This means that relationships within the department tend to be close and personal. The department head does not deal with employees known only by a personnel number, but with individuals who are well-known to the entire department. This knowledge may make it easier for a supervisor to allocate tasks in a way that takes advantage of each person's strengths, but it may also make it difficult for the supervisor to maintain the distance that is necessary to appraise employees' performances objectively. It may also tempt a supervisor to inappropriately discuss administrative decisions or problems. These kinds of discussions can easily turn into gossip and undermine the supervisor's effectiveness. Finally, employee familiarity may create situations in which an individual uses the sympathy generated by a personal problem to manipulate the supervisor into allowing an unequal distribution of the departmental workload.

Another complication that results from the small size of the children's department is the distinction of the professional status of librarians from the clerical staff. In many library systems clerical staff remain in one library or branch for many years and build up seniority. Professional staff tend to move between branches or library systems. As a result, many young professionals find themselves working in a department where the clerical staff may be 20 or more years their senior and have many years of experience in the department. The skills learned through professional education may not be as evident as the clerical staff's intimate knowledge of the branch collection and the local community. It may be difficult in this situation for the supervisor to gain the confidence of staff members and persuade them to follow administrative leadership. Anyone moving into a situation like this should be careful to show respect for the clerical staff's knowledge. At the same time, the young professional must not downplay the broader base of skills learned through professional education and association with the wider library world. Together, professional and clerical staff can make valuable contributions toward effective library service.

In addition to their small size, library departments differ from many businesses because they dispense service on a nonprofit basis. Measuring the productivity of an employee or a department is difficult without a tangible product. In most manufacturing plants, a supervisor's success can be measured by the number of products produced. In a library, however, the increased skill of staff members in answering reference questions or selecting books may be extremely difficult to measure. A supervisor's success in creating a productive work environment may be revealed only slowly through an increase in the use of services and an anecdotal record of users' perceptions. The lack of immediate, measurable results may be discouraging in the short term, but eventually a well-run department should be demonstrably more effective.

Personnel Supervised

The personnel supervised by a department head may include librarians, library assistants, clerical staff, pages, and others, such as maintenance or security staff and volunteers. Each level of staff requires a somewhat different type of supervision.

Supervision of professional staff is often carried out on a collegial basis, with regular meetings, discussion of problems, and decisions that are frequently made by consensus. One of the goals in supervising and training librarians is to enable them to develop the skills necessary to take positions as department heads in other branches or libraries. Sharing background information about policies and decisions helps librarians to understand the reason for, as well as the procedures of administration. It also enables them to follow the spirit as well as the letter of institutional goals.

Library assistants and clerical staff need to know some of the background reasoning on library policies. However, their primary need is for information that will help them do their jobs, not participate in administration. This is not necessarily true of nonprofessional staff who may become candidates for professional education. Discussing library policies may encourage these individuals to enter the profession. But for the many library assistants who prefer to remain as nonprofessional staff, technique and procedures take precedence over general policies. This does not mean that supervisors should teach nonprofessionals rote tasks. Many clerical tasks, such as registering new borrowers, are governed by specific procedures. An individual will probably carry out these procedures more efficiently if he or she understands their purpose. Sometimes supervisors spend too much time teaching procedures without explaining the policy they support. Although this saves time, mistakes become more frequent when someone tries to carry out a rigid set of procedures without understanding their purpose and recognizing when they should be modified.

In most libraries, pages are high school students in their first job. Many of them are not familiar with the demands for punctuality and continuous work during their shifts. Some pages find it difficult to understand that they are expected to work when scheduled and that unexplained absences are unacceptable. While direct supervision of pages is often the responsibility of a senior member of the clerical staff, the department head is responsible for setting policy and for maintaining overall supervision. Pages usually lack interest in the inner workings of the library or library policy. However, their supervisor should make them feel important to the efficient operation of the department, while all library staff should treat pages as respected members of the staff.

In some libraries the issue of using first or last names causes a problem. Pages are usually called by their first names, but sometimes are expected to address other staff by their last names. This distinction may seem natural in some communities because of differences in age or job status, while in other communities it is unacceptable.

Supervisors should guide and monitor the conduct of pages in all departments of the library and should be alert to possible interpersonal tensions involving pages. Whenever possible, requirements that have no direct bearing on job performance should be avoided. If the pages' behavior, dress, or manner of work seem to create a problem in the library, a general staff discussion may lead to an acceptable consensus on standards. Staff members often more willingly accept decisions in which they participate, than regulations handed down from an administrator.

For the most part, the library's central administration supervises maintenance staff. The department head typically makes requests for specific tasks, such as changing a light bulb or moving a bookcase, through established procedures. Complaints about maintenance are also usually handled through regular channels. Problems with maintenance staff often result from misunderstandings about responsibility for specific tasks. A department head should try to obtain information about what is considered routine maintenance, what are acceptable special or emergency tasks, and what department personnel are expected to handle themselves. These categories can vary widely from one library to another. As with other personnel, maintenance staff generally work best in a department where their work and expertise are respected and acknowledged. Even such a simple thing as addressing maintenance personnel by name can help promote cordial relationships.

Communication Within the Department

Effective supervision depends on good two-way communication. The manager must not only express information about library policies, procedures, and plans, but must also listen and understand staff members' comments, ideas, and complaints.

Clarity

Almost all speakers believe that what they are saying is clear and blame any failure of communication on the listener. However, supervisors must accept the fact that many oral and written messages lack clarity, even for an attentive listener or reader. Several reasons may lead to a lack of clarity in communication.

Overestimating Background Knowledge

Supervisors sometimes forget that a staff member does not have all of the information necessary for understanding a statement or request. "You'd better check the condition of our Chinese language titles because we may have extra funding available at the end of the budget year" is not a useful directive for a new librarian. To do the job, the new librarian needs to know when the budget year ends and whether to check only books or include serials and videos. When giving this directive, the department head should briefly discuss the timing of the budget and the possibility of receiving extra funds. The department head should write out the criteria for checking the materials and a definition of the materials to include. This information is more effective in written than in oral form because it is probably too detailed to remember easily.

Using Jargon

Unusual words and words that have a special meaning in a particular work situation are often incomprehensible to outsiders. Such words should either be explained to those who may not understand them or altogether avoided. A supervisor who asks a new page to "straighten up the chapter books" or to "remove the books from the OPAC tables" may get a look of blank incomprehension.

Failure to communicate because of overestimating background knowledge or using jargon will occur less frequently if the department head takes the time to discover whether the listener understands what is said. Simply asking, "Do you understand?" may be ineffective because an employee may not wish to reveal his or her ignorance. However, asking "Is that clear?" may help the listener to express a lack of understanding because the emphasis is on the clarity of the statement, rather than on the capacity of the listener to understand. Sometimes a lack of understanding is better detected through facial expression or body language than in what the listener says. It may be useful to repeat the message using different words or expand the statement to provide more information. Asking the listener to repeat the message can help ensure that it has been understood, but only if the listener restates the original message; people can parrot words without understanding them.

Long-Windedness

While some managers fail to communicate because they do not give enough information, others bury the message in a glut of extraneous information. When giving directions, it is almost always best to omit alternatives. A manager might say, for example,

> "I want you to move the children's videos. They are too close to the reference desk. I had thought of putting them under the window in the picture book corner, but they shouldn't be in direct sunlight, and the little children might damage them anyway. So it would be best to put them in the space between the easy readers and the parents' collection. Anyone who is old enough to borrow them can easily find them, and whoever is at the reference desk will be able to keep an eye on them."

The person who is to move the videos may have difficulty sorting out what is to be done. Background information should be given only when it is useful; otherwise directives become confusing.

Organization

Good organization can help to make complicated messages more under-standable. One rule of thumb that is sometimes suggested is to tell people what you are going to say, say it, and then tell them what you said. In practice, this means that when giving directions or explaining policy the manager must first clarify the subject of the discussion: "Today I want to explain the plans for our summer reading program." Then the manager describes the regional or system-wide plans. The manager might end with a statement, such as "Now that you know the general outline of our plans, we can discuss the implementation in our branch. Does anyone have a suggestion as to how this will work here?"

This kind of organization does not stifle discussion, but channels it in useful directions. Staff members will understand the overall structure of the policy, procedure, or plan and will not waste time trying to create solutions from scratch, but be able to select useful ideas. Although impractical ideas and plans may still be suggested, the group, as a whole, will have some guidelines as to what is feasible.

A similar type of organization can be used in training a new employee. For example, the statement "Today I will explain how our overdue system works" would be followed by its explanation and concluded with "That's the general outline of our procedures. Helen Chung will be able to answer specific questions. Are the overall procedures clear now?" It takes practice to learn how much detail should be included in an explanation, and organizing the message will help make it clear despite how brief or detailed the specifics are.

Barriers to Communication

Sometimes the attitude of a supervisor becomes a barrier to effective com-munication. One such attitude is the "That's impossible" reaction. If a new staff member suggests that picture books should be interfiled with the fiction collec-tion, this may be the supervisor's first reaction. This will not only kill the suggestion but will also reduce the likelihood that other ideas will be presented in the future. Discouraging input from members of a department is a bad management technique; no one person can have all of the ideas that might improve services. Any idea that is brought forward should receive courteous attention. And each staff member deserves a response that affirms the validity of making suggestions, even though the specific suggestion may be rejected.

Making a joke or a flippant comment about ideas presented also discourages communication. If a department head laughs about the new smoking regulations, for example, staff members may fail to recognize that they are expected to abide by the rules. If a librarian jokes about pages' or colleagues' suggestions, all communication with them is likely to end. It is sometimes difficult to distinguish between being amusing and being rude or even insulting. As a rule, it takes time for a new staff member to understand when a supervisor is joking. Therefore, it is usually best to treat serious matters seriously until a good working relationship has been developed. Although a light touch can make a workplace more friendly and pleasant, heavy-handed humor, practical jokes, and sarcasm should be avoided. Needless to say, any jokes that make fun of particular ethnic, racial, disabled, age, or gender groups must be avoided. They can lead to lawsuits and loss of employment.

Format of Communication

Managers communicate both orally and in writing. Most communication within the department will be accomplished by talking, sending e-mail messages, or writing memos. These methods serve different and complementary purposes.

The great advantage of face-to-face communication is the opportunity for feedback. The manager not only hears what the listener has to say, but also can observe his or her body language and facial expressions. A manager should not be so intent on what he or she is saying that the listener's reaction is ignored.

The manager should maintain eye contact when talking to a single person. When speaking to a group, the manager should look around and try to include each individual in the bond of communication. Being aware of the listeners enables the speaker to notice signs of disagreement or boredom. In the kind of informal communication that takes place within a department, disagreement or boredom should be immediately acknowledged. The manager might say, for example, "You seem to be troubled; am I wrong in saying that we have a vandalism problem?" or "Have you heard all this before? Perhaps we should move on to discuss solutions instead of talking about the problem." By openly recognizing signs of communication failure, the manager allows the listeners to keep the discussion moving. No real communication occurs when an individual or group is addressed by someone without having an opportunity to respond.

When the person responds, the manager should listen closely and pay attention to what is said. No matter how irrelevant or trivial the response may seem, the manager owes the staff member the courtesy of listening. On the other hand, it is not necessary to listen at length to obviously unhelpful responses. Most staff responses are worthy of attention either because they contain useful ideas or because they reveal a misunderstanding. Judicious listening enables a manager to recognize the speaker's ignorance of library policies or goals, dissatisfaction with procedures, or conflicts with staff members. While a manager may not be pleased to discover these problems, he or she will be a more effective manager when informed of them.

While face-to-face communication has the advantage of allowing for amplification of ideas and immediate response, written communication has the advantage of precision and permanence. When an important issue is to be discussed, both oral and written communication may be needed. A preliminary oral discussion allows for the free flow of ideas and suggestions or the airing of complaints. A written follow-up enables each participant to read and remember what was discussed and the decisions that were made. Most managers have notes taken during a staff meeting or group discussion. It is also useful to take notes during or immediately after an important discussion with an individual. Using the notes the department head can put the major points into a statement that both parties can review.

Written communication within the department is appropriate for announcing changes in library policy, such as new regulations for borrowing CD-ROMs. In addition, written communication is useful for giving details that may be easily forgotten if merely told to a staff member, such as the library's holiday hours or the procedures to be followed when a child loses a book. Departmental memos are used as reminders of deadlines or special events, such as the deadline at which requests for vacation must be received or the date when the mayor is to visit the library. No important communication should be given solely in oral form; inevitably at least one staff member will be absent or will forget even the most important announcement.

The principles of clarity and organization that hold for oral communication apply equally to writing. Brevity is desirable, as most staff members quickly scan memos; very few read to the second page. The memo should include contact names and locations for staff members requiring additional background information. Jargon and clichés should be avoided. The message should be stated succinctly, usually in a style similar to spoken language. For example, do not write:

> All personnel are requested to pay strict attention to the regulations about allowing food in the public areas of the library. An increase in the incidence of insect pests has been noted by the maintenance staff. This has required more frequent use of pesticides and has increased the workload for maintenance people. Children and their parents should be advised of the existence of our policy and told that infringement will result in the loss of library privileges.

Instead, write:

> Please remember that no food is allowed in the public areas of the library. Roaches have been seen in the children's room during the past month. If you see children or parents eating or carrying food into the library, ask them to take the food outside and eat it there. Children who persist in bringing food into the library will be denied entry.

The telephone is not ordinarily used for communication within a library department, except when staff members call to say they will be unable to come to work. The person taking such a call should note the absence and its reason. It is important to have this information in writing and to note whether a follow-up is expected. For example, a staff member may call to report that she is ill and has an appointment with her doctor to see what treatment is required and how long she will be unable to work. In this case, the manager has reason to expect a follow-up telephone call. If the call is not received by the next day, the department head should see that the staff member is called and that the expected length of absence is determined. Sometimes a telephone call involves an absence that is specified in the employment agreement, such as a certain number of days allowed for a death in the family. In such cases, the supervisor should send the staff member a letter clarifying the length of time allowed for the absence. This should be done in a way that indicates the supervisor's sympathy with the staff member's loss, but it is important that the individual understands the library's expectations. Misunderstandings frequently arise when such information is only given orally or when the supervisor assumes that an individual is aware of the particular policy.

Most libraries use electronic mail for much internal communication, but more often between departments, rather than within one department. Individuals working on different shifts in the department may use e-mail, which can be valuable if a staff member occasionally works at home. Further discussion of this and other types of communication within a library system is included in Chapter 9.

Making Decisions

Making decisions is one of the manager's most important jobs. Few things harm an organization more than a manager who evades decisions. In fact, it is a compliment when a manager is called decisive. Everyone wants to make correct decisions, but most choices are between better and worse, rather than right or wrong. In most cases, making any decision is better than vacillation. If a choice must be made whether the storyhour should be for three- to five-year-old children or for four- and five-year-old children, either decision would enable the library program to move forward. Not making a choice might result in delaying the program, annoying parents, who must call back later to register a child, or killing the enthusiasm of the librarians who are eager to plan the program. Any of these results is more detrimental than making the "wrong" choice.

One of the first issues involved in a decision is selecting the individual responsible for making it. The person who makes decisions exercises power but may also be blamed or reprimanded if the decision has unpleasant consequences.

Some decisions in libraries are made by the Library Board or the CEO. The Board has the legal responsibility for the library and must approve major policy decisions. Many operational decisions are delegated to the CEO, who may in turn delegate some of them to department heads. The management style of the chief administrator and the expertise and experience of the department heads determines the degree of delegation. In some libraries, the head of Adult Services is perceived as being more powerful than the head of Children's Services and may be given the power to make more decisions. The head of the children's department cannot demand more power, but he or she can demonstrate a readiness to become a decision maker by being willing to make decisions, to stand by them, and of course, by making them successful.

When an administrator talks to the department head about a decision, it is important to clarify exactly what kind of input is desired. Is the department head being asked to give input into a decision, make a recommendation, or make the decision? Decisions may be joint decisions, individual decisions, or executive decisions.

Joint Decisions

Some decisions within a department should be made by the entire group or by a sub-group or committee. To start the decision-making process, the manager should explain to the staff whether they are being asked only for suggestions or if the group will make the decision. Group decisions are most appropriate when a group of employees must accept a decision and the time limit for making it is fairly long. In a children's department, for instance, a group might decide how to allocate work to minimize the disruption caused by major repairs to the library building. Each individual is likely to know best how the repairs will affect a particular job. Allowing each staff member to suggest ways for coping with inconvenience will minimize general resentment. The manager will not be seen as the person who handed down decisions that cause inconvenience.

Individual Decisions

Some decisions that affect only individuals, not the overall running of the department, are best made by the individual. The time at which each staff member takes a coffee break or lunch break is not crucial, as long as the department is adequately staffed at all times. The same is often true of vacation scheduling or the sequence in which many tasks are completed. The manager can often leave such decisions to the individuals, themselves. This allows the staff members to control aspects of their work that may be important to them, which in turn will make them feel better about their jobs. Flexibility encourages people to take ownership of a job and to develop a sense of responsibility for handling it.

Executive Decisions

Not all decisions can be made by individual staff members or by a committee. The department head should be prepared to make many of the major decisions. Specific steps that a manager can take to make an effective decision include:

- Review the information. Identify the exact choices. If documentation is available, read it. If you need to ask people about their plans or ideas, do so with an open mind.

- Evaluate and weigh the pros and cons, not just in terms of the staff's desires or the department's traditional stance, but also in terms of how the CEO or outsiders might evaluate the results. Are there political implications to one solution or another? Will some community group feel underserved? Is it important to make the decision immediately or is time available for discussion and deliberation?

- If possible, allow time for deliberation. The greater the change, the more expensive or time consuming it will be; therefore, more time should be allowed for making the decision. Timing is important, and delay can sometimes allow the impetus to slip away. But at the same time, a leader should not be pressured into making a premature decision.

- Consider possible negative consequences growing out of the decision. Think about the attitudes and values of people who will be affected. Consider the power of precedent. Does the decision fit in with the normal procedures of the organization? Consider whether a decision will cause a unique opportunity to slip away. Think about whether a decision is being delayed because of a desire for perfection.

One tool to help the manager make a decision is to organize the information in a decision table. For example, one of the department's objectives may be to increase the use of the library by non-English-speaking children. Several ways are available to do this. The department might buy more materials in different languages, institute storyhours in different languages, or initiate a publicity campaign in the ethnic communities. After identifying the possibilities, the manager should investigate the cost of each option. Then the manager might invite opinions from some staff members. The final decision will probably rest with the department head. Factors that weigh in the decision will be costs (including staff time), availability of expertise (especially for the storyhours), and knowledge of the needs and wishes of the community. The manager might create a decision table similar to figure 4.1 on page 50 to organize this information.

A chart of this kind will not make the decision, but it should help the department head to consider the possibilities and their consequences. The initial choice may be modified or changed in time. One component of decision making is monitoring results, so that appropriate modifications can be made to the option.

Sometimes a department head may carefully and reasonably make a decision, but, nonetheless, later realize that it was the wrong decision. A manager must know when to reverse a decision but should try to avoid vacillating. If a decision must be changed, the manager should calmly consider the alternatives and try to decide the next move before widely discussing the change. In announcing the reversal of a decision, the department head should explain as clearly as possible the reasons for the change and should try to avoid being overly apologetic or dwelling on the fact that a mistake was made. All managers make mistakes. An important aspect of leadership is to be able to acknowledge a mistake and to move quickly to remedy the situation.

Objective: To increase use of library by new Spanish-speaking immigrants.

Strategy	Will it accomplish objective?	Is it cost-effective?	Negative impacts?
Buying more Spanish language materials	Only if the community knows they are available	Could be managed out of book budget, but no money for publicity	Resentment on part of users of existing multilingual collection. May not be able to maintain size of English language collection
Holding Spanish storyhours	Will probably attract the community	If volunteer storytellers can be found, cost would be reasonable	May not be able to maintain interest unless Spanish materials are available
Try to develop co-operation with schools and borrow materials for the summer months	Would attract readers if the schools publicize availability of materials in the summer	Expense would be minimal	Might disappoint users when the materials return to the schools in the fall
Publicity campaign about library services	Should bring people into library, but would they accept the all-English services?	Flyers to schools and a talk on community television would fit within public relations budget	Might disappoint new patrons who are unable to use the services provided in English

Fig. 4.1. Decision Table.

Recruiting and Retaining Staff

At a library, children need help in choosing books and other materials and learning how they are used. Good staff who understand children's needs and are enthusiastic about serving children are the key to good services. More than half of a library's budget is generally spent on staff salaries, so the investment in recruiting and retaining the best possible staff is great.

Sources for Staff

Although all staff members play an important role in providing services in a children's department, it is the professional staff who set the tone and direction of services. Professional staff members are recruited from library schools that offer an American Library Association-accredited program. The number of accredited schools in North America has declined in recent years, but the number of graduates has increased (Dalrymple 1997, 33). The value of a degree in information studies is recognized by corporations, government departments, and other organizations, so libraries compete against many other potential employers for the best library school graduates.

The work of a children's librarian is not visible in everyday life or in the media, so not many young people make it a career goal. One way of increasing the pool of applicants is for librarians to publicize the importance and interest of the work. Some libraries have had success in working with schools to present talks at career days and to provide information for guidance counselors. Providing information about the profession of children's librarian at high schools and colleges can help to recruit a diverse group of young people.

The message to take to young people should include the challenges and rewards of working with children in a library. To one children's coordinator, ". . . work as a youth services librarian offers a career with the potential for creativity, variety, and independence" (Salvadore 1995, 75).

Candidates for recruitment into the field are sometimes found among the library pages, clerical workers, and patrons. Many librarians first became interested in the profession as a result of a part-time library job while attending school. Department heads should be alert to signs of interest among pages and clerical workers and find time to discuss with them the possibility of pursuing professional library work. Occasionally parents will discover, during trips to the library, that they might enjoy becoming a professional in the field.

Process of Hiring

When a new position has been approved by the library board, the department will work with the chief librarian and the library's personnel officer to find the most appropriate person for the position. In almost all library systems, job openings are posted first within the system and, often, the municipality. If no suitable candidate is available within the system, an advertisement is placed in library journals, and recruitment may occur at conferences or library schools.

Any advertisement for a public library position must meet government standards for fairness and follow the format approved by the municipality. It should also be specific enough to encourage only qualified applicants to respond. A few words about the community and the library may arouse interest among applicants. Studying the advertisements published in recent issues of *American Libraries* or other journals, such as those shown in figure 5.1 may provide ideas for its phrasing.

Interviewing

In large library systems, preliminary screening of applications for a job is usually carried out by personnel staff. In smaller libraries, the chief librarian and the head of the children's department may review applications. Whatever the procedure, the person in charge of children's services should be closely involved in selecting new children's librarians. Experience in children's services is the best background for understanding the demands of the job and the candidate's suitability.

Most libraries prefer to interview five or six candidates for each open position. If many of the candidates are from out-of-town, some of the interviewing may be conducted by telephone; however, personal interviews are preferable. Sometimes a library conference offers an opportunity to conduct interviews with several candidates. Preparation for an interview includes a close review of the application and the checking of references. Interviewers should consider procedures and decide whether interviews will take place individually or in a group. In some library systems the personnel officer will conduct a preliminary interview and then pass on the most promising candidates to the head of the children's department and the chief librarian. Other libraries prefer a more informal group meeting with three or four librarians present.

CHILDREN'S LIBRARIAN. West Dublin Public Library seeks a dynamic, enthusiastic librarian to develop the children's department of a newly renovated branch library. The individual will have responsibilities for collection development, coordination of programming, staff training and supervision, and direct public service. Candidates should have a commitment to and interest in serving children, an ability to plan and evaluate age-appropriate programs, familiarity with both print and electronic resources as well as computer technology and applications. The minimum requirements are an ALA-accredited MLS degree and 2 years of professional experience. West Dublin is a town of 35,000 located in one of the most scenic areas of New England. The community is dedicated to maintaining high quality educational and cultural activities. Annual salary range is $27,554–$33,678. Applicants may call 203-568-9977 or write to **Personnel Services, West Dublin Public Library, 700 Pine Street, West Dublin MA 06764**.

YOUTH SERVICES LIBRARIAN. Green Valley Public Library, Green Valley, Ohio. This person manages youth services for a four-branch library system in an active community of 120,000 people. An enthusiastic and energetic individual is needed to initiate and coordinate creative youth programming including summer reading programs, school visits, computer services, and storytelling. People skills are important as the library works with other community groups in providing a wide range of services to a growing population. Requirements include an ALA-accredited degree and five years of public library experience. Salary range is $31,435–$34,780. Excellent benefits and opportunities for further education. For application, call, write or e-mail: **Human Resources Department, Green Valley Public Library, 25 Portal Road, Green Valley, Ohio 44152; 216-473-8000; publib@gvalley.org**.

Fig. 5.1. Advertisements for Children's Librarians.

The interview should always be held in a private, welcoming atmosphere, such as an office or meeting room. Water and often tea or coffee is usually provided for the candidate. This allows the interviewers to establish a pleasant, friendly atmosphere. A few minutes of small talk can help to ease the way into the more formal interview.

Both the interviewers and the candidate use the interview as an opportunity to learn more about each other and to assess how well they might work together. When interviewing several candidates for a job, it is useful to ask the same question of each candidate so that comparisons can be made. At the same time, each candidate should be allowed to talk freely and to express ideas that may move each interview in a slightly different direction.

The interviewer will want to open the conversation by briefly describing the job and the objectives of the interview. The next step is to ask questions that elicit information about the candidate's background and experience. Open-ended questions are the most useful because they allow the candidate to expand upon areas of interest and expertise. In other words, try to avoid asking questions that can be answered with "yes" or "no."

All questions in a job interview must be designed to elicit information relevant to the position. A number of areas are off-limits because they are too personal. All questions must conform to the guidelines issued by the Equal Employment Opportunity Commission. Examples of prohibited questions include the following:

- How old are you?
- Are you a U.S. citizen?
- Are you healthy?
- Do you smoke?
- Are you married?
- Do you have children?
- Do you have plans to become pregnant?
- What are your child care arrangements?
- What is the occupation of your spouse?
- What kind of discharge did you receive from the military?
- Have you had any major illnesses in the past five years?
- Have you ever been treated for drug addiction or alcoholism?

In general, all non-job-related questions are prohibited. Some specific questions about physical abilities are acceptable, including the following:

- Can you meet the attendance requirements of this job?
- Can you perform the functions of this job with or without reasonable accommodation?
- Can you describe or demonstrate how you would perform these functions? (Russell 1997, 11)

Before making a hiring decision, librarians should scrutinize the job application and check all references provided. An applicant may be asked to explain any breaks in the employment record. A rise in the reports of violence in libraries has led some administrators to recommend that a criminal background check should be made of all potential employees (Willits 1997), although few libraries routinely do this. In some jurisdictions, employees are fingerprinted after being hired, and a background check is done at that time.

Careful notes should be taken during each interview so that comparisons can be made between the candidates. After allowing a few days for consideration, all of those involved in the interviewing process should discuss each candidate's interview. If the group disagrees on which candidate was the strongest, a second interview may be necessary. Eventually, a decision is made, and the successful candidate is offered the job. As soon as the position has been accepted, the unsuccessful candidates should be thanked for their applications and informed that they were not chosen.

Orientation of New Staff

For permanent, full-time employees, the department head usually conducts the introduction to the department. If another person is designated to do this, the department head should meet and welcome the new employee as soon as possible. Part-time employees, especially pages, are often introduced to the library by the member of the clerical staff who supervises their work. The department head should personally meet and welcome each new page.

Orientation to the physical environment is important because libraries are complex organizations. Every employee should know the location of the library's various departments and services, all entrances and exits, and staff lounges and facilities, as well as the location of other branches in the system. A floor plan of the library may help to orient new employees. Within the department, new employees need to know the location of various sections—the reference, picture book, and program areas—as well as photocopying and computing equipment, meeting rooms, public access washrooms, and telephones. It is easy for a person who has worked for several years in a particular building to forget to mention some of these facilities. A checklist can serve as a reminder of information to be covered during the tour.

Introducing a new employee to the department staff, as well as to relevant people outside of the department, is as important as giving the building facilities tour. The new employee should be introduced to each person who works in the department, and notes should be made to ensure that off-duty staff members will be introduced to the new employee as soon as possible. Receiving a welcoming and personal introduction to the department, as opposed to being thrust into a new situation without knowing coworkers, can make a crucial difference in shaping the newcomer's attitude about the job.

Social customs, such as contributing to a coffee fund, taking a turn at bringing refreshments, or having an annual staff potluck supper should be explained at this time. Details, like identifying those responsible for making coffee in the morning and describing where employees are expected to park may not seem important, but they make a difference in establishing friendly working relationships.

The time involved in teaching the procedures that a new employee is expected to master varies with the position. A new page may be quickly taught to shelve and check in and out materials, while a new librarian will spend many weeks learning different aspects of his or her job. Whatever the level of training, the department head should make sure that it is effective. Simple procedures should be clearly described and then demonstrated. The new employee should be allowed to watch someone perform the task and then to practice it. Because few people can remember oral instructions over time, a written description of the procedure should be available for future reference.

Staff Retention

Because library jobs are complex and demanding, the loss of a staff member causes difficulties throughout the department. A library manager should work hard to ensure that all staff members find their jobs challenging and satisfying. Staff members will then be less likely to look for other employment and more likely to provide excellent service.

Continuing Staff Training

Because libraries are constantly introducing new practices or modifying old practices, staff training must be continuous. Some additional training, especially for professional staff, takes place outside of the library at conferences and workshops. An effective administrator encourages staff members to attend such meetings because they offer training in specific skills and the discussion of new ideas. Meeting colleagues from other libraries or other professions often leads to such an exchange of ideas, which can result in broadening the scope of a library's work. A problem exists when a staff member chooses to attend workshops in only one area—storytelling or puppetry, for example—and resists suggestions that a course in computer software might be more valuable. Most library departments need staff members who are proficient in a variety of skills, and one of the tasks of the department head is to encourage a broad-based, rather than narrow, continuing education program.

Large library systems sometimes provide staff training for children's librarians within the system. This may be directed by a youth services coordinator, or each branch may take a turn planning a workshop. Depending on the budget, these workshops may be directed by outside experts or conducted internally, providing an opportunity for library staff to exchange ideas. In either case, meeting to share ideas about programming or services is generally beneficial. The practice should be encouraged on a regular basis. The stimulation of new ideas can enliven a department's services and prevent staff burnout.

No matter how extensive the opportunities for continuing education outside of the department, some staff training will take place within the department. In recent years this often occurred as new technology was brought into the library. When a library is planning a major change, such as installing a new computer system, careful thought should be given to staff training. The usual practice is to have outside experts instruct a small group of library staff members. Those staff members can train other staff members until, eventually, everyone can handle the new technology. All staff members must have the opportunity not only for instruction, but also for sufficient practice so that they become comfortable with the system. A department head may wish to require that all employees use new equipment frequently because those who do not practice at least twice a week tend to lose their computer skills. After the skills have been mastered by all staff members, others will have opportunities to use the computers.

Even when the technology being introduced is not a major change, such as the introduction of public Internet access in the children's department, staff training should be carefully planned. An enthusiastic introduction by a sales representative or a staff member can encourage a receptive attitude among staff members. Each individual should be given ample time to practice using the equipment until he or she feels comfortable with it. Staff members are bound to show various degrees of interest in computers, but few people are completely opposed to their use. All staff members who might be called upon to help patrons with the computers must become comfortable using them. When one or two staff members are allowed to become the resident computer experts and monopolize the facilities, service usually suffers. Because computers are standard equipment in most children's departments, the department head should expect all appropriate staff members to be able to use them and to know when service calls must be made.

Not all staff training involves technology. Changes in the community may make it desirable to offer continuing education sessions about working with different cultural groups, persons with disabilities, or the aging. Legislative changes may mandate training in copyright restrictions or handling fines. Social conditions may make it necessary to teach staff members better security measures. The library administration may decide how to deliver this training, or it may leave the decision to the discretion of the department head.

The principles of teaching involve introduction, motivation, explanation, and reinforcement. Methodology may include showing videos, bringing in experts, giving a talk at a staff meeting, or handing out written material. To be effective, most training should include two or more of these methods. It is important that staff members believe the training is necessary. A well-produced film or video, or an authoritative outside speaker is usually more persuasive than the department head or another staff member, unless the staff is already convinced of the importance of the subject. Discussing the issue with staff members and asking questions reinforces the lesson. If a video is used, a facilitator should try to elicit questions and discussion afterward. Written material is often ignored when it is the sole method of information dissemination, but it is useful for reinforcing information given in another format. If the training includes suggested actions, such as the way to react to a hostile intruder, role playing makes the learning realistic and memorable. Anything that actively involves the learner is likely to be remembered better than a lecture or other passive presentation.

Testing is rarely an acceptable way to assess what the staff has learned, but reminders can be effective. Short questions and answers in the staff newsletter or on the bulletin board, especially if they are phrased in a humorous way, can remind staff of what they heard at a workshop. In addition, printed materials, videos, cassettes, and other individual learning tools can be made available to staff for reinforcement.

Administrators suggest most of the topics for continuing staff training, but it is a good idea to ask staff members what kind of training they would find useful. Sometimes managers are unaware of staff members' concern.

Effective Meetings

Although many employees complain about having to attend meetings, they feel short-changed when not informed about library developments. A good manager tries to hold meetings that are informative, effective, and achieve the goals of the organization. Meetings can accomplish many different objectives, which include the following:

- share information
- solve problems
- eliminate time-consuming repetition in individual sessions
- generate ideas
- gain cooperation
- promote team spirit and consensus
- lessen impact of rumors
- assign responsibilities and initiate action
- provide training in new techniques and provide staff development activities (McCallister and Patterson 1997, 59)

The most effective meetings are usually planned in advance. First, a manager should determine whether a meeting is the best way to accomplish the desired objective. If the primary goal is to inform staff about a change in procedures or personnel, sending a memo or e-mail message might be more effective than calling a meeting. Meetings are an effective way to generate discussion and raise questions. If the purpose is to introduce a policy decision that might be controversial or appear threatening to some staff, a meeting is probably the best way to introduce the subject.

A written agenda should be prepared for most staff meetings so that individuals know what to expect. Usually the agenda should be circulated to participants about one week before the date of the meeting. In addition to the date, time, place, and the items to be discussed, it is often useful to include information about the type of meeting—decision making, planning, reporting. Background material should be sent out with the agenda, as well as suggestions about bringing other items. If guests will be attending the meeting, it is courteous to let staff know their names and the reason for their presence.

Organizational cultures vary in the degree of formality of meetings. In some libraries, participants sit comfortably in a circle of chairs, and coffee and cookies are provided. In other systems the setting is a formal board room and water is the only refreshment. A manager should try to balance between maintaining a formal style that might be perceived as intimidating and a laid-back meeting that degenerates into a cozy social event and accomplishes little. Staff members usually appreciate comfort, but they also prefer a well-organized and efficient meeting that allows them to get back to work in a timely manner.

Before the meeting starts, arrangements should be made to have a recorder keep minutes. Action minutes—recording decisions, rather than their discussion—will be sufficient for regular meetings. If controversial items of particular importance are to be discussed, it may be preferable to tape a portion of the meeting for future reference.

The manager should start the meeting on time, to encourage staff members to arrive promptly. Most staff meetings do not require elaborate parliamentary procedure, but the chair should ensure that each participant has a chance to speak and that no one is intimidated or silenced. The chair should also see that the agenda is followed and that the discussion does not wander. If the majority of the attendees want to discuss a particular topic further, a future meeting should be organized.

At the end of the meeting, the chair should summarize the decisions and agreed follow-up actions. The minutes should be written and distributed either on the library LAN or in paper copy as soon as possible.

Increasing Employee Job Satisfaction

Financial benefits to library staff are strictly limited by city administrators who make the salary decisions for all employees. Unlike many managers in profit-making organizations, the library manager usually has little control over how library salaries are allocated. This is particularly true in a unionized library.

Managers in public sector organizations should be aware of the ways in which nonmonetary rewards can be used to recognize employee achievement. Libraries benefit when employees are happy in their jobs and "nonmonetary rewards can intensify the employees' desire to succeed and can promote employee self-esteem" (Padilla and Patterson 1997, 35).

One of the most popular nonmonetary rewards is flexible work scheduling. Flextime allows employees the freedom to plan work schedules that fit their life patterns. Because the library is a public service organization, this freedom is limited by the need to have the library staffed during busy hours of the day and days of the week. Even working within these constraints, however, a manager can often find a way to allow employees some voice in their scheduling. Ordinarily, allowing flextime would be a decision made for the entire library, rather than one department, but it is an important enough issue for a manager to advocate on behalf of all staff.

Another way in which managers can help to increase employees' job satisfaction is to provide opportunities for career development. This can take many forms, such as job rotation, so that staff develop competencies in several areas; training courses or workshops; or the encouragement of participation in professional associations. Sometimes a manager can enhance an employee's enthusiasm for the job simply by listening to suggestions and being open to new ideas. Showing respect for an individual's ideas encourages job commitment and benefits both the employee and the library.

Celebrations of achievement through public recognition of a completed project or particularly outstanding service enable employees to feel that their work is appreciated. The only danger of this kind of recognition is that it may lead some employees to feel that the manager has a few favorite employees whose work is more valued. If a department head wishes to recognize achievement, he or she must be sure that all individuals have an equal chance to be honored. A star system, in which some employees are highly visible and others work in obscurity, can foster an unhappy and discontented work environment. A balanced approach should allow each employee's strengths to be recognized and encourage greater job commitment.

Handling Conflict Situations

Many managers prefer to believe that relationships within the department are friendly and supportive; they are often shocked and unprepared when a conflict erupts. Unfortunately, no matter how well a department is managed, disagreements between staff members or between a staff member and the department head occur. A department head should not react as though disagreements were a personal attack or a reflection upon individual management styles. Instead, the conflict should be treated objectively, as a normal part of life within any institutional setting.

Encouraging Effective Work Habits

Most library departments are small enough for all employees to fall under the direct supervision of the department head. Sometimes a second level of management oversees clerical assistants and pages. The small size allows direct relationships and frequent opportunities for face-to-face meetings among all staff members. The department head in this situation wants to be friendly and approachable, but this goal may conflict with the need to maintain an efficient work flow.

Library personnel often have greater flexibility than workers in factories or large offices. For example, a new staff member who informs the department head that she has instructed her eight-year-old son to telephone her every afternoon as soon as he arrives home from school may be encouraged by the department head to receive this call. If one day the department head notices that three patrons are waiting for the attention of this staff member, who is on the telephone giving detailed instructions to her son about which play clothes to wear, the supervisor is likely to feel that library service is suffering. What is the most effective form of intervention?

The supervisor may solve the immediate problem by offering to help the patrons, thinking that the telephone call will probably end soon. More direct discussion is needed. The supervisor should speak privately to the staff member to ensure that the situation does not reoccur.

During the discussion, the supervisor must first obtain the exact explanation. If it was a crisis, and the telephone call had to be extended, the incident might be overlooked. Anyone can occasionally have an emergency that disrupts their workday. It is more likely, however, that the telephone calls have become longer or more frequent because either the employee or the son enjoys them. If the child has fallen into the habit of calling three or four times during the afternoon to ask about one thing or another, it is unlikely that the employee is operating as efficiently as possible.

The supervisor must then set limits on the calls and see that the employee adheres to them. A warning may be sufficient to remind the employee of other obligations, which should reduce the number and length of calls. The supervisor must unobtrusively observe whether the librarian is spending an unacceptable amount of time on the telephone. It might be desirable for the child to call another library employee, with whom he will not be tempted to talk to for long, to say he has safely arrived home. If the child needs to talk longer with his mother, the employee might be encouraged to schedule her break, or even her lunch hour, when the child returns home. Then the longer conversations may be conducted in the staff lounge. It may also be possible for the mother to communicate with her child by e-mail, as long as the time involved is not excessive.

A less desirable way to ensure that employees do not spend too much time on personal phone calls is to limit phone use to library business. Employees may see this as rigid and unfair because many rely upon their business telephone to make necessary personal calls. As long as such calls do not interfere with library business, there is no real reason to outlaw them. A supervisor should try to consider employee's concerns and not deny them resources that can make their lives more satisfactory without adversely affecting library operations.

Most employees recognize that the library has a right to maintain working efficiency. They accept limitations on their behavior, as long as they believe that the entire staff is being treated in the same way. In fact, a manager who does not require appropriate work habits is not likely to be respected and liked as well as one who enforces reasonable and fair regulations. The department head may maintain close, friendly relationships with staff but owes it to the library to maintain effective library service.

Whether the problem is librarians surfing the Internet instead of helping patrons, pages talking with other high school students at great length, or circulation clerks making inappropriate comments about children's book choices, the principles are the same. The supervisor should first ask questions to assess the situation—whether it is a unique occurrence or a habitual pattern. Then the supervisor should privately interview the employee. The supervisor should always treat the employee with respect and try to understand the reasons for the problem behavior. Steps that are taken to resolve the problem should be based on changing the behavior, not on punishing the individual. The supervisor should explain why the behavior is a problem and describe appropriate behavior. Finally, it is up to the supervisor to suggest a solution. Usually it is better to suggest a different behavior, rather than prohibiting problem activities. A clerk who makes disparaging comments about the books children choose might be advised to give each child a book list, suggesting that they read some of them.

A summary of the discussion should be recorded in writing for the staff member's personnel file. After choosing a solution the supervisor must observe whether the undesirable activities cease. If the behavior reoccurs, the supervisor should have another meeting with the staff member and follow up by sending the individual a written description of the original solution. An employee must be fired if his or her behavior does not meet library standards. To terminate employment, a complete written record must be kept of the employee's unsatisfactory performance and of all of the attempts made by the supervisor to resolve the problem with the individual.

Handling Grievances

Unionized libraries have a series of agreed steps to be taken when an employee has a complaint concerning a management decision. A department head should be familiar with the union contract and aware of the steps to be taken when a formal complaint or grievance is filed. Many of the steps taken under union regulations are similar to those followed in any library grievance situation.

The supervisor must take each complaint seriously and listen to the employee's point of view. Occasionally a supervisor reacts to a complaint as if it were an idle comment. For example, a clerical staff member tells the department head that his vacation has been scheduled for August when he wanted it in early July. If the supervisor says something, like "Oh well, the beach is better in August. You'll get a better tan," the employee's unhappiness and sense of grievance will grow. The supervisor's friendship with staff members should not interfere with their role of manager and responsibility for mediating between the library administration and the staff.

After allowing the staff member to explain the grievance, the supervisor may need to ask other staff members about the facts of the case. Were the vacation schedules drawn up without working out overlapping requests? Did the circulation clerk fail to tell the pages that they could go on their breaks? Has one librarian been assigned to work every Saturday for a month? Was a new circulation assistant scolded in front of library patrons? No decision should be made until the accuracy of the charges has been determined. Often, complaints based on misunderstandings disappear when the facts are made clear.

If one employee treats another badly, the department head should try to rectify the situation and ensure that it does not reoccur. If someone did not receive the required break time, nothing can undo that action, but an apology and perhaps some extra break time will help to make up for the mistake. The supervisor's most important task is to correct the person who made the mistake and to firmly impress upon him or her that it should not happen again. Again, the supervisor should have a private discussion with the individual, explain why the action was inappropriate, and request a change in behavior. A written account of this interview should be placed in the employee's personnel file, in case similar events occur in the future.

A supervisor should try to find out how similar grievances have been handled in the past. A new supervisor can do this by looking at personnel records or talking with a personnel officer or the chief librarian. Current procedures should not make a sharp break with tradition. Staff members expect the library's response to be consistent with past practice.

It is better to prevent grievances than to have to deal with them. The supervisor should try to be sensitive to the mood of the department—not only among the librarians who spend a great deal of time together, but also among the clerical staff and pages. Is there bickering, snide commenting, or a set of cliques? These often indicate that the staff members are divided and that trouble may be growing. Tension often increases when libraries undergo changes; a large growth in community population or substantial building renovations, for example, can foster an increase in complaints.

When these conditions prevail, the department head should make special efforts to develop a good staff spirit. Also, the department head should request additional staff members or budget increases if the workload is growing. If the staff believes that the department head is trying to make work conditions more satisfactory, they are likely to feel better about their jobs. A manager who is seen to be working fairly and consistently to increase the library's effectiveness and who treats staff members with respect is likely to have fewer problems with grievances than one who appears to be remote and uninterested in or unaware of staff problems.

Security Issues and Common Problems

Threats to library security and damage to collections and buildings are frequently reported in the library press. The value of assets in libraries, especially computers, has increased in recent years, leading to a greater risk of theft; the presence of disruptive patrons in some libraries has forced changes in library security (Arterburn 1996); and natural disasters, such as fires, earthquakes, and storms, continue to plague a certain number of libraries each year. Such problems may be rare in any particular library, but they do occur. This does not mean that a department needs to become a tense, high-security area; an atmosphere of relaxed awareness rather than anxious suspicion is usually appropriate. In general, problems can be divided into two groups: those resulting from natural or manmade physical emergencies and those caused by dealing with people.

Although problems occur in even the best-run library, sound planning can minimize the damage they cause. Every library should have a policy, approved by the library board, that explains how various emergencies should be handled. These plans need to be reviewed and updated frequently, but no matter how often they are changed, every department should have a current copy of the plan readily available for all staff (Baltimore County Public Library 1987). Like general policies, contingency plans are often kept in a loose-leaf notebook available in each department for quick and easy reference. All staff members should be aware of the contingency plans and should know what is expected of them in various situations.

One Person in Charge

A basic principle of good administration is that at any time the library is open, one designated person should be in charge. One of the weaknesses in the emergency procedures of many libraries is their failure to specify the staff member in charge when an emergency occurs (Curry 1996, 182). This can lead to confusion and may put a staff member or patron in danger. Normally, the person in charge is the department head or another professional staff member.

During meal hours, coffee breaks, or on Sundays or evenings, when the professional staff may not be on duty, someone in the department should be made responsible for observing and handling emergencies and notifying the proper authorities if something dangerous occurs. Most minor problems, such as a leaking roof or broken furniture, can be handled by contacting the maintenance staff promptly or taking such common sense actions as putting a wastebasket under a drip in the ceiling. The major reason for having one individual officially in charge of the department at all times is that when a more serious problem occurs, staff members immediately know to whom they should report.

The individual in charge of the department should also be aware of any unusual happenings. These include building emergencies, such as a power outage, fire, or flood; medical emergencies; and criminal activities (theft, vandalism, or assault). A gray area of eccentric behavior on the part of patrons—sleeping, eating, talking aloud, or behaving in a bizarre or inappropriate fashion—may or may not reach a crisis level. Another common problem is loud or boisterous behavior often, but not always, caused by children or teenagers. The individual who is in charge of the department should be alert to possible problems and should monitor situations.

Reporting Problems

When a problem occurs in the department, it should first be reported to the building supervisor. Quite frequently a difficulty in one department is noticeable throughout the building, but this is not always true, especially if a department is somewhat isolated from other departments. The senior building administrator should be notified whenever the department implements emergency procedures. If a problem is not serious, the report may appear in a memo after the event. The branch head or chief librarian should be told about all unusual occurrences in every department.

Communication is one of the keys to avoiding crises in libraries, especially those involving problem patrons. Unless the librarian in charge of a department is aware of past patterns of behavior, he or she may be caught unawares by an unexpected crisis. An example of this is cited in an article in which a staff member becomes emotionally upset as the result of having a patron persistently stare at her (Curry 1996, 186–87). An earlier discussion at staff meetings of the patron's behavior and the distress it was causing a staff member might have avoided an unpleasant incident.

From the building level, the chain of command moves up to the library system. Any problem that necessitates calling in outside authorities should be reported to administrators at the system level. A continuing series of lower-level problems, such as disruptive children or teenagers is usually considered a matter for systemwide monitoring. Often, problems in one branch move to another; good communication can help prevent their spread.

Support from community resources, such as the police and fire departments, utility companies, and occasionally schools or other social agencies, is needed for many problems. The library's contingency plans should indicate when outside agencies should be notified. Need for the fire department is usually the easiest decision to make, because any indication of possible fire requires this attention. Knowing when to call the police or another agency is more difficult and should be covered in the library's contingency plan.

Developing a Contingency Plan Document

Developing plans for appropriate action in emergencies requires input not only from the library staff, but also from outside agencies. While the general principle of emergency response may be similar for many library systems, the implementation may vary considerably, depending on local conditions. It is important to know the way in which local agencies, such as the police, medical, and fire services, prefer to be informed of emergencies and which is the appropriate agency to be notified of particular occurrences.

The contingency document will probably be divided into sections dealing with physical emergencies, medical emergencies, and problem patrons. Each section may be written by a committee of staff members in consultation with appropriate outside agencies. Each section should consist of the general principles governing the event (emptying the building quickly in case of suspected fire, for example) and then a list of the specific procedures to accomplish those goals. The phone numbers of emergency contacts should be included. While the principles of dealing with emergencies may remain relatively constant, the specific procedures must be reviewed and updated at least twice a year and whenever a change of personnel occurs in a relevant department.

After the planning document has been drafted, it should be reviewed by the library administration, appropriate civic agencies, and the library board. The board will give final approval to the document and take responsibility for actions carried out under the plan. Individual librarians who are acting in accordance with the accepted contingency plans are thus relieved of liability for injuries that might occur during an emergency.

Common Emergencies

Fires, storms, power outages, and medical emergencies are some of the most common disasters that affect libraries. Less sudden, but equally serious problems, can be caused by insects and animals. To avoid severe consequences from each of these problems, planning, preventive action, and emergency reactions are necessary.

Fires

Although most libraries are in fire-resistive buildings, the danger of fire still exists. Fire can damage materials and cause injuries. Consultation with the library's insurance agents will be necessary for developing plans that deal with fire emergencies. In addition to contingency plans, libraries should have available preventive measures, including:

- fire alarms or detection systems that relay to a fire station;
- fire extinguishers located in areas where small fires might occur (around electronic equipment, wastebaskets, etc.);
- signs adjacent to fire exits advising the staff and public what steps to take in an emergency; and
- fire drills for the staff to prepare them to take appropriate action when a fire occurs.

Actions to be taken when the fire alarm sound or a fire is discovered may vary depending on the local situation, but the first priority is to evacuate the building. Patrons must be urged to leave the building immediately without stopping to pick up clothing or other possessions. School-age children are usually familiar with fire drills in school and will usually follow directions given by an adult in authority in such situations. Patrons with disabilities and preschool children, especially if they are not accompanied by an adult, need attention. Some children with disabilities cannot hear alarms and some cannot see where danger lies. These children can be partnered with another child or with an adult who can lead the way to safety. Children in wheelchairs may be able to walk with assistance or can be carried outside. Wheelchairs should be left behind, unless an exit without stairs is immediately available. Very young children should be led or carried out of the building. The librarian must be sure that every child is included in the evacuation. After a room has been emptied of people, the door should be closed but not locked.

Once outside of the building, children should be kept in a designated area until emergency personnel indicate that it is safe to reenter the building. If the building remains dangerous for a period of time, older children should be encouraged to go home. The librarian will have to arrange for preschoolers and children with disabilities to be picked up by parents or taken home by volunteers.

Storms

Plans should be made to cope with severe storms—blizzards, tornadoes, or hurricanes. Someone on the library staff should monitor weather reports so that any storm warnings will be passed on to administrative staff. A decision to close the library is usually made by the chief administrative officer, although occasionally the children's department may urge patrons to go home before the library is closed. Children should not be encouraged to leave the building if the storm threat is severe enough to endanger them on the street. During severe electrical storms or incidence of high winds, children are probably safer inside the library.

In regions where tornadoes occur, the library will have designated areas where patrons should be taken when the event is imminent. Everyone on staff should know the procedures to be followed when a storm occurs. Regular storm drills should be a part of continuing training for library staff.

Medical Emergencies

Medical emergencies affecting either staff or patrons must be handled quickly and decisively. The kinds of emergencies that can occur include heart attacks, seizures, psychotic episodes, choking, falls, and injuries ranging from a paper cut to a gunshot wound. Less acute medical problems arise when a child in the library develops a fever, a rash, or begins vomiting. The best contingency plan for medical emergencies is to have as many staff members as possible trained in first aid techniques. For staff members who do not take formal courses, brief training in emergency procedures should be periodically given at staff meetings.

The staff member who is in charge of the department when a medical emergency occurs must immediately decide what procedure to follow. Most communities have emergency telephone members to call for help when a serious medical problem occurs. If doubt about the seriousness the problem exists, it is better to be overcautious than careless.

While waiting for medical assistance to arrive, the library staff should keep the affected person comfortable and isolated from curious patrons. The department should have a blanket to keep the person warm and a first aid kit. Only immediate first aid should be administered. This includes resuscitation if breathing stops, treatment for choking, and stopping dangerous bleeding.

When a child in the library appears to be sick but does not require emergency treatment, the librarian must use judgment in deciding the action to take. If the child is with an adult but appears to have a contagious disease, the adult can be asked to take the child out of the library for the sake of other patrons. Similarly, if the child is with a sibling or other children, the librarian may suggest that they go home until the child feels better. If the child is alone and appears to have a fever or to be ill, the librarian may call the child's home and suggest that a parent or other adult fetch the child.

Animals and Other Creatures

Most libraries require pets to be left outside the building, except perhaps for special programs. (Guide dogs for patrons with disabilities are an exception to this rule.) Dogs that are tied outside the building can be a nuisance if they bark and can become a problem if the owner leaves them for too long, especially in bad weather. If an animal is obviously uncomfortable, the child should be asked to take it home and to return to the library at another time. Children need to be encouraged to treat their pets humanely.

A variety of wildlife—birds, bats, skunks, raccoons, mice, stray cats, and squirrels—may occasionally be found in the library. Sometimes a bird or animal that has blundered into the building will leave quickly if given the opportunity (through an open door or window). If this does not happen, the animal control department should be called. A wild animal may carry rabies and can endanger staff and patrons. Unless a staff member has special expertise, it is unwise to try to catch a wild animal without help. Obviously, children should never be encouraged to try to catch wild creatures. At best, amateurs may frighten the creature and cause it to injure itself in attempting to escape; at worst, they may kill the animal or cause it to attack a person. Most animals that invade a library will stay out of the way of people, if not disturbed, and can be left in peace until the authorities arrive.

Some pests that invade libraries do not create immediate emergencies but pose long-term problems. Insects that attack books are not a major problem in most children's departments, where turnover is high. Household pests, such as ants, roaches, beetles, and silverfish, are generally kept in check by regular pest control and good maintenance.

Allowing food in public libraries can invite insect infestations. The most effective way to avoid these situations is to enforce firm rules against food in the library, which may not fit with library priorities. Several public libraries now have a designated area where patrons can obtain coffee, soft drinks, and snacks. These facilities are extremely popular with patrons who have grown used to bookstore cafes. It is probably wise, however, not to allow food to be eaten in the children's department. If a program for children features food, it should be confined to a limited area that is cleaned soon after the end of the program.

Problem Patrons

Because the library is a public institution, it must provide open access for all members of the community. But because not everyone in a community uses the library for the same purposes, some patrons can cause problems. These problems range from the minor irritation of noisy babies to the serious threat of would-be rapists or drug dealers. Librarians must know how to deal with these diverse difficulties.

Unattended Children

Children who come to the library for periods of time before or after school each day while their parents are at work are often called latchkey children or self-care children. While the presence of these children in the library offers librarians an opportunity to encourage the reading of books and the use of other materials, the length of time that the children spend in the library may cause problems. Often, these children have been told by their parents to remain in the library until someone arrives at home to take care of them. This means that after school and on holidays, a number of children may be confined to the library when they would rather be doing something else. Although they may not be disruptive, many of these children are not content to read or use library materials during their entire time at the library. A lack of other kinds of activities may lead them to start playing boisterous games or loudly socializing. If Internet access is available, they may tend to monopolize the computers; thus keeping other children from using them.

Most children's librarians are committed to providing the best possible service to latchkey children. In recent years, several studies and conference programs have focused on the library's response to these children (Dowd 1989). Several libraries have tried to meet the needs of these children by providing organized after school and school break activities. Providing these services requires both staff time and money. If a library is hard-pressed to offer conventional services, it will probably not want to take on additional duties. Some libraries have posted signs requiring that all children under a specified age must be accompanied by an adult, but this leaves children within walking distance of the library unable to visit it as often as they would like.

The increasing numbers of unattended children in libraries over the past few years has led a number of libraries to develop and publicize policies concerning the library's responsibility toward them. Policies may include a statement, such as the following:

> If an unattended child is being disruptive, is habitually left unattended for long periods of time, or is deemed to be at risk of coming to harm (as in the case of a child being left unattended when the library is ready to close), an effort will be made to locate the responsible parent, guardian, or caregiver. If necessary, appropriate law enforcement or child protective authorities will be notified to take custody of the child (Allen County Public Library 1996).

Because providing after-school services for school-age children is a community-wide issue, it may be wise for the library to seek a cooperative arrangement with other agencies. For example, the library could provide programming one afternoon a week, with the understanding that other community groups will organize programs for the other four afternoons.

Disruptive Children

A growing problem in many children's departments are young children who come to the library with an adult but are not effectively supervised. The youngest of these are preschoolers who are told to stay in the children's room while their caregiver looks for books in the adult department or leaves the library for a short time. Sometimes a three- or four-year-old can browse contentedly in the picture book section for an hour or so, but younger children are likely to start pulling books from shelves, crumpling pages of magazines, or interfering with other children who are reading or playing games.

The only recourse for the library staff is to prevent the child from continuing disruptive behavior, while watching for the return of the adult who brought the child. A polite but firm explanation that young children cannot be left alone in the library may prevent future occurrences, but sometimes more serious action is needed. The child may be taken to the adult, or the adult may be told that they will be denied use of the library unless the child remains under supervision. To make this treatment effective, the library staff must be vigilant in watching for potentially disruptive preschool children who accompany adults.

Older children frequently like to work on school projects or homework in groups. This often causes considerable noise but is not a problem if it does not disturb other patrons. However, when children begin fighting or pushing and shoving each other in a disruptive way, the librarian has to take some action. The first step is a reprimand and a reminder that the library should be a place where everyone can carry on their activities in peace. A second warning should include the statement that if the behavior does not stop, the individuals involved will have to leave the library. If this is unsuccessful, the children should be asked to leave with the provision that they may return when they are prepared to behave appropriately.

If the same group of children continues to be disruptive, they may be barred from using the library for a period of time—a week, for example. Barring children from the library should be done with caution, because public libraries are meant to encourage, not discourage, use. Sometimes groups of children who are not allowed into the library will hang around outside and harass library users. If the situation persists, it is usually best to try to gain the group's cooperation by meeting with them to discuss causes and possible solutions to problems. Allowing the youngsters to have some say in developing library rules may help to make them cooperative patrons. If the children habitually use the library, it is clear it is where they want to be. The library should make it possible for children to use the library without disrupting service to others.

Serious Delinquency

Occasionally children or teenagers go beyond merely causing annoyance or disruption of services. Vandalism may take the form of defacing books and other materials or damaging or defacing the library building or grounds. If the culprits can be identified, their parents should be notified of the activities. If this does not put a stop to the vandalism, the police must be called. Police generally take damage to the building or grounds of the library more seriously than damage to materials. Persistent tearing or marking up of books can be a serious problem, but it is often difficult to trace the offender. Carefully monitoring materials as they circulate can narrow the field of suspects and lead to identification of the offender. Usually, if the offender is a young person, notifying the parents and requiring payment for the damage are the most effective deterrents to further vandalism.

Theft of books or other materials, such as cassettes and compact discs, which are particularly vulnerable, can be a major issue. Even with an effective security system, a library can expect to lose a certain percentage of materials each year: two to four percent loss has been suggested as the average (Lincoln 1984). When loss numbers are higher than this, librarians should try to institute more effective measures of security, depending on the type of material stolen. Cassettes, compact discs, computer disks, and videos are frequently kept behind the desk. The patron selects from the empty cases on display and when the transaction is made, receives the actual item. This helps to cut down on the loss of material from the shelves but does not solve the problem of borrowers who fail to return items. Days or weeks of amnesty sometimes produce a flood of overdue materials, but many librarians feel that amnesty is unfair to patrons who return materials on time. No comprehensive solution is probably available to the problem of theft. Alerting the community to the severity of the problem through media releases may gain community support. If the problem becomes severe, local police officials or security consultants can sometimes suggest preventive measures. Certainly the police should be notified if there appears to be systematic or widespread theft of library materials.

In addition to the common problems of vandalism and theft, some libraries have problems with the use or distribution of illegal drugs in the library. While these offenses are most often perpetrated by teenagers or adults, school-age children are sometimes involved. Librarians can minimize the opportunity for drug dealing in the library by making sure that all areas of the children's department can be monitored by the library staff. Bookshelves and seating should be arranged so that the library staff can observe the entire room. Washrooms should be kept locked and the key given to individuals on request. Except for young children, only one individual at a time should use the washroom, and the staff member should keep track of the length of time any one person has the key. These precautions may seem excessive in a small neighborhood branch library but are sensible in an urban setting.

Problem Adults

Most adults who use the children's department of a library do so either because they are accompanying children or because they are interested in children's materials. Occasionally, however, adults' behavior in the children's department may be questionable. Some public libraries, especially those located in the downtown areas of large cities, have made it a policy not to allow adults to remain in the children's department unless they are accompanying a child. Adults who wish to consult materials from the children's department are asked to use them in another area of the library. This approach may be necessary in some urban libraries, but most smaller systems prefer a more open policy. In most libraries, adult use of the children's department is considered acceptable, and parents, teachers, and students of children's literature often use the collection. Generally, librarians should assume that every individual has a reason for using the library and may do so unless his or her behavior impinges on the rights of other patrons. At all times, the person in charge of the department needs to be alert to potential difficulty (Baltimore County Public Library 1987).

Children's librarians should be aware that pedophiles who wish to meet young children are attracted to places where children congregate. The precautions mentioned above—making all parts of the department visible to library staff and limiting access to the washrooms—tend to discourage such individuals. Nevertheless, librarians should notice adults who are using the children's room and be especially wary if an adult approaches a child who did not come into the department with him or her. Frequently the child's reaction will indicate that the adult is a family member, but if it appears to be a stranger addressing the child, the librarian should intervene. This can be done unobtrusively by offering to help the child, thus forcing the adult to come up with a plausible explanation for his or her actions. Usually this will be enough to frighten a person away if the intention is to harm the child.

Many children are trained at a young age to be wary of strangers who could harm them. Books and courses that "streetproof" children are popular with parents in many communities. Sometimes, however, children have difficulty knowing whether an adult in the children's department works in the library or is a stranger. For this reason, many departments provide name tags for staff members; children know that these adults can be trusted. This can be especially important for male children's librarians, because most children are taught to be more suspicious of men than women.

In contrast to adults who like children for the wrong reasons, some adults are annoyed or irritated by children in the library. If a children's department is adjacent to the adult department, especially if the sound insulation is poor, the children's voices may be heard in the adult department. Some adults are disturbed by this noise, especially if they are trying to work. Often the problem can be solved by physically rearranging the library, so that the tables where adults might work requiring concentration will be farthest away from the children's area. Adult browsers will probably not be disturbed by the children's noise. Added sound insulation, including carpeting or sound baffles, such as felt or fabric hangings, can also be useful in reducing noise.

The library staff must set limits for noise in the children's department and not allow unreasonable demands for silence. A reasonable buzz of noise and conversation, punctuated occasionally by short periods of wailing or crying, is acceptable. Other patrons must learn to accept these sounds. An adult who is particularly irritated by noise could be offered the use of headphones to block out sound.

Children running around the adult department, shouting exuberantly or crying for long periods, are disturbing to others. Librarians can require that school-age children restrict their noise to an acceptable level. Adults accompanying young children who cry for an unreasonably long time can be asked to take noisy children outside until they have quieted down. In any public facility, the comfort of the majority of patrons and staff must be given due consideration.

Intellectual Freedom and Censorship

The development of the Internet has added a new dimension to discussions about intellectual freedom and censorship. The idea of children being able to access unmonitored information from people and organizations all over the world concerns many parents. When Internet access becomes available in public libraries, parents and other adults are concerned about what their children may see, read, and hear. Librarians must be aware that professional associations have debated these issues for many years and that respect for intellectual freedom is a basic professional commitment. An official document of the American Library Association (ALA) states: "Freedom of expression encompasses the freedom of speech and the corollary right to receive information. These rights extend to minors as well as adults" (ALA 1996a).

Access to electronic information is only the most recent development that has caused controversy in the ongoing discussion of intellectual freedom and its relationship to children. From the beginnings of public library service to children, arguments have occurred about the amount of freedom children should be given in choosing books. Recordings, films, videos, and Internet access have been added to libraries, but books are still the major target for complaints about library materials. As a public institution in a pluralistic society, libraries have an ill-defined relationship with children. Unlike public schools, they are not compulsory and not charged with providing formal education. Because they are funded by tax money, libraries are not free to cater entirely to majority taste but are expected to provide services that are, in some sense, a social good. They must offer recreation and entertainment to entice children to use their facilities but, at the same time, serve as quasi-educational and cultural institutions.

The philosophical basis of censoring children's materials is that because children do not have the knowledge or power to choose books and other materials for themselves, adults must do it for them. Many adults believe that children are likely to accept false information and values that are presented to them in books and other media. Most parents, librarians, and teachers want to give children materials that uphold generally accepted social values such as honesty, compassion, and tolerance, as well as love of family, community, and country. These values are widely held throughout society; authors, publishers, and printers tend to produce materials that reflect these values. Librarians, most of whom make their materials selections from mainstream selection aids, find that their choices rarely cause controversy. Nonetheless, ideas and values change over time and differ among various social groups, so there are always some materials on which people do not agree. Almost every librarian has heard objections raised to materials at one time or another, and the number of complaints has not diminished (Wirth 1996, 44). How librarians handle these objections can have a marked effect on the library's relations with the community and on the effectiveness of its programs.

Areas of Concern

Censorship attempts generally reflect four areas of concern, although these areas sometimes overlap. The first involves "family values," a term that is used by many people who want library materials to reflect a traditional pattern of marriage and sexual behavior. Some parents and other adults do not want children to read books that deal with unconventional sexual behavior. Picture books that portray a homosexual lifestyle, such as *Daddy's Roommate* (Willhoite 1990) have been challenged in a number of jurisdictions in North America.

Materials that adults consider damaging to traditional religious beliefs may draw objections. These materials may be characterized as promoting secular humanism or as being antireligious. Some parents object to materials about witchcraft and the occult; even the classic *Halloween ABC* (Merriam 1987) has drawn fire.

Political views are an area of concern to adults who object to books and other materials that might be considered communistic or socialistic. In the past, some books about the Soviet Union and the United Nations were challenged, although these concerns seem to have abated in recent years.

The fourth area of concern is minority rights. Some adults object to materials that they see as perpetuating stereotypes or as critically portraying a particular group. The popular *The Indian in the Cupboard* (Banks 1981) has been questioned on these grounds. Some libraries have had challenges to the alleged gender stereotyping in sex education books such as *Girls and Sex* (Pomeroy 1981).

In discussing censorship, it is important to remember that most adults agree about the type of material that should be provided for children. The boundaries of what is acceptable for children are constantly changing, however, and the materials that expand the boundaries, dealing frankly with topics formerly forbidden, are the ones that may cause problems. Different groups within society also have different standards for the subject matter and language of children's materials. Libraries, as public institutions, must respond to criticism from any community group. Librarians, through their associations, have sometimes stated that they oppose all forms of censorship, but with rare exceptions, they choose from a limited body of materials that has been preselected for children. Within the context of that selection, censorship issues can be seen as a continuing force in developing a community's sense of what is acceptable for children to read, hear, or view. The threat posed by the Internet is that material made available on it is not monitored by any publishing company or selection committee. The identity of the individuals posting material on the Internet may be unknown, and the materials themselves change from hour to hour. These materials, thus, pose a special problem to librarians protecting intellectual freedom.

Censorship attempts may occur when a minority of the population does not share a widely held belief and objects to materials that reflect that belief. People who believe in a literal interpretation of the Bible may object to materials that discuss evolution. When the number of objecting adults is small, the challenges are more of a nuisance than a threat to the library collection. On some issues, individuals on both sides may believe they represent the majority of community opinion. Individuals may object to having points of view different from their own reflected in the library collection, on the grounds that "everyone" shares their attitude toward profanity, sex, evolution, and politics. It can be difficult to persuade these individuals that other people in the community have different values.

Some people may object to a book or other material that portrays behavior contrary to their norms, even though such behavior may be common. Examples would be the use of irreverent or obscene language or incidents of shoplifting or vandalism by children. Even though the behavior may be condemned or shown as inappropriate in the context of the materials, the mere treatment of the behavior raises objections.

Many adults believe that if public institutions, including libraries, do not provide materials about unacceptable behavior, children will remain unaware of such behavior. A librarian committed to intellectual freedom takes the position that children should be made aware of a variety of behaviors and ideas, both good and bad, so that they will be able to evaluate them and to make informed choices. These two beliefs rest on different assumptions about the nature of reading and using materials, so conflicts between the proponents of the two beliefs will always occur. The battle over censorship is a continuing one in a democratic society and librarians should make an ongoing commitment to intellectual freedom.

Issues of Internet Access

An increasing number of public libraries in North America are connecting to the Internet. A 1996 report reveals that public libraries in the United States have made impressive gains in connectivity: from 21 percent of public libraries connected to the Internet in 1994, to 44 percent connected in 1996 and a projected 76 percent connected by March 1997. In terms of public access to the Internet, public libraries went from 13 percent providing public access to the Internet in 1994, to 28 percent in 1996, and to a projected 50 percent by March 1997 (National Survey 1996). Although great discrepancies still exist in the provision of Internet services in various libraries, the trend to universal access appears to be accelerating.

Internet access for library patrons raises a number of intellectual freedom issues for librarians. Receiving the most attention is access to inappropriate material for young people, including sexually explicit material, hate literature, and antireligious materials. Most library materials are selected after librarians have reviewed them or read their reviews. Material on the Internet is not monitored. Anyone with the proper equipment can mount a website, and librarians cannot preview material before it is accessed by the patron. The library is, therefore, unable to reassure parents or children that the information acquired on the Net is accurate, unbiased, and reliable. Internet access presents a new set of problems for youth librarians.

The ALA policy on Access to Electronic Information clearly states that "users should not be restricted or denied access for expressing or receiving constitutionally protected speech" and "the rights of users who are minors shall in no way be abridged" (ALA 1996a). The responsibility for limiting children's access to electronic information lies with the parents, not with the library.

Although librarians do not monitor patrons' use of the Internet, they have a legitimate interest in encouraging responsible use and have tried different systems of doing so. The most controversial method is to install filtering software that blocks access to websites considered inappropriate. However, according to one critic, "Installing blocking and filtering software on Internet terminals may seem like an easy way to appease concerns about children accessing controversial information, but these tools put librarians in the role of censors, and undermine young people's rights to access information" (Champelli 1996). The filtering software is an imperfect method because it works on the identification of specific words or terms on a website. Thus, some librarians have reported that a website devoted to breast cancer was blocked from access, as well as sites that include the word *sex*, even when used in sites concerning sex education.

Another approach that is taken by many librarians is to provide lists of appropriate websites where children can find information relevant to their school assignments or other interests. Because the amount of time that each child can spend on the Internet is frequently limited by library policy to a half hour or an hour, children can locate sites useful for their information needs but do not have time to cruise the Net aimlessly and find objectionable materials. Librarians can also provide copies of suggested Internet guidelines for children that will help parents set limits on home use of this medium.

At its 1997 annual conference, ALA announced the start of a parent education campaign to offer advice and suggestions to parents about their children's use of the Internet. Brochures are available from ALA's Public Information Office for distribution in libraries. At the same conference, the ALA Council passed a resolution affirming that the use of filtering software by libraries violated the "Library Bill of Rights." Children's librarians should be aware of these developments and keep up with evolving professional standards that affect their work.

The best way to keep up with discussion on the use of the Internet in public libraries is to subscribe to children's librarians' listservs (see Chapter 17). Topics discussed on listservs include the issue of adult patrons who observe children viewing sites they consider objectionable. Complaints about the materials that other library patrons are using are not generally considered valid, but the visibility of computer screens has made them an object of interest to many adults. Websites are accessed in a more public way than most library materials, thus making them more vulnerable to complaints. Some libraries have arranged computer terminals close to a wall for the privacy of the individuals using them. Many issues of this sort can be expected before Internet access in public libraries becomes a standard and accepted practice.

The second intellectual freedom issue with the Internet is respecting the rights of content providers. Much of the information posted on the Internet is copyrighted and neither text nor graphics should be downloaded and used as part of an assignment without giving credit to the author. Youth librarians should display rules for the fair use of electronic information and instruct patrons about appropriate behavior. Many libraries have developed guidelines for the acceptable use of the Internet. One example of such a policy is shown in figure 7.1.

Disclaimer

The Internet and its available resources contain a wide variety of material and opinions from varied points of view. Users need to be good information consumers, questioning the validity of the information. Not all sources on the Internet provide accurate, complete or current information. The user is the selector in using the Internet with individual choices and decisions. The Internet is not monitored by any entity. Users may encounter material that could be considered inappropriate.

Parents of minor children assume responsibility for their children's use of the Internet through the Library's connection. Parents and children are encouraged to read *Child Safety on the Information Highway* and *My Rules for Online Safety.*

The Library expressly disclaims any liability or responsibility arising from access to or use of information obtained through its electronic information systems, or any consequences thereof.

Internet Acceptable Use Standards

All electronic traffic originating from the Indianapolis-Marion County Public Library Connection shall be in accordance with these *Acceptable Use Standards.* Failure to abide by these standards may result in the loss of Internet privileges.

Acceptable Use

Use of the library's Internet Connection shall be guided by the following principles:

1. Respect for the privacy of others.

2. Attention to the legal protection provided by copyright and license to programs and data.

3. Consideration for the security and functioning of computer networks and systems.

4. Library staff may limit PC access time if other library patrons are waiting for access to PCs.

Unacceptable Use

1. It is not acceptable to use the Indianapolis-Marion County Public Library Connection for any purposes which violate U.S. or state laws, to transmit threatening, obscene or harassing materials, or to interfere with or disrupt network users, services or equipment. Disruptions include, but are not limited to: distribution of unsolicited advertising, propagation of computer worms and viruses, and using the network to make unauthorized entry to any other machine accessible via the network. Illegal acts involving the Library's Internet Connection may be subject to prosecution by local, state or federal authorities.

2. Users may not represent themselves as another person.

3. Users shall not develop programs that harass other users or cause harm to other computer systems. Examples of such programs are computer "viruses" and "worms."

4. It is assumed that information and resources accessible via the Internet are private to the individuals and organizations which own or hold rights to those resources and information, unless specifically stated otherwise by the owners or holders of those rights. It is therefore

Fig. 7.1. Acceptable Use of the Internet Policy. Reprinted by permission of the Indianapolis/Marion County Public Library.

not acceptable for an individual to use the Library's Internet Connection to access information or resources unless permission to do so has been granted by the owner or holder of rights to those resources or information.

5. Malicious use is not acceptable. Use of the Indianapolis-Marion County Public Library Connection and any attached network in a manner that precludes or significantly hampers its use by others is not allowed.

6. Unsolicited advertising is not acceptable.

7. Computing resources shall not be used to access pornographic materials.

8. No purchase may be made via the Internet Connection. There is no security for credit card numbers or account numbers in the Library's software.

Modifications to These Standards

The Indianapolis-Marion County Public Library reserves the right to modify these standards at any time.

Return to Main Menu

Indianapolis-Marion County Public Library
Post Office Box 211
Indianapolis, IN 46206

http://www.imcpl.lib.in.us/

Intellectual Freedom and Professional Ethics

The defense of intellectual freedom is an important aspect of professional ethics for librarians. The American Library Association's "Statement on Professional Ethics 1981" includes the injunction "Librarians must resist all efforts by groups or individuals to censor library materials" (Lindsey and Prentice 1985, 64). Libraries exist to provide access to information, not to restrict it. Because intellectual freedom is a central issue in librarianship, many professional organizations have adopted statements concerning librarians' behavior in its regard. The ALA's Office for Intellectual Freedom has prepared extensive reviews of the historical background and issues involved in intellectual freedom (ALA 1996b). The basic intellectual freedom document of the ALA is the "Library Bill of Rights," reprinted in figure 7.2.

Library Bill of Rights

The American Library Association affirms that all libraries are forums for information and ideas, and that the following basic policies should guide their services.

1. Books and other library resources should be provided for the interest, information, and enlightenment of all people of the community the library serves. Materials should not be excluded because of the origin, background, or views of those contributing to their creation.

2. Libraries should provide materials and information presenting all points of view on current and historical issues. Materials should not be proscribed or removed because of partisan or doctrinal disapproval.

3. Libraries should challenge censorship in the fulfillment of their responsibility to provide information and enlightenment.

4. Libraries should cooperate with all persons and groups concerned with resisting abridgment of free expression and free access to ideas.

5. A person's right to use a library should not be denied or abridged because of origin, age, background, or views.

6. Libraries which make exhibit spaces and meeting rooms available to the public they serve should make such facilities available on an equitable basis, regardless of the beliefs or affiliations of individuals or groups requesting their use.

Adopted June 18, 1948; amended February 2, 1961, and January 23, 1980, by the ALA Council.

Fig. 7.2. Library Bill of Rights. Reprinted by permission of the American Library Association.

In addition to the general principles of intellectual freedom, some issues apply specifically to children. Article 5 of the "Library Bill of Rights" states: "A person's right to use a library should not be denied or abridged because of origin, age, background, or views." In order to clarify the ALA position on access to library materials, the ALA Council adopted an interpretation of the "Library Bill of Rights" called "Free Access to Libraries for Minors," shown in figure 7.3.

This basic statement about children's right to use the library has been amplified by interpretations approved by ALA. The position on access for children and young people to videotapes and other nonprint formats is: "Policies which set minimum age limits for access to videotapes and/or other audiovisual materials and equipment, with or without parental permission, abridge library use for minors" (ALA 1997). A similar interpretation is included in the document "Access to Electronic Information, Services, and Networks" approved by ALA Council at the 1996 Midwinter Meeting (ALA 1996a). Each of these documents is a powerful weapon for the librarian in combating attacks on library materials.

Free Access to Libraries for Minors

An Interpretation of the LIBRARY BILL OF RIGHTS

Library policies and procedures which effectively deny minors equal access to all library resources available to other users violate the LIBRARY BILL OF RIGHTS. The American Library Association opposes all attempts to restrict access to library services, materials, and facilities based on the age of library users.

Article V of the LIBRARY BILL OF RIGHTS states, "A person's right to use a library should not be denied or abridged because of origin, age, background, or views." The "right to use a library" includes free access to, and unrestricted use of, all the services, materials, and facilities the library has to offer. Every restriction on access to, and use of, library resources, based solely on the chronological age, educational level, or legal emancipation of users violates Article V.

Libraries are charged with the mission of developing resources to meet the diverse information needs and interests of the communities they serve. Services, materials, and facilities which fulfill the needs and interests of library users at different stages in their personal development are a necessary part of library resources. The needs and interests of each library user, and resources appropriate to meet those needs and interests, must be determined on an individual basis. Librarians cannot predict what resources will best fulfill the needs and interests of any individual user based on a single criterion such as chronological age, level of education, or legal emancipation.

The selection and development of library resources should not be diluted because of minors having the same access to library resources as adult users. Institutional self-censorship diminishes the credibility of the library in the community, and restricts access for all library users.

Librarians and governing bodies should not resort to age restrictions on access to library resources in an effort to avoid actual or anticipated objections from parents or anyone else. The mission, goals, and objectives of libraries do not authorize librarians or governing bodies to assume, abrogate, or overrule the rights and responsibilities of parents or legal guardians.

Librarians and governing bodies should maintain that parents—and only parents—have the right and the responsibility to restrict the access of their children—and only their children— to library resources. Parents or legal guardians who do not want their children to have access to certain library services, materials or facilities, should so advise their children.

Librarians and governing bodies cannot assume the role of parents or the functions of parental authority in the private relationship between parent and child. Librarians and governing bodies have a public and professional obligation to provide equal access to all library resources for all library users.

Librarians have a professional commitment to ensure that all members of the community they serve have free and equal access to the entire range of library resources regardless of content, approach, format, or amount of detail. This principle of library service applies equally to all users, minors as well as adults. Librarians and governing bodies must uphold this principle in order to provide adequate and effective service to minors.

Adopted June 30, 1972; amended July 1, 1981; July 3, 1991, by the ALA Council.

Fig. 7.3. Free Access to Libraries for Minors. Reprinted by permission of the American Library Association.

The responsibility for restricting children's access to certain materials in libraries rests with parents. Most libraries today accept the principle of free access for all patrons to all parts of the collection. If parents want their children to take materials only from the children's department or other designated areas, they should inform the child. With young children who visit the library primarily with their parents, this does not become an issue because parents can easily discourage children from taking out material of which they disapprove. Babysitters, day care workers, teachers, and other adults who accompany children to the library also frequently monitor children's choices.

When children begin to use the library on their own, they may select materials of which their parents disapprove. For this reason many challenges to materials are made by the parents of school-age children. Some libraries have printed notices distributed with new library cards informing parents that the responsibility for restricting access rests with them and not the library. This notification is useful in defending the library but does not prevent complaints. Parents often believe, quite justifiably, that if they prohibit certain types of materials, their children might be tempted to seek them out deliberately. They prefer to have the library restrict access, rather than do it themselves. Librarians must convince parents that the library has a responsibility to purchase materials for the entire community—adults as well as children—and that materials objectionable to one group are often acceptable to another.

Although parents have the major role in protecting their children from undesirable materials, libraries do accept responsibility for selecting materials that are generally accepted as appropriate for children. Objections from parents or other individuals or groups should be treated seriously as indications of community beliefs and feelings, even though they may seem to the librarian to be completely baseless. Psychological studies of people who feel strongly that library materials need to be limited to those that agree with their viewpoint often indicate that these individuals have authoritarian personalities. That is, they have a dogmatic and simplistic approach to censorship and see it as a way of controlling the behavior of other people (Fine 1996). The library's position on intellectual freedom must be explained and defended as a positive attempt to provide a wide range of information and recreational materials within the norms of current social acceptance.

School Media Centers

Because school media centers are parts of a compulsory educational system, they are more vulnerable to censorship attempts than public libraries. Some school librarians justify not buying controversial books on the basis of their availability in public libraries. Adults who succeed in having books removed from curricular use or from school libraries may later attempt to have them removed from public library shelves. The best defense against this is for school and public librarians to work together to defend intellectual freedom in all libraries.

Dealing with the Community

One way to cope with attempts at censorship is to avoid them, but this must not be accomplished by practicing timid selection. Instead, patrons and the rest of the community should be made aware of the kinds of materials the library provides and the reason for their provision. All librarians should be familiar with the guidelines of the ALA's Office for Intellectual Freedom and should stay abreast of professional literature on the subject, such as through the ALA's bimonthly *Newsletter on Intellectual Freedom*. The ALA also publishes helpful materials that librarians can use in devising strategies for coping with complaints (Reichman 1988; ALA 1996b). Workshops at conferences or within the library system can help to make librarians, trustees, and members of the public more sensitive to issues of intellectual freedom. When a number of censorship questions arise within their state or region, libraries should seriously consider planning this kind of educational training. Models are available for effective workshops (Schexnaydre and Burns 1984).

Dealing with Concerns About Library Resources

As with any public service, libraries receive complaints and expressions of concern. One of the librarian's responsibilities is to handle these complaints in a respectful and fair manner. The complaints that often concern librarians the most are those dealing with library resources or free access policies. The key to handling these complaints successfully is to be sure the library staff and the governing authorities are knowledgeable about the complaint procedures and their implementation. As normal operating procedure, each library should maintain:

- a materials selection policy;
- a library service policy;
- a clearly defined method for handling complaints;
- in-service training;
- lines of communication with civic, religious, educational, and political bodies of the community;
- a vigorous public information program on behalf of intellectual freedom; and
- familiarity with any local municipal and state legislation pertaining to intellectual freedom and First Amendment rights.

These procedures will not preclude receiving complaints from pressure groups or individuals, but they will provide a base from which to operate when concerns are expressed. When a complaint is made, the librarian should listen calmly and courteously. Everyone in the community has a right to express a concern. Good communication skills can help the librarian explain the need for diversity in library collections and the use of library resources.

If, after discussion, the person is not satisfied, advise the complainant of the library procedures for handling statements of concern. If the person makes a written complaint, inform the administrator or governing authority (usually the library board) of the complaint. Promptly send full, written information about the nature and source of the complaint to the immediate supervisor, so that appropriate individuals can be briefed without delay. The complainant should receive a prompt written reply.

If the complaint becomes a public issue, the library should inform local media and civic organizations of the facts and enlist their support. The person or group making the complaint should not be allowed to dominate community information sources.

Contact the ALA's Office for Intellectual Freedom and the state or provincial intellectual freedom committee to inform them of the complaint and to enlist their and other agencies' support.

Several organizations, including the ALA and the National Council of Teachers of English, have published forms that can be used by libraries to obtain a written record of a citizen's request that a library reconsider its decision to provide certain materials. The ALA version of this form is reproduced in figure 7.4.

Dealing with Specific Groups

More requests to reconsider material are received from parents than from any other group (Jenkinson 1986). Many of these requests grow out of parents' natural desire to instill in their children the values they consider important. They may object to materials that suggest religion is not a necessary part of life or that particular groups of people are inferior or superior to other people. Whatever the particular viewpoint, the librarian should respect parents' feelings but insist on following professional procedures in dealing with the complaint. The key to dealing with parents is the phrase, "It is the parents—and only parents—who may restrict their children—and only their children—from access to library materials and services," contained in the ALA statement "Free Access to Libraries for Minors" (ALA 1996b). The library has a responsibility to provide a variety of materials; some of them may offend one parent but be strongly upheld by others. Many parents will see the force of the argument that if a book is removed at the behest of one parent, other books, which they may prefer, could be removed on appeal from other parents. No one individual or group—no matter how vocal—can be allowed to dictate the selection policies of a library that serves the entire community.

Occasionally individuals other than parents request the removal of materials from a children's collection. Many adults are not familiar with modern children's books and are shocked by the topics covered and language used in them. Often a calm discussion about the books or other materials will help to resolve these issues. Children occasionally object to materials they believe will be harmful to children younger than themselves. These objections give a librarian an opportunity to explain the concept of intellectual freedom and to talk about the reasons that the library provides a wide range of materials.

Organized groups sometimes try to have certain materials removed from libraries. Occasionally these groups have coordinated plans and use sophisticated techniques for gaining publicity and community support. If such a group becomes active in a community, it is helpful for libraries to share information about the way the group operates. In these circumstances, professional associations can be

Request for Reconsideration of Library Resources

[This is where you identify who in your own structure, has authorized use of this form—Director, Board of Trustees, Board of Education, etc.—and to whom to return the form.]

Example: The school board of Mainstream County, U.S.A., has delegated the responsibility for selection and evaluation of library/educational resources to the school library media specialist/curriculum committee, and has established reconsideration procedures to address concerns about those resources. Completion of this form is the first step in those procedures. If you wish to request reconsideration of school or library resources, please return the completed form to the Coordinator of Library Media Resources, Mainstream School Dist., 1 Mainstream Plaza, Anytown, U.S.A.

Name _____ Date _____

Address_____

City _____ State _____ Zip _____ Phone _____

Do you represent   Self   Organization?

1. Resource on which you are commenting (please specify):

Book   Textbook   Video   Display   Magazine

Library Program   Audio Recording

Newspaper   Electronic information/network

Other

      Title_____

      Author/Producer _____

2. What brought this resource to your attention? _____

3. Have you examined the entire resource?_____

4. What concerns you about the resource? (use other side or additional pages if necessary)

      _____

5. Are there resource(s) you suggest to provide additional information and/or other viewpoints on this topic?

      _____

Revised by the American Library Association Intellectual Freedom Committee June 27, 1995

Fig. 7.4. Statement of Concern About Library/Media Center Resources. Reprinted by permission of the American Library Association.

helpful. Usually the group does not represent a community majority, but it can become so vocal that its support seems greater than it is. Publicity in the local newspaper or on radio or television can help to raise public support for the library.

Besides requesting the removal of certain materials from libraries, people may sometimes insist that other materials be added to the collection. Most patron suggestions for additional materials are welcomed by librarians, but occasionally, patrons request materials that are not appropriate for the library. Usually these are religious materials that individuals or groups believe should be in the library. It is sometimes difficult to explain to people unfamiliar with library procedures that guidelines are in place for selecting materials, and that certain standards must be met. A selection policy that outlines the kinds of religious materials that will be included in the collection is helpful. A statement commonly used in selection policies disallows sectarian material; this policy statement often rules out the kinds of materials individuals or groups wish to donate. It should be made clear that gifts must meet the same standards as purchased materials.

When Censor and Librarian Agree

Occasionally librarians are embarrassed to discover that they agree with an objection raised by a library patron. This can occur when shelves have not been weeded and outdated and offensively sexist or racist materials have been found. Such materials should be reconsidered in the light of current selection policies, and if they do not meet standards, they should be discarded or moved to the adult collection to represent a historical point of view. Material that a librarian finds offensive, but that has been recently selected through the usual channels should not be removed. The selection process in a library represents the overall library viewpoint, rather than that of any one individual, so some controversial selections will always be made.

A study by Jenkinson found that 12 percent of the materials questioned in public libraries were removed from the library (Jenkinson 1986). Other materials were retained but restricted to adult circulation. A more recent survey found that nearly 90 percent of libraries reported that, since 1990, no items had been removed because of a community request (Wirth 1996, 44). This finding indicates that, on average, less than one complaint in 10 results in the removal of materials. In cases where materials were removed, either the librarians agreed that the material was offensive or they did not want to become involved in an argument. Removal or restriction is the easiest way to resolve a censorship challenge, but it is also the most dangerous. Once librarians have given in to the people who want to limit library materials, they have abandoned the responsibility for maintaining their professional standards and ethics. "If the keepers of books, journals, films, compact disks, and software do not vigilantly defend free expression and intellectual freedom, who will?" (Hauptman 1988, 66). While parents and other community members have a right to challenge materials in the library, they do not have the right to take away the professional responsibilities of librarians. A strong stand against unwarranted interference with library practices is a way for a library to retain the respect of the community as a professional institution.

Organizing Special Events

Like other public institutions, libraries sponsor special events to offer patrons experiences outside of the normal library services, to inaugurate a new service, or to celebrate historic milestones. Occasions to celebrate may include any of the following:

- opening of a new branch
- inauguration of Internet service
- gift of a special collection
- the visit of an author, illustrator, or performer
- book sales
- storytelling festival
- art, craft, or historical exhibit
- public lectures

These events focus attention on the library and can attract beneficial publicity. To take advantage of the public relations value of these events, it is important that they be carefully planned.

Special events take considerable time, planning, and funds, so no library department can expect to host many of them. On the other hand, they provide invaluable publicity for a program and generate excitement among patrons and staff. A department head may wish to host at least one special event every six months to call attention to departmental activities. Among the most popular and effective events for children's departments are visits by an author or illustrator. This chapter will focus on such visits, but the principles discussed here are applicable to other special events.

Preparation

The first decision to be made about organizing a special event is its objective. Even events that are initiated outside of the department, such as the opening of a new branch, can be shaped to serve the department. If events are not well planned, the department may not receive good publicity and may appear in an unfavorable light.

The purpose of many events is to attract the largest possible crowd and to gain as much publicity as possible. In this way, residents who do not ordinarily use the library may be encouraged to attend the event and become library users. Events, such as branch openings, where the objective is to introduce as many members of the community as possible to the new facility, are examples of these large-scale special events. A constant movement of people through the building enables residents to learn how to get to the library and to view the facilities. Programs that encourage people to linger, such as films or storyhours, might cause overcrowding and prevent some people from entering the building.

A different kind of event—the visit of a children's author, for example—aims to provide a more intensive but smaller program. If the author writes difficult books for older children, it would be unwise to send out press releases inviting all children in the community to attend a reading. This would inevitably attract families with preschool children who would not be interested in the program and might be noisy and disruptive. The objective in this case would be to invite children of a suitable age who would be able to have an exciting, reasonably close interaction with the author.

The objectives of special events include the following:

- attracting as many people as possible
- attracting people of all ages
- attracting as many children in a particular age range as possible
- offering a specific group within a community a chance for an enriching experience
- attracting parents or professionals working with children
- attracting community leaders
- attracting members of a particular ethnic group
- attracting media—newspaper, television, and radio reporters
- attracting library workers from outside of the community

Initial Planning

If a department decides that it is time to arrange a special event, such as a visit from an author or illustrator, the first step should be brainstorming about the choices. Staff members and the children themselves can be asked which author or illustrator they would most like to have visit the library. (Be prepared for some impossible choices, such as Louisa May Alcott or Walt Disney.) Choosing a visitor whose books are popular with the library's clientele ensures a large audience, but widely popular authors may be difficult to schedule and to afford.

Authors and illustrators with some connection to the community may be easier to attract than national figures. If the visitor lives within a short distance of the library, both costs and time commitment will be minimized. Some authors who once lived in or visited the community may be particularly interested in participating. Other attractions are the author's regional interest or a relationship to an ethnic group within the community. Try to think of the reasons the visitor would want to visit a community, as well as why a library would invite him or her.

If after considering the possibilities, the staff agree that a nationally known figure would benefit an event, consider joining with other groups in the community to sponsor a visit. This not only limits the cost that each participating group incurs but also gives the visitor a wider audience and greater marketing potential for the visit. Schools, universities, bookstores, community or religious groups, and museums may be contacted as potential partners.

After drawing up a pool of potential candidates, talk to librarians who have heard each potential visitor speak. Colleagues who attend state and national conferences may have information, as can other librarians and teachers in the area. Library listservs, such as PUBYAC, also provide a forum for gathering opinions about the appeal of potential speakers.

Before investigating the specifics of a visit, check whether the library has the potential visitor's books. If necessary, the collection can be updated before the visit, but it is usually best if patrons have had time to read the books before the visit.

After obtaining the chief librarian's approval, the department head can proceed to implement the visit. Contact can be established through the publisher, whose representative will want to discuss the proposed dates, the type of presentation, the honorarium, and other costs to be covered. Be realistic and honest with the publisher about the amount of publicity that the event will receive, the size of the anticipated audience, and the number of the author or illustrator's books that are likely to be sold. All parties concerned should have realistic expectations for the event.

Constructing a Budget

During the initial stages of planning for a special event, the librarian should prepare a preliminary budget. It is not much different from the budgeting for regularly scheduled programs, but extra forethought should be given to major events. Occasionally a special event may appear to be free or inexpensive, but the costs in money and staff time can quickly mount. It is useful to estimate the costs before a final commitment is made, because the decision whether to have the event is based on the importance of the objectives in relation to costs.

Direct Costs

Direct costs can be divided into preparation, the event itself, and post-event completion. Preparatory costs include publicity (design, layout, printing, postage, and fees) and arrangements (telephone, postage, equipment rental, and costs of staff meetings). Event costs include honorarium and transportation; extra staffing (guards and janitorial staff if the event is held after hours); refreshments; programs; and photography. Post-event costs include cleanup, additional staff, and post-event publicity. A detailed analysis of building a budget for an author or illustrator's visit can be found in *Inviting Children's Authors and Illustrators* (East 1995).

Staff Time

Staff time for special events is frequently underestimated. Because the time spent in preparing for and carrying out the event must be taken from other duties and has a dollar value, it is a good idea to estimate its expected value. Cost of staff time can be estimated by the categories of workers carrying out tasks.

A department head will usually work the full day of the event, plus spend some time in preparatory meetings. Librarians will devote the equivalent of three or four days in correspondence, preparing publicity, supervising preparations, and attending meetings, as well as the full day of the event and the following half day for wrap-up. Clerical staff often spend the equivalent of one week's time preparing for a special event. Because clerical staff time is less expensive than professional time, as many tasks as possible should be allocated to them. Decisions should be made concerning which usual tasks can be postponed or eliminated for the time being.

Using Volunteers

One way to reduce staff time spent on special events is to use volunteers. Members of a Friends of the Library group will sometimes devote a great deal of time to a special event, especially if routine work is balanced by the opportunity to meet a well-known person. Older children and parents of library users are sometimes willing to contribute time to mailing publicity, decorating the children's room, or preparing and serving refreshments. In addition, adult volunteers may be willing to meet visiting dignitaries at the airport and to entertain them for a few hours while the library staff is busy with other preparations.

Although volunteers are not paid for their work, they should receive other rewards. Often the opportunity to meet an admired author or other guest is the major impetus for volunteering, but librarians should try to add other incentives. Librarians owe volunteers the courtesy of including them in planning sessions and listening to their suggestions. A volunteer who has given considerable time to welcoming and entertaining a guest might like to be included in publicity pictures and be mentioned in publicity releases. The volunteer would almost certainly appreciate an invitation to a luncheon or dinner for the guest. Any program prepared for an event should list the names of volunteers. The librarian's opening or closing remarks should mention volunteers who have given considerable time to the project. After the event, each volunteer should receive a letter of appreciation from the librarian. Children who help with a visit might be given a small gift, such as a paperback copy of a visiting author's book. Gracefully acknowledging the library's gratitude to volunteers will help to ensure a continuing supply of help for future events.

Publicity

Many large library systems have public relations or publicity departments that prepare press releases and arrange media contacts for all library events. The department head, however, is usually most knowledgeable about the specific audience for particular events and should keep the publicity department informed about all related details. Well in advance of the date when the department is to host a visit, the librarian should prepare information about the visitor, including background, publications, and potential audience. Many children's authors write for a particular age group, and the target for publicity might be the parents of preschoolers, day care personnel, or middle school teachers, depending on age level. Some authors write about a particular ethnic background; this can give an indication of community groups that might be particularly interested. A visiting performer, such as a magician, might be of interest not only to children but also to local entertainers or magicians; an artist or craftsperson will appeal to adults in craft classes, as well as to children. The more potential audiences that can be identified, the greater the event's likely impact.

In a small library, the librarian may be asked to prepare news releases. The key to writing a successful release is to be clear, concise, and lively. The release should open with the most important, eye-catching information, so upon seeing it, a person will not toss it aside without realizing its potential interest for readers. The first two or three short paragraphs are crucial because many newspapers cut news releases from the bottom up to shorten them. Therefore, important information, such as the date and time of the performance should never be placed at the end of the release, but near the beginning—usually immediately after the first, attention-getting sentence. Figure 8.1 shows a sample news release.

Newspapers and radio and television news programs often want more information about a project described in a news release. A librarian should be prepared to accept telephone calls from local media people and be able to give enthusiastic accounts of the upcoming program. It is useful to have biographical information about a speaker or performer available beside the telephone, so that queries can be answered quickly and knowledgeably. If the information requested is not immediately available, a follow-up telephone call should be made as soon as possible. Media people work on short deadlines, and a story may not be covered if the library does not supply details promptly. Requests for interviews with a librarian about the program, either in person or on the telephone, should be encouraged. Not only does the program receive greater publicity, but the library's reputation as an informed and responsive institution is enhanced.

White Lake Public Library

410 Silver Ranch Road
North Canyon, New Mexico 88932
Tel: (505) 666-7234
Fax: (505) 666-7269

Nelson J. Peterson, City Editor, *White Lake Journal*
473 Main Street, North Canyon, NM 88932

Contact: Agnes Geary, Children's Librarian
Tel: 666-7236 fax: 666-7269
E-mail: axg@publib.org

FOR IMMEDIATE RELEASE

Popular children's author Miguel Cortez will read excerpts from his recently published adventure story, *Ghosts of Riding Ridge*, at the White Lake Public Library on Sunday, February 17, 1998 at 2:30 pm. Children six and over as well as parents, grandparents, and other adults are invited to attend the reading.

The author of more than fifteen books for children and adults, Miguel Cortez is also well-known as a storyteller and historian. In recent years Mr. Cortez has established himself as an expert on the history and legends of silver mining. He is currently working on a television series about the history of mining in North America. In addition to his reading, Mr. Cortez will answer questions about his television writing and his historical research. Audience members who have tales to share about mining in this area will be invited to participate. Earlier this year Mr. Cortez received the Golden Arrow Award for notable achievement in historical writing.

Copies of Mr. Cortez's books will be on display at the library. Children may bring their own copies of his books for autographing.

###

Fig. 8.1. Sample News Release.

Media representatives, both writers and photographers, should be invited to attend any special event. If an event is particularly visual—involving a magician or artist, for example—the invitation should mention that feature.

The library's website is one of the most important places to post a notice of an upcoming event. Frequently, the publicist for a publishing company can provide biographical material and photographs to be mounted on the site to provide background for the announcement of the visit. Photographs of the visitor, the book jacket, or illustrations add greatly to the attractiveness of a website announcement.

Electronic notices sent to libraries and schools in the region, as well as to bookstores, community groups, and appropriate listservs, are effective. Besides informing potential attendees, these notices also let other librarians know the speakers and topics that might be available for other visits.

In addition to the media, community groups may provide effective publicity, especially in large cities or suburban areas where no appropriate local media outlets are available. Librarians may send news releases and flyers to schools, day care centers, churches, social or ethnic organizations, day camps, bookstores, and any other gathering place that seems appropriate. Volunteers may distribute flyers door-to-door in large housing complexes or post them in supermarkets, coin-operated laundromats, and shopping malls. An eye-catching and inexpensive flyer can be designed by the library's graphics department or by a librarian with access to computer graphics programs. The flyers may incorporate children's designs if time is available to run a contest or program to elicit drawings.

The most obvious pool of potential attendees for a library program is people who use the library. Large posters should be placed in both the adult and children's department several weeks before the program. Flyers should be displayed on the circulation desk or a publicity table near the library entrance. Circulation clerks should place small publicity pieces in each book circulated for the month preceding the event. Notices to parents are especially useful in informing about programs that may be of interest to them or their school-age children. The entire library staff, not just those in the children's department, should be aware of coming programs and be able to provide information about them. To facilitate this, the department head can post notices in the staff lounge, print announcements in the staff newsletter, send e-mail messages through the library network, and mention forthcoming programs at staff meetings.

Staff Preparation

Any special event that requires extra staff effort will probably go more smoothly if staff members believe the event is worthwhile. To increase enthusiastic cooperation from staff, many of them should be involved in its planning. Staff members will be more willing to undertake an event they see as a united effort than one that the administration forces upon them. Many staff members, from librarians to pages, will have ideas about publicizing and facilitating an event. Persons who are interested and willing to take responsibility for specific tasks should be encouraged to do so, with the department head coordinating the overall plans. One person might design publicity materials, another coordinate distribution of publicity, a third supervise physical arrangements (e.g., seating, cloak room, and decorations), and a fourth arrange housing for the guest. Distributing tasks among a number of persons lessens the burden on any one individual, although it means the department head or a designate must monitor progress in each area.

Because time spent on a special event is taken away from regular duties, the department head should discuss which regular tasks must be carried out and which can be postponed. The department head and staff should agree in advance on priorities. In a large department, the agreement should be put in writing to avoid later arguments or recriminations.

Volunteers should be recruited about six weeks before the event. By this time, library staff will have made the major decisions, but time will still be available to solicit ideas for details. Many volunteers, both children and adults, cannot make firm commitments of time more than four to six weeks in advance, so recruiting volunteers too early may cause some to drop out later.

Usually volunteers are recruited from regular library users or Friends of the Library groups. Because the staff has frequent and informal contact with these individuals, the librarian need only make informal inquiries until an appropriate number of volunteers are found. Occasionally, the librarian may ask an organization or group to volunteer for a particular program. Recruitment on this level requires a more formal approach, through telephone calls or letters to a contact person in the group.

No matter how volunteers are recruited, it is usually a good idea to follow up verbal communication with a written note about the expected activities. Note the specific dates and time: "taking tickets between 2:00 and 3:00 p.m. on Sunday April 18" or "distributing flyers to the Heather Hill retirement residence on April 10," for example. Putting agreements in writing will make it easier for volunteers to remember what they have promised, and for the library staff to identify the other tasks that need to be done.

The department in charge of the special event must inform the chief administrator about all plans, since programs are normally cleared through the administrative office. The chief librarian should be invited to attend the program and to welcome attendees. Because a special program in the children's department can cause extra work for staff members in other departments, other staff members should be informed of the event, so that they can plan their schedules accordingly. Most staff members appreciate at least being invited to programs, even if many of them will not attend.

Handling Visiting Celebrities

Several months may elapse between making arrangements for a visit and the final event. The visitor should be kept informed, in writing, of all plans as they develop. The department head will probably speak to the visitor by telephone several times in order to confirm housing and speaking arrangements. All such telephone calls should be followed up by a letter, so that no misunderstanding will occur. The publicist from the publisher's office should be copied on all of these letters. Details, such as the location, travel arrangements, housing, honorarium, and billing procedure should be clearly explained. If the program is to be taped, or photographs are to be taken for the library, written permission should be obtained. At least two weeks before the visit, a detailed itinerary should be sent to the visitor.

Many out-of-town authors or performers expect a staff member or volunteer to meet them at the airport. If the library cannot provide this service, the visitor should be given clear instructions regarding the ground transportation to take and directions to their destination, such as to a hotel or the library. When a visitor is to drive to the community, clear directions—preferably a map—should be sent well in advance. If the visitor arrives close to mealtime, clear information should be given about the arrangements made for a meal. It should never be assumed that visitors prefer to make their own arrangements for housing and meals. Occasionally, a visitor may be housed at a private residence. Some visitors prefer this arrangement because it is more personal than a hotel, but the host should ensure that the visitor has enough privacy to prepare the program and to prevent fatigue from constantly meeting new people.

The department head should try to meet the visitor as early as possible, either at the airport, hotel, or private home. This first meeting will give the librarian an opportunity to discover the guest's personal requirements. Some speakers prefer solitude for several hours before their presentation; others prefer to visit the library or a local attraction. Most visitors want to see where they will speak and to check equipment, such as computer equipment, overhead or slide projectors, and microphones.

Most meals, except for breakfast, provide opportunities to introduce the guest to library staff or community members. One staff member or volunteer should be responsible for the visitor during each meal. This person should ensure that the meal meets the visitor's preferences as to type of food and drink, including dietary restrictions. The staff member or volunteer must also ensure that one or two guests do not monopolize the visitor's attention and that the meal does not drag on and tire the visitor.

During the visitor's stay, whether it is for a day or for a weekend, a designated contact person should be available to answer the visitor's questions and handle contingencies. These may range from laundry, dry cleaning, or a midnight pizza, to the loss of cash and valuables, an illness, or an accident. The visitor should never feel friendless while visiting a library community.

On the day of the presentation, the visitor should be taken to the library with time to spare. Even the most sophisticated speaker can develop stage fright and want the reassurance of being close to the scene of the event. Equipment and facilities should be retested just before the event. Every effort should be made to meet the needs of the speaker, whether for solitude, the company of several people, or a glass of water.

The end of the program can mark the beginning of a difficult period for the speaker. No matter how successful the event and how warm the applause, the speaker may experience a letdown. The host librarian should try to alleviate this by ensuring a follow-up. If a reception is planned, the speaker should be guided, so that he or she is neither monopolized by a few guests nor ignored.

After the public reception the speaker should be taken out to a meal or for a drink to allow the excitement of the occasion to subside gradually. Even famous and sophisticated speakers may feel uncertain after a performance and wonder whether the occasion was a success. They enjoy hearing that the library appreciates the speaker and is happy with the event. Librarians may hesitate to praise a famous guest, assuming that the visitor knows that he or she was a success, but everyone likes to hear well-earned praise and appreciation.

Finally, the department head must see that the visitor is paid as soon as possible after the event. If receipts are needed for expenses, the host should remind the guest to present these before leaving. If, for any reason, payment might be delayed, the letter of appreciation sent to the guest after the event should mention the reason and provide a date by which payment can be expected. The library's financial officer will handle the processing, but the department head should be sure that the honorarium and expense money are paid. It is embarrassing for a speaker to have to write to an institution to remind them of an unpaid obligation.

Following Through

Assign the task of cleaning up after the event before the day itself. Maintenance staff will do most of the cleaning. If volunteers are expected to help clean up, they should know this well in advance. Staff members should have specific assigned tasks; cleaning up usually runs more smoothly if the department head participates. As part of the cleanup, remove all outdated notices about the program from bulletin boards.

Immediately after the event, send a news release to local media. The event's publicist can write the release in advance, adding final details after the event. The library should send out the release, even if local media representatives attended the program. The release can help reporters prepare their final copy and may result in an extra story. News releases should be sent to regional and state library publications and to national publications, if appropriate. Good publicity helps the library.

The notice on the library's website should be changed to reflect the completion of the program. Photographs of the event are an attraction, especially if some patrons discover themselves in the pictures. A list of the speaker's books should remain posted so that audience members will remember which ones they want to read.

The department head should write letters of appreciation immediately after the event. In addition to thanking the speaker, the department head should write to thank a publisher or bookseller who has helped with the program, as well as the library's volunteers. Memos of appreciation to staff members who worked on the program are appropriate; copies should be placed in employees' files so that their efforts can be acknowledged in an annual review.

The department head should prepare a written report of the event, even if it is not required by the administrator. The library staff may find a file of procedures for special events useful in planning future programs. The report should describe the planning process, the time commitment, any problems that arose, and ideas and suggestions for improving the event. An abbreviated version of this report can be sent to the chief administrator, and some sections can be incorporated in the department's annual report.

Integrating Children's Services in the Library System

Public libraries, like many other public institutions, are constantly scrutinized and asked to demonstrate their value to the taxpayers they serve. Chief administrators of libraries represent the institution to governing bodies and are responsible for justifying every aspect of the library's work. Children's department heads, therefore, must be sure that the administration and other staff members are aware of the department's programs and services.

For many years, children's services were considered "the classic success of the public library" (Leigh 1950, 100), and children's librarians often felt no need to justify their activities. The situation has changed during the 1990s, and as one writer expressed it, "today, even this nominal success is being challenged by changes and new situations in the public library's external environment" (Willett 1995, 26). These economic, social, and demographic shifts make it necessary for children's librarians to be sure that administrators and colleagues within the library system are aware of the work being done in their department.

Libraries are complex organizations that are divided into a number of departments, each one of which has a different function. Some of these departments form an operating chain; for example, the acquisitions and technical services departments receive orders for materials from the public service departments, acquire and prepare the materials, and deliver them to the ordering department, which provides public access to them. The result is that the acquisitions department is aware of the materials being provided in the public service departments. Other departments operate in parallel fashion and may have little interaction with one another. Adult services, especially in large libraries, may operate quite independently of the children's department, and its staff may be unaware of changes in either children's materials or services. This isolation is dangerous for both departments, because the library must be seen by the public as a unified service.

Building Awareness Within the Library

The fundamental reason why the children's department should maintain close contact with other library departments is that without such contact, service eventually suffers. Adult and children's services are complementary, and individuals will at various times draw on both departments. Most library users are introduced to the library through the children's department. If those services are successful, children become users of adult services. The patron's transition between departments should be easy; this is better accomplished when the departments work closely together.

Besides providing better service, pragmatic reasons dictate that the children's department promote awareness of its objectives and services within the library. When budgets are allocated, the importance of children's services should be apparent to administrators and other people in the system. Some children's librarians seem to feel that if they work hard and provide good programs and materials, the rest of the library staff will naturally notice their achievements. Unfortunately, individuals are usually so busy with their own work that they often miss the activities of other departments. Changes, in particular, are likely to go unnoticed. In a large library, the children's department must conduct an ongoing program of publicity to avoid having staff members in other departments view the children's department as providing essentially the same materials and services it did five or 10 years ago.

Because of the specialized nature of the work and the physical isolation of some children's departments, its personnel may be unfamiliar with staff members in other departments. Staff tend to have more respect for others' work when they know the people who are involved in it and share some knowledge of its associated difficulties. For this reason, the head of children's services should encourage staff members to attend social events, staff and committee meetings, and other all-library activities.

Children's services personnel should make the most of opportunities to become known to other staff members and to impress upon them the value of the children's department. They can do this by developing informal contacts with staff members in other departments and by participating in general library work. Children's staff should volunteer for committees and show an interest in the activities of all library departments.

Service on library committees is an important way for staff members to work together on issues that affect the entire library. Children's librarians who demonstrate expertise in technology or reference service and who offer sound suggestions about solving library problems earn the respect of colleagues. Their organizational abilities and clever ideas can be demonstrated in committee work. When the library staff comes to know children's librarians as bright, well-rounded professionals, they are more likely to respect the work of the children's department.

Children's librarians must do more than remind other staff members who they are and what is happening in the children's department. They must also convince others of the value of their work. It is important to avoid the "cuteness trap"—being seen as a nice person who has a fun job working with cute little children, making cute little puppets, telling cute little stories, and reading cute little picture books. If staff members from the children's department sit in the staff lounge and discuss the number of paper pumpkins they made that morning, other staff members may believe that the work of the department is trivial. Every department has its share of nonprofessional work, but the reasons for the work are professional. Instead of commenting only on trifles, librarians should mention some of the program's goals—the knowledge of shapes and colors that children gain from handling the pumpkins, for example. Obviously, a coffee break or lunch hour is not the time for giving a lecture on child development, but it is wise to be aware of the stereotypes that may be reinforced by talking only about the details, rather than the rationale of the programs.

Types of Communication

Informal Communication

Informal communication is a continuous process among colleagues in the workplace. While some of the communication may be about nonwork subjects, much of it will concern the job. Informal communication with administrators, especially in a large library system, will be less frequent, but still likely to be a part of the job. Much informal communication is face-to-face, but telephone conversations, memos, and e-mail are also part of the overall picture.

One way to have effective informal communication is to choose the channel that your listener prefers. Some administrators encourage staff members to drop into their office to talk over some problem or event. Others prefer a telephone call or a memo, which leaves them with a permanent record of the conversation. All colleagues have similar preferences, and communication is more likely to be satisfactory if their preferred method is chosen.

Face-to-Face Communication

When delivering a message or making a suggestion that may be controversial, a face-to-face meeting offers the advantage of providing immediate feedback on how the message is received. The listener's expression and body language, as well as the communication itself, will indicate whether the idea is welcomed or questioned. One of the basic principles of communication is that listening and watching are as important as speaking. If the person being addressed starts fiddling with desk implements or looking away, it may be wise to suggest that you present your idea in writing. If the listener begins frowning and moving restlessly, comments may be elicited even before the message is finished. A face-to-face encounter must allow for two-way communication if it is to be effective. Unheeding insistence on presenting a message is inappropriate. The key to effective face-to-face communication is to invite comments and interruptions and to respond to them without losing the train of thought.

Several factors can make face-to-face communication less effective than it might be. One is the "I know I'm right so don't try to tell me" attitude, which may be assumed by either speaker or listener. People who have made up their minds and refuse to listen to other suggestions cut off communication from the beginning. People tend to refuse to listen to messages that appear threatening. A children's librarian who has spent years honing her puppetry skills may be shocked to hear a chief librarian say "I don't think that we should continue giving puppet shows. They take too much staff time." If the puppeteer refuses to listen or to consider the chief librarian's point of view, the situation will become even worse. Instead, the children's librarian should listen carefully to the suggestion and respond to it seriously. When the librarian is upset by the idea, the best reaction is to ask for time in which to prepare a response, either in person or in writing.

In talking with an administrator, a department head should be watchful about the style in which information is presented. Recent research on the ways in which men and women express themselves in work situations suggests that many women undermine their authority by the way they talk. Women, more often than men, speak indirectly (Tannen 1994): "I think it would be a good idea for us to hire a library clerk to replace the library technician who is leaving," instead of: "I've decided that we can save money by replacing our library technician with a clerk and assigning some of the technician's work to our professional staff."

Frequently, women make themselves sound even more tentative by ending a statement with a rising voice as if asking a question: "A series of storyhours in the playground this summer might attract new users to the library[?]." Tannen believes that women speak this way because they are trained to seek approval, rather than to announce decisions. The result is that the female manager appears to be indecisive and asking for direction, rather than making a statement. A department head should try to speak in a businesslike way that sounds neither apologetic nor aggressive.

Telephone Calls

Telephone communication shares many of the advantages of face-to-face communication because feedback is immediate, questions can be raised, and explanations be immediately given. On the other hand, it is impossible to see the listener's body language. The speaker has to develop sensitivity to small clues, such as silences and clearing of the throat. Chief librarians and other administrators usually have secretaries to screen their calls, but many librarians do not; for the latter a call may interrupt an important task or duty. When calling, ask if it is a convenient time. It is better to call back when the individual can give the phone call his or her full attention than to talk to a person who is distracted by other duties. When receiving calls at an inconvenient time, ask if the call can be returned at a more appropriate time. Communication suffers when either person is trying to cope with more than one thing at a time. Of course, if a call is to be returned, it must be done as soon as possible. Playing telephone tag is annoying and can sabotage communication. Some people may find it worthwhile to set aside a certain time for telephone calls—the first hour in the morning, before the department is busy, for example—so that telephone calls can be taken or returned without undue distraction.

Because telephone calls are often sandwiched between other activities, they may be easily forgotten. When a call is received, it is usually wise to make notes about the caller, the date, the subject, and any action to be taken. These notes will be reminders of promises and agreements. When an important agreement is reached on the telephone, it is often best to follow it up with a letter formalizing and recording the decision.

E-mail and Faxed Communications

E-mail capability is available in most library systems. E-mail messages may be categorized as something between a telephone call and a memo. They can be sent quickly and informally to anyone else on the system, but the speed of the response depends on how often the other person uses the system. Like a telephone message, they require little effort and are easier and faster to send than a letter. Messages can be printed out so that a record of them exists, but if a message is ephemeral, it can be erased. Because e-mail does not interrupt other people and can be read at the receiver's convenience, it has become an important medium of communication, but it has its drawbacks. You can usually count on individuals to open their regular mail, but e-mail messages sometimes languish unread. Many e-mail systems indicate to the sender when a message is received. For those systems that do not, courtesy requires that the receiver let the sender know that the message was received. One basic safety measure is to archive any important message sent or received electronically.

The use of fax machines to send written messages is increasingly important. This quick and relatively inexpensive way of sending memos, letters, or other documents has revolutionized communication in many organizations. Because fax documents are written before being sent, the sender has a record of the message. Some formal documents, such as those with legal status, are not official in a faxed version, so the original document may need to be sent later by mail.

Formal Communication

Memos

One of the most frequently used forms of communication in any organization is the memo, a form that can range from quite informal to formal, depending on the subject and format. Most administrators have found memos an efficient way of keeping in touch with the activities of various departments within the system. A department head will usually keep the chief librarian informed by memo of activities within the department, potential problem issues, suggestions for library procedure changes, and requests for increased budgets or other services.

As previously mentioned, a face-to-face meeting or telephone call that results in a decision or a solution to a problem should be followed by a memo that serves as a permanent record of the decision. The department head will refer to memos when problems persist and when reports are to be written. For this reason, the department head must be sure that all important departmental issues are covered in memos. Because memos are generally filed by subject, it is best if each memo is devoted to only one subject. Otherwise, the less important issue contained within the memo may be lost or ignored.

When memos serve as documentation for decisions, they become formal communications. Whenever a memo dealing with an important issue is circulated, a copy should be kept in the department files for verification. This is particularly important if it deals with a request for action. If, for example, an agreement has been reached that an additional row of shelving is to be installed, it is important to record the date of the agreement by filing the memo. If the action is not taken within a reasonable period of time, the department head can follow up with a reminder as shown in the sequence of memos in figure 9.1.

TO: Rosa Moraga, Chief Librarian

FROM: Su-Ellen Blackman, Children's Department

DATE: April 12, 1998

I am glad that you are pleased with the selection of shelving for our new Homeschooler's corner. The new shelving will blend in well with existing decor and should be more durable than the other models we examined, without being more expensive. We are looking forward to having our new section ready for the opening of school in September.

TO: Rosa Moraga, Chief Librarian

FROM: Su-Ellen Blackman, Children's Department

DATE: July 14, 1998

As noted in my memo of April 12, we have been hoping to have our new Homeschooler's corner ready for use by the opening of school this fall. While the majority of our books are processed and ready to be shelved, we still do not have the required shelving. I have called R. W. Simmons Library Supply Company several times but have not received a satisfactory explanation for the delay.

TO: Rosa Moraga, Chief Librarian

FROM: Su-Ellen Blackman, Children's Department

DATE: August 20, 1998

Thank you for contacting R. W. Simmons Company and sending me a copy of your letter of July 19. The bookshelves finally arrived and were installed yesterday. I hope that you will be able to attend the coffee hour on September 23 at 4:00 p.m. which will mark the official opening of the Homeschooler's Reading corner. Mary L. Wabinski, President of the Homeschool Association of Northern Michigan, will be the guest of honor.

Fig. 9.1. Sequence of Memos.

Any memo that deals with a personnel problem should be filed in the individual's personnel file. These memos serve as important reminders to supervisors when they prepare performance assessments and are invaluable if disciplinary measures need to be taken. Memos of commendation are also important for writing performance assessments or recommendations for employees who may be applying for other positions.

If difficulty is encountered obtaining answers to memos, consider investing in business forms that provide space for an answer on the same page that the message is written. Some of these forms come with a copy sheet, so that if the memo is returned by mail, both the sender and receiver have records of the original memo and the response. More frequently, the response is sent by fax, which automatically provides a copy for both sender and receiver.

Although it is important to keep files of certain types of memos, the number of memos circulated in any large organization will soon clutter the records department unless they are regularly weeded. Memos that refer to specific events or ephemeral matters should be removed from the files at regular intervals. Many memos are written on computers, and the machine files as well as paper files, should be regularly deleted. Clogging a computer's hard disk with memos about a temporary problem is unnecessary. One paper copy of each memo in an archives file is sufficient.

Letters

Letters circulated between departments in the library system are more formal than memos. Letters are used to document changes in status, such as promotions, increases in salary, formal reprimands or commendations, and resignations. Because letters give the title and position of the writer and recipient, they are preferable to memos whenever the document may need to be shown to others outside of the library system.

Reports

Another type of formal communication that is common in a library is the written report. Many of the principles of writing any report are the same as those for annual reports, which are discussed in Chapter 10. Reasons for preparing a report include such things as requesting funding for a particular project, preparing for a new building or a renovation, or investigating new types of media or programming.

Reports should be well organized, clear, complete, and persuasive. Frequently, the writer of a report must assimilate a great deal of background information before preparing even a short report. However, time should not be wasted in reading everything that can be found on the issue. Most people find it useful to start by preparing an outline of the points to be covered. A number of books and software programs can help those who find it difficult to construct an outline.

While reports should cover all of the important points, they should be concisely written. Pages of prose should not obscure the basic facts an administrator needs to make a decision. Usually, a report should start with an administrative summary (written after the report is completed), which includes the most important factors to be considered and the recommended action. The report itself should include the following:

- a brief introduction giving the situation that led to the decision to write the report;
- an explanation of the factors that must be considered;
- facts and figures to support the argument put forth;
- suggestions for action implementation;
- appendices providing sources of information, documentation, and amplification of issues.

The presentation of the report should be as professional as possible. Desktop publishing programs can produce different typefaces and a variety of graphics that can strengthen the effect of the report. While the administrator's decision will be influenced more by content than by format, a clear, crisp presentation conveys the impression that the author is a competent professional who has probably been as careful in assembling the facts as in presenting them.

Cooperating with Other Departments

Most of the methods of communication discussed in this chapter take place between the administrator and the department. It is also important to communicate frequently and effectively with other departments in the library. Face-to-face communication is the most important method of communication, and in a small library, it may be all that is needed. Sometimes, however, people are lulled into a sense of security because they talk with members of other departments on a daily basis. If the conversations cover general topics, rather than work-related ones, other librarians may not know much about the actual affairs of individual departments. For this reason, memos concerning events and projects should be sent to other departments, noted on the library LAN, and posted on well-read bulletin boards.

In large libraries where members of one department may see staff from other departments only infrequently, it is even more important that written communications be widely circulated. Staff meetings can be opportunities for talking about projects and issues within departments, in addition to the more general topics. Librarians in children's departments should be sensitive to the flow of power within the library system and should try to tap communication channels to the decision makers. This should be done on both an informal and formal level. The head of a children's department should make himself or herself known to all of the other department heads. If department heads eat lunch or have coffee breaks together, the head of the children's department should try to be included. It is not always easy at the beginning for the newest and often the youngest member of the management team to be accepted by others with more experience, but the effort is worthwhile. A department that is isolated is often seen as less important.

In any busy library, staff members work hard at their individual jobs and have little time to observe the activities of others. One of the tasks of a department head is to make it easy for others in the library to remain aware of what is going on in their department. Good communication techniques keep pathways open to administrators and staff members throughout the library system.

Systemwide Coordinators of Children's Services

The task of coordinating children's services throughout a library system is the traditional job of the children's coordinator. The early leaders of children's services, such as Anne Carroll Moore at the New York Public Library and Lillian H. Smith at the Toronto Public Library, selected the children's staff, set policies for book selection, conducted in-service training, and acted as spokespersons for children's services throughout the system. The position, while subordinate to that of the chief librarian, was almost parallel because children's services were often left almost entirely in the hands of the children's coordinator. Because children's services were generally seen as successful, they did not often require or receive intense scrutiny by the chief administrator.

With the cutbacks in funding to public libraries during the 1970s and 1980s, the number of coordinators of large public libraries decreased. Some systems failed to fill the positions when a coordinator retired, while others moved the children's coordinator to another position (Rollock 1988, 54–55). While this trend seems to have been reversed to some degree, a shortage of coordinators still exists in many states (Willett 1995, 78), and the role of the coordinator has been redefined in many library systems.

Patterns of Coordination

Coordinator as Executive Officer

Children's coordinators who act as executive officers are responsible for seeing that high-quality children's services are maintained and for representing these services both inside and outside of the library system. The coordinator's office makes decisions about policy and hiring and handles relations with state or provincial library departments. A good part of the work may involve writing funding proposals, responding to legislative initiatives, and lobbying. The coordinator also represents children's services to schools and other community groups and is usually the library's representative at meetings with school administrators or community groups.

Coordinator as Adviser

In recent decades, a number of large library systems developed more decentralized administrative patterns in order to make library branches more responsive to local community needs. One way to do this was to allow branch heads to exercise greater control over the collections and services in their branch. Allowing a system coordinator to determine the children's collection and programming policies led the branches to decisions that might not serve their unique situation. For this reason, some library systems redefined the coordinator's role to that of adviser to children's librarians. Under the new system, individual departments made final decisions subject to the approval of branch heads, rather than coordinators.

While this change may be seen as mainly a change in administrative charts, it had observable effects on library systems. In one large library, for example, the reorganization meant that branches could buy materials that were not on the coordinator's selection list. Librarians hired for children's positions were interviewed by representatives of the personnel office and the branch librarian, but often not by the coordinator. Systemwide book selection meetings were abandoned as were most staff training events. Children's services in various areas of the city began to differ considerably from each other, depending on the philosophy of the staff within the particular branches.

Tasks of a Children's Coordinator

Personnel

Personnel decisions are among the most important aspects of organizing a department. A first step can be writing job descriptions for the staff of children's departments. Job descriptions indicate whether staff members are expected to spend on-the-job time reading reviews, professional materials, and children's books. They also define which tasks should be handled by a professional, clerical, or other staff person.

Preparing job descriptions is an important task for many coordinators. Although staff members sometimes believe that having a job description limits flexibility, these documents serve several useful purposes, such as

- providing library managers with a formal document outlining what they can expect staff members to accomplish;
- communicating current performance expectations to job incumbents and future expectations should staff members seek promotion;
- offering information about what aspects of performance will be evaluated during employee appraisals;
- justifying disciplinary actions for failure to perform duties;
- protecting the library against unfounded allegations of discrimination (Carson et al. 1995, 69).

The basic information included in a job description should include the position title, the department in which the job is located, the position of the person to whom the employee reports, a statement of the duties of the position (often including the percentage of time allocated to each), the equipment used to perform the job, physical demands of the job, and the supervisory requirements of the position. The date of the job analysis that led to the description should also be included. Figure 9.2 is an example of a typical job description for a children's librarian.

MEMPHIS SHELBY COUNTY PUBLIC LIBRARY AND INFORMATION CENTER

JOB DESCRIPTION

POSITION TITLE: Librarian I   EFFECTIVE DATE: Dec., 1992

AGENCY: Children's/Main   REVISED DATE: May, 1996

JOB GRADE: E4   JOB CODE: 21223

SCOPE:
Under the direction of the Senior Agency Manager, provides public information services in the areas of adult and children's reference, readers' advisory, collection development and programming; provides programs for organizations and participates on library and community committees.

ESSENTIAL JOB DUTIES/RESPONSIBILITIES:
1. Supports the Library's mission, policies, goals and objectives through provision of professional library service which incorporates interview and retrieval processes and the provision of programming and other activities.

2. Provides information services from department resources including computer databases and specialized files where present; conducts user-focused reference interviews emphasizing listening and feed-back and assessment as well as information search and delivery; provides reader's advisory primarily for children and their caregivers.

3. Assists with development of a children's collection for the department which reflects the collection development policies and practices of the system; uses Collection Development Officer and Youth Services Coordinator as resources.

4. Implements and assists with organization of visitation to neighborhood schools and day care centers; provides programs for class visits to the library; and participates in networking with schools and other youth services agencies for cooperative programming development. Regularly rotates on day care service through schedule on delivery vehicle, Training Wheels.

Fig. 9.2 continues on page 110.

Fig. 9.2. Example of Job Description. Reprinted with permission of the Memphis/ Shelby County Public Library and Information Center.

5. Performs activities in assigned areas of responsibility, which may include ordering materials; maintenance of specialized files; development of procedures; assistance with system-wide activities; compilation of information/statistics for reports; and training of others.

6. Coordinates and directs the work of other staff and volunteers as required; identifies problems with performance and recommends solutions; assists with agency training functions; serves as the person-in-charge as designated.

7. Participates on library and community committees as assigned.

QUALIFICATIONS AND SPECIAL SKILLS:
Master's degree in Library Science from an ALA accredited library school or Master's degree in early childhood education or child development from an accredited college or university; experience in a public library working with young children preferred; must be able to work flexible schedule which includes evenings and weekends, and work in a collegial environment as a team member. Experience in giving training workshops for adults/caregivers highly desirable.

Position requires excellent oral and written communication skills and the ability to apply principles of library and information science in a public library setting. Must have the ability to work successfully in a customer service oriented environment.

Proficiency in personal computer skills, PAC on computer terminals and all basic office equipment required. Valid Tennessee driver's license and at least two years of unrestricted driving experience and a good driving record; must be able to obtain Class F Tennessee driver's license.

WORKING CONDITIONS/EQUIPMENT USED:
Works primarily in a temperature controlled public building. Occasional travel within United States and frequent travel within Shelby County. Must have ability to operate personal computers and basic office equipment. Must be able to drive The Training Wheels mobile unit. Position requires some standing, sitting, stooping, bending, stretching and lifting 20 lbs.

DISCLAIMER:
The above statements are intended to describe the general nature and level of work being performed by people assigned to this position. They are not intended to be construed as an exhaustive list of all responsibilities, duties and skills required.

Materials Selection

One of the major tasks of the coordinator is establishing and maintaining selection policies (see Chapter 3). If the library does not have a written selection policy, the coordinator should assign its preparation a top priority. If a selection policy is already in place, the coordinator makes sure that it is periodically reexamined and updated. The mechanism for this may vary from one library to another, but most systems appoint a committee to solicit suggestions and to pass on those suggestions that seem appropriate. The coordinator normally chairs this committee and sees that its decisions are carried out.

Selection policies are written in general terms that must be interpreted for specific occasions. The coordinator should maintain a record of interpretations as they are accepted by the chief administrator or the library board. Some of these interpretations should be integrated into the policy at its next revision; others may remain as part of the record of administrative decisions.

In most library systems, the coordinator not only clarifies selection policy but also coordinates the selection procedures. Some libraries have book selection meetings where staff members evaluate materials sent by the publishers. The coordinator normally prepares and circulates a list of all of the materials available for evaluation at such a meeting. Reviews of each item, either from selection journals or written by a staff member, may be circulated or made available at the meeting. The coordinator asks individuals to present oral reviews of specific titles that are either particularly interesting or potentially controversial. These selection meetings, while planned primarily for materials selection, also allow staff to discuss professional information, integrate new staff into the group, air problems, and discuss areas of concern. A coordinator tries to ensure that the atmosphere is informal enough to encourage communication and that the meeting is long enough to serve these purposes.

Selection meetings may be impracticable when a system is unable to provide examination copies of a sufficient variety of materials. Some regional libraries organize an examination center where libraries can send staff members. Sometimes only the coordinator goes to the examination center. In other libraries, materials selection may be made on the basis of reviews and lists compiled by the coordinator. Most children's librarians prefer to examine the materials themselves, but the coordinator in consultation with other staff must decide which method is best for a particular library. Whatever method is chosen, the coordinator usually makes sure that staff members receive information on time and that their choices are efficiently handled.

Perhaps the most troubling aspect of the coordinator's responsibility for materials selection is handling complaints that are made by parents, teachers, or others. Most complaints are made at the branch level, and they may be handled satisfactorily by the children's librarian and the branch administrator. Information about the incident should be shared with the coordinator. Only by knowing the complaints that are made and how they are handled can the coordinator remain aware of community feelings about the library.

When a complaint is not settled satisfactorily at the branch level, the coordinator should be involved in handling the issue. While the chief administrator and library board have the final responsibility, the children's coordinator can amass the documentation necessary to defend the item. Wide background knowledge about children's materials is helpful in dealing with complaints about specific items.

Guidelines for handling censorship attempts are an important part of library management (see Chapter 7). The children's coordinator should ensure that effective guidelines are in place and that all children's services staff are aware of them. Preparing for complaints and learning procedures for handling them are an important part of ongoing staff development. The coordinator's role will be much easier if each step of the procedure has been competently handled.

Programming

In some library systems, the children's coordinator sets programming policy for all children's departments. Such policies include

- target groups to be served (by age or other category);
- general objectives of programming;
- level of personnel involved in programming;
- approximate amount of staff time spent on programming.

After these policies are agreed upon, the coordinator helps children's department personnel to develop programs that fit within the policy guidelines.

One of the advantages of centralized programming is that publicity and program materials can be efficiently shared among branches. If one brochure about programs is produced for the entire system, more money can be spent on designing and producing a professional-looking product. A coordinated listing of programs covering all branches can also be mounted on the library's website.

In another common model of program organization, the coordinator works with children's librarians to work out policy and to coordinate programming. The goals and objectives of programming may vary from one branch to another, as will target groups and possibly the personnel involved. The coordinator works with each branch to help the staff achieve the branch objectives. In this model the role of the coordinator is more supportive than directive.

Library systems frequently coordinate programming for summer reading programs. The savings that result from centralized production of publicity and other materials make it possible to achieve high visibility across the community. Because the summer reading program is often the most widely publicized children's program in the library, the individual or committee that plans themes and implementation must spend considerable time on the project. A successful summer program often involves the cooperation of schools, businesses, and other community agencies, so it offers good public relations opportunities, as well as provides valuable reading experiences for the children. Many coordinators regard planning the annual summer reading program as a major part of their overall responsibility for publicizing the role of the children's department. Some states or regions develop program themes used by all libraries in a given area. Each coordinator works on part of the planning, and the development and implementation of the overall program continues throughout the year.

When outside groups or individuals are brought in to present programs, the coordinator is usually the person responsible for handling the details of inviting, scheduling, and handling the visit. Some library systems regularly arrange a special program, puppet show, magician, or theater group for holidays. Other opportunities for outside programming present themselves when an author or illustrator visits the region. A coordinator should take advantage of these opportunities to plan events that will both raise the library's profile and offer good programming.

Budgeting

The coordinator is often responsible for determining the budgets for the branches or advising branch managers on budget decisions.

When the children's coordinator sits on the budgeting committee, he or she can influence the total amount of funding available for children's services across the system. The coordinator's task is to present the needs of children's services reasonably and persuasively in the context of the overall system budget.

After the overall budget allocations are made, the coordinator works with the branch heads and the children's departments to determine how the budget will be spent at the branch level. Needs and services vary from one branch to another. It is the coordinator's task to ensure that the children's department receives an equitable share of the branch budget, so that appropriate materials and services can be provided. The children's department staff in each branch can benefit from the coordinator's assistance in presenting their funding needs to branch heads.

Some systems do not include the coordinator in basic budget decisions. Instead, the coordinator's role is limited to advising children's librarians on budget decisions. Some coordinators find that busy children's librarians do not always take an appropriate interest in budget matters. It is easy for staff of a children's department to become so overwhelmed by handling their normal workload that they avoid spending time on budget decisions. A wise coordinator will insist that in the long run, setting budgets is more important than most other tasks, and that the time spent on budgeting will strengthen the department.

Working Without a Coordinator

Most small, and even many medium-sized library systems do not have children's coordinators. At many libraries with one or more branches, the head of the children's department in the main library is responsible for the tasks of a coordinator. These tasks include coordinating programming and materials selection, representing children's services to the library board or other groups, and sometimes participating in personnel hiring. This system often works well, at least while the system remains small, but there are disadvantages in not having a full-time coordinator. The head of any children's department is involved with branch responsibilities much of the time. The freedom to travel in the community, to meet with educational or business groups, and to visit schools and other institutions is limited. It is difficult to achieve a high profile for library children's services, unless a coordinator is available to spend time outside of the library.

Some systems have a committee of children's librarians that carries out tasks that would otherwise be handled by a coordinator. In a small system, each branch would have a representative on the committee, while in a larger system, the branches may rotate membership. A committee of six to eight individuals is probably the largest size that can be effective. Some committees are chaired by the senior member; others rotate the chair among members. At regular meetings, usually monthly, the committee decides on program plans, discusses problems, and agrees on systemwide publicity. Subcommittees of one or two members can carry out specific tasks between meetings. Although a committee structure always presents some problems in administration, this system can work well when colleagues cooperate and respect one another's professional views. It is certainly preferable to making no attempt at coordinating children's services throughout a library system.

Annual Reports in Various Formats

The annual report is the major public record of a library's performance. Its purpose is to keep the community and other libraries informed about library operations. It is also the chief source of historical information about a library. Lillian H. Smith's annual report for the Toronto Public Library provides a vivid picture of children's services at the beginning of the twentieth century.

> Children to the number of 9,180 have been present at the 180 story hours held regularly at the branches during the year with the exception of the months of June, July, August and September. These figures do not include the informal story hours which are carried on at the request of the children when the heaviest part of the day is over. At three branches a division of the story groups was made, the younger children coming Saturday morning to the ever popular fairy tales, legends, and nature stories, while the older children at a different hour find equal enjoyment in the achievements of heroes and historic events as recounted by the Children's librarian (Toronto Public Library 1913, 12).

The annual reports being prepared today will serve future historians as sources of information about public libraries at the beginning of the twenty-first century. In the interests of maintaining an accurate yearly account of a library's activities, librarians should recognize the importance of preparing careful annual reports.

Types of Annual Reports

Many reports are produced for mounting on a library's website, as well as in traditional print format. This innovation has meant a change in the style, but not the purpose of reports. The length and format of annual reports vary from one jurisdiction to another. Some localities have legal requirements for the form and content of the report, while others leave these decisions to the library administration. Legal requirements must be observed; often, however, these requirements are minimum standards, and additional information can be added. Some libraries provide only the most general statistical and factual material; others incorporate anecdotes, statistics, and illustrations. It is useful to look at reports produced by other libraries and those available on the Internet before choosing the department's approach. Figure 10.1 shows a sample children's services section from an annual report.

Because annual reports are management tools, the decisions about the individual responsible for preparing the report and the form it should take are important. In some libraries, the chief executive officer compiles the report on the basis of information supplied by the various departments. Each department submits information to the administrator but has little input regarding format and detail. In other libraries, responsibility is more widely distributed. The departmental sections of the report may be written by each department, and the results compiled by the chief administrator; or a committee of department heads or others may work cooperatively on the report.

The head of children's services may have little chance to influence or change the accepted practice in preparing annual reports. As with most management work, however, the greater the input to the system, the stronger the manager's position. Whatever the overall plan, the head of children's services should probably try to influence the type and amount of information submitted and provide input on the content and design of the report.

The format of the annual report can vary from a sober, official-looking compilation of data to a professionally designed piece of graphic art that looks like an advertising brochure. Many libraries produce the report in more than one format: a formal report for the library board, a shorter version for the public, and an online report for the library's website. The target audience should determine the format. A library board typically wants a full report including all the appropriate statistics and facts. The high quality of graphics available on the Internet and in publicity pieces has heightened the expectations of board members for well-designed and well-presented information, but most of them are willing to contend with a report containing a spread of figures. Members of the general public, on the other hand, will not usually take the time to read anything but a brief annual report in which the statistics are presented in graphic format. Preparing material so that it is useful and accessible to both of these groups and also serves as a historical record is a challenging task. The time and effort spent in planning and preparing for the compilation of the annual report can pay dividends in the form of increased public visibility and good publicity for the library's services.

"Castle ReadMore is the best summer reading game to date."

The 1995 summer reading game, "Castle ReadMore" was the most popular in the history of the Etobicoke Public Libraries. Children across Etobicoke (and their parents too!) loved the adventure. Participation in the game increased by 17% over 1994.

"Castle ReadMore is the best summer reading game we've done to date," states Mom, Hedy Ann Tammerk, "...even my five year old was able to guess the riddles. All three kids wanted to zoom through to the finish. It surely does promote reading and library use."

Each of the three children, (*pictured to the right*), enjoyed different categories. But they all loved the game and enjoyed helping to free "Eeple" from the Castle's dungeon.

"What is the game this summer?" asked Kristian, the youngest of the kids. It seems that everyone is anxious to "Go for the Gold" in this summer's Reading Olympics.

Reading Made Fun

Etobicoke Public Libraries Makes Reading Fun was a year-long public relations campaign designed to encourage children ages 6 to 10 to read and use the library. Under the overall campaign umbrella, three interrelated programmes were produced that had a common recognizable element - Eeple - (Etobicoke Public Libraries), the Court Jester.

Eeple provided a fun image which promoted participation in Read to Succeed (a grade 4 outreach programme), the Summer Reading Game and the Reading Festival. The components of the three programmes offered versatility to branches so that each could tailor supporting activities to promote library service.

page 5

(From left:) The Kuld children Silvi, 10, Kristian, 5 and Erik, 8, enjoyed participating in Etobicoke Public Libraries' 1995 summer reading game, Castle ReadMore.

Eeple proved to be a great hit with children. 3,788 kids took part in the Read to Succeed programme, 4,569 children participated in Castle ReadMore and over 250 attended the Reading Festival.

Etobicoke Public Libraries' court jester, Eeple, hams it up with Arthur and D.W. Aardvaark and Peter Rabbit at the Reading Festival.

Fig. 10.1 continues on page 118.

Fig. 10.1. Children's Services Section of Annual Report. Reprinted with permission of the Etobicoke (Ontario) Public Library Board.

The Reading Festival

Saturday, September 23 was the day that the Etobicoke Public Libraries (EPL) celebrated reading, literacy and the library at its second annual Reading Festival.

The event marked the end of this year's popular summer reading game, Castle ReadMore. Children who completed the game were invited to be knighted at the Festival. Over 250 children led by Eeple, the game's court jester, were knighted by Sir Thomas of Cresswood from Medieval Times Dinner and Tournament. They were dubbed "a knight or lady of the realm."

Author and cartoonist Ben Wicks delighted children by inviting them to the stage to help him draw.

Heather Brown, 14, and Lindsey Murrell, 11, from Road to Avonlea appeared on stage in costumes from the show.

Raptor entertains the kids at Etobicoke Public Libraries' 2nd annual Reading Festival with "gym-dino-nastics."

CITY TV personality Oliver Walters emceed the Festival and Etobicoke actor Robin Dunne read the children a story.

Salome Bey, affectionately known as "Canada's First Lady of the Blues", shared excerpts from her work in progress, RAINBOWORLD.

Kids were delighted when the Raptor mascot appeared. He told the story of "How the Raptor Came To Be" and entertained the kids with "gym-dino-nastics" and basketball moves.

All of these stars donated their time in support of literacy and the library.

photo by The Etobicoke Guardian

Children were "knighted" and dubbed a "knight or lady of the realm."

Author & cartoonist Ben Wicks shared a story with some of the children who attended EPL's 2nd annual Reading Festival.

page 6

Preparing the Report

Collecting Data

In some respects, the preparation for an annual report continues throughout the year. Statistics concerning acquisitions and circulation are automatically compiled by the library's computer system. Statistics about programs, program attendance, and class or other group visits should be input into departmental files whenever such an event takes place.

Also, the department should keep a file, in both electronic and paper format, of all the publicity material produced within the department. Such a file is useful as a historical record, a source of ideas for future programs, and as material for the annual report. In addition to the publicity materials, a brief report of the program, including anecdotal accounts of the occasion, can be used for generating annual report material. Press releases about library activities and newspaper reports of programs or services should be saved. Photographs are especially important because they often contain information that is not recorded in written form—the people who were present, the setting, and visual details of the occasion.

If the department head sets up a file labeled "Annual Report" and makes a habit of saving material that might be useful for the report, he or she will be able to gather many useful bits of information that might otherwise be lost. Instead of thinking of the report as a once-a-year chore, the librarian should consider it an ongoing responsibility. Then, when it is time to compile the report, the basic materials will be readily available, and the task will be much less daunting.

No matter how much material is collected throughout the year, additional information must be collected shortly before writing the report. Important changes in the department, such as retirements, resignations, and new staff appointments should be documented. Building or department renovations or additions need to be noted. Major physical rearrangements of the department or the addition or deletion of particular types of collections such as games, toys, or artifacts warrant mention. Information about these changes should be gathered in one place to facilitate the preparation of the report.

Involving Other Staff Members

In large departments, the report may be written by a committee. Committee members may include all of the professional staff or only two or three department members. Writing a report by committee usually means assigning various sections of the report to different individuals, circulating the drafts for comments and suggestions, and seeking group approval for the final draft. This can be a time-consuming process, but it involves several staff members in the department's yearly work and can lead to a more complete and balanced report.

In small departments, one person, most often the department head, usually assumes responsibility for writing the annual report. Frequently, that individual solicits input from other department members. While the backbone of the report may consist of prescribed statistics and factual material, it is often possible to include additional information that reflects a fuller sense of the department's activities and accomplishments. Suggestions for additional information may come from any staff member, so it is in the interest of the report writer to ask for ideas. Invite suggestions for changes and improvements by circulating a draft copy of the report. No one knows more about the department than its staff; their input can make the difference between an effective report and one that is merely technically correct.

Writing the Report

Overall Plan

Annual reports should tell a story. One effective annual report starts with the words "This is a story about one year in the life of a big city's library system. It is a story about growth and change . . . and success and the people who create that success" (Mississauga 1996, 1). Instead of thinking of the report as a random collection of facts and figures, the writer should analyze the material, decide what the information conveys, and organize the facts in such a way that the reader understands the message. Few people care about or can even understand numerical data unless they are arranged in a meaningful way.

What is the message that the report is trying to convey?

"This has been a great year, capped by the opening of our new branch library."

"We have had unexpected budget problems this year, but our fundraising efforts have been successful and we expect next year to be better."

"Moving to the new building caused a lot of turmoil, but our services are still effective."

"It has been a pretty good year overall, although there are problems in a few areas."

Once the basic message is clarified, the report is easier to prepare. The pieces will fall into place as they are arranged in a logical and cohesive order.

Some basic items should be included in every annual report:

- major achievements
- highlights of the year
- changes, including new materials, staff, and programs
- problems (frankness depends on the report's use)
- future plans

Four different audiences have an interest in the type of services provided by the children's department. One audience is the children's department staff, including clerical staff and pages. As a rule, every member of the department's staff can affect services, so it is useful for them to know about the library's progress and to feel that they have a role to play in its success. Another in-house audience is the library administration and staff in other departments. The chief administrator needs to know the department's affairs through formal reports, as well as informal communication. Other staff members also need to know the activities of the children's department. The larger the library, the more formal communication is needed. Funding bodies, specifically the library board, are concerned with services within each department. Finally, outside groups, including the community in general as well as parents, teachers, and the children themselves are part of the department's public.

The report's format may allow some informal information to be included along with the statistics. Anecdotes that highlight services and clarify the meaning of the statistics get the message across and linger in people's minds. Each anecdote should be brief and make a point. These anecdotes are often used by local newspapers or other media in stories about the library's annual report. They may also favorably impress local government funding agencies.

Graphics

When gathering information for the annual report, it should be determined whether any of the information can be presented in graphic form. Few people enjoy looking at rows of figures. If these figures can be presented in a more eye-catching way, they will have a much greater impact. They will stick in people's minds and make points more emphatically than if they are hidden in tables or in dull paragraphs of text.

Pictures can be used effectively in print and electronic versions of a report. The best way to show how much children enjoy using the books in your collection is to take a picture of children reading like the picture shown in figure 10.2. Photographs can be inexpensively scanned and integrated into a word processing program for text or for mounting onto a website.

Fig. 10.2. Photograph Scanned into Report.

Comparisons can be shown in various types of graphs. An increase in the proportions of children who are registered library users can be depicted in a bar graph (see figure 10.3). When developing a graph like this, try several different formats for the graph until the one that shows the information most clearly is found.

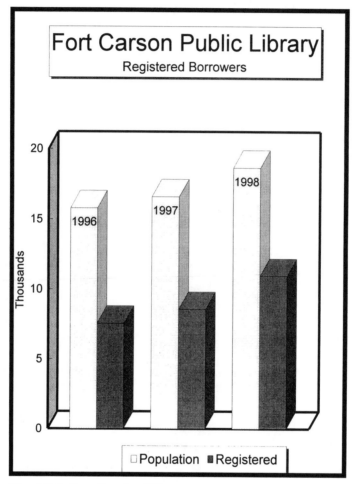

Fig. 10.3. Bar Graph of Borrowers.

Another kind of comparison that lends itself to graphic representation is the department's performance across time. Information about the increase in circulation after opening a new building can be presented as a line graph (see figure 10.4).

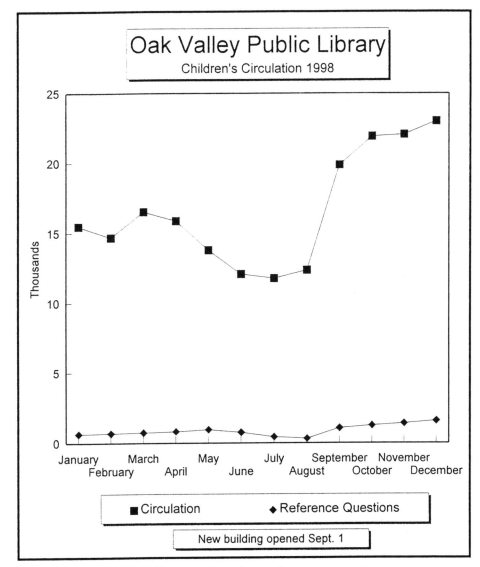

Fig. 10.4. Line Graph Showing Circulation Increase.

Another way to present material simply and clearly is to describe a person or activity in terms of average statistics. An average patron may be described as follows:

In North Auburn, the average child with a library card

- visits the library 27 times a year
- uses electronic resources during every visit
- attends six programs a year
- borrows 46 books a year

This method can be used to construct an average program, or the average day of a staff member, as follows:

In Lilacville, the typical children's librarian

- recommends 18 books a day
- talks with three parents and 30 children a day
- instructs seven patrons in the use of the computer resources a day

---

The ways in which to use a profile are limited only by imagination.

Tailoring Reports to Different Groups

The department head will want to distribute evaluative information to several groups. Each group requires a different approach. The author of a report should consider how much and what kind of information is appropriate for each audience.

The children's department staff will be interested in the complete report. The department head should arrange a staff meeting to discuss the report and its implications. The chief administrator also receives the full report. The department head should discuss the report with the chief administrator. This discussion should cover the results, problems (including sensitive issues that might not be included in the report), and future plans. The department can give other library staff a summary of the report at a staff meeting. The funding agency should receive a précis of the report and an oral report. Outside groups often receive a version of the report that is developed for distribution to the public. This is also the version that is usually posted on the library website. Press releases and speaking engagements at schools or community groups may also be appropriate.

Oral Reports

The annual report is only the beginning of the reporting process. Almost each presentation of the information is accompanied by an oral report. These oral presentations raise some problems.

When reporting to someone in authority or to a group of people, the presentation should be carefully prepared. Both of these situations often make librarians tense. Although the librarian may have written the report and knows it very well, he or she should review and jot down notes on the points to be made in each oral presentation. Even if the notes are not used, the act of writing them down helps to fix them in memory. Each point should be numbered, so that as they are presented, they can be mentally checked off. This mental checklist ensures that no points were forgotten. If the meeting is informal, keeping track of the points can be accomplished by uncurling a finger each time one is made.

Oral presentations supplement the written report—all of the information in the written report should not be included in the presentation. The concentration should be on the highlights—outstanding successes or problems, or future plans. People remember less information from an oral presentation, so the number of points should be limited to no more than 10.

Reports to the Public

Some libraries, especially larger ones, have a public relations staff that prepares information for distribution to the community. Most public relations staff welcome suggestions from departments as to events or information to publicize. The release of a library's annual report may spur newspapers or other media to contact the library and ask for additional information about services. This is more likely to happen if the report is visually attractive and interesting and if media people are presented with materials that make it easy for them to dramatize the information.

In dealing with the public, remember to catch people's attention and to try different channels.

Catch People's Attention

Information from the library enters a vast sea of media information. Few people find a library story intrinsically exciting, so the highlights must be chosen and presented in a way that draws attention. If the department's priorities include unusual and innovative services—services to homeless children, Internet access, or literacy programs—they should be emphasized. This will keep the media from focusing on traditional library programs (see Chapter 13).

Try Different Channels

The more ways in which the library's report is made available, the larger audience it is likely to have. Having the main points of the annual report available in timely fashion on the library's website reaches an audience in the community that is already committed to using the library. This version of the report may also be read by librarians in other parts of the country or around the world. However, not all of the potential patrons of the library are accustomed to surfing the Net. Press releases should be sent to local media outlets, and the librarian may ask to be invited to radio and television talk shows. A short précis of the annual report should be made available in the children's department for parents to pick up when they come in for programs or materials. Copies should be sent to local schools to let teachers know the services and materials that are available. The release of the annual report is an occasion for calling attention to the library's services. Many day care centers, parent-teacher associations, religious groups, and parenting groups like to have librarians talk to them about the resources and services of the children's department. With careful planning the annual report may be used not only to publicize the services but also to improve them through increased community support.

11

Preparing Budgets

Constructing a budget requires a great deal of time and effort, but, if carefully prepared, a budget is an important means of organizing library services. As organizational instruments, budgets help librarians determine priorities and achieve goals and objectives. According to Prentice (1996, 20), "Budgeting and planning are, or should be, parallel activities. The budget should be seen as a plan with dollar figures attached." A department's budget indicates the resources that will be needed to meet the department's goals and objectives. No matter how ambitious the proposed objectives are, they will become realities only if they are funded.

Libraries generally have two major types of budgets: the operating budget and the capital budget. Capital budgets deal with one-time expenditures, such as building a new library or making major renovations. Managers at the departmental level deal most often with operating budgets—the allocation of funds for the ongoing activities of the department.

Who Prepares the Budget?

In most public libraries, budgets are developed by a committee headed by the library director or someone designated to act as financial officer. The membership of the committee may vary, but most often it includes all of the department heads or program directors. Whether the manager of children's services is included depends on how the job description is phrased and how the organizational chart is drawn. In some libraries, children's services are represented by the head of a public services department, which includes both adult and youth services. In other libraries, the branch heads take part in the budget-planning process, and they make decisions about the budget for children's services within their branches. The manager of the children's department may be asked only for input about spending for the current and following year.

Because the budget is such an important document, the individuals involved in its preparation have the power to make influential decisions. A department head should seize the opportunity to have as much input into these decisions as possible. A department that is represented on the budget committee will be more autonomous than one that simply accepts the budget handed down by a branch or department head.

Even if the head of the children's department is not part of the group preparing the budget, he or she can prepare a budget proposal to present to them. According to one experienced librarian, "Do not sit back like a victim who has no control and must simply take what is given" (Deerr 1995, 16). One way to increase the chance of being appointed to the budget committee is to be aware of the processes and knowledgeable about departmental needs. At the very least, anything connected with preparing budget reports or requests should be top priority for the department head.

Because the budget is the library's fundamental planning tool, it is also a political instrument. For this reason, it is important to present a convincing case for suggesting budgetary changes. Almost all new budgets are presented within the framework of previous budgets, so the parameters of the current requests are set by their extent. A proposal to double a department's budget because someone suddenly realized how much could be done with more money is likely to be rejected. Instead, budgetary changes should be realistic increments of the current budget. The department head must support each suggestion or request by carefully documenting the need for the increase. If the library system is operating under a flat budget, this will mean cutting back on some programs when new ones are added.

Changes are apt to be slow and based on past experience. Some administrators suggest that new ideas be repeatedly mentioned in a budget, so that the governing board will come to accept and fund some of them. A proposed budget increase that is turned down one year may be proposed again and accepted the following year.

A budget grows out of the department's goals and objectives; meeting department goals and objectives justifies budget requests. A manager should be able to defend budget requests on the basis of meeting the objectives set and approved by the administration. This holds true regardless of what budgeting system the library uses.

Types of Budgets

Budgets can be prepared in various formats. Many states and provinces mandate which budget format public libraries must use. In other jurisdictions, the local municipality selects the budget format to be used by all departments, including the public library. For use within the library, however, budgets may be reformatted, and more detailed breakdowns may be added to enable administrators to track trends and changes.

The types of budgets most often discussed are line-item budgets, planning and programming budgets, and zero-based budgets. Most libraries do not use any one type in its pure form and may, in fact, use different types for external and internal use.

Line-Item Budget

The line-item budget is the most traditional and commonly used type of budget. Most people are familiar with line-item budgets because they are often used for personal budgets. Because it is simple, a line-item budget can be prepared by an inexperienced person, based on the past year's budget. In a line-item budget, amounts are listed for each item of expenses:

Books	$115,000
Periodicals	$ 7,000
Salaries	$195,000

These figures are not clearly related to programs or services but are based on the expenditures of previous years or on information about what other libraries spend. This type of budget makes it easy to see how the money is spent, whether the budget has been met, or whether spending is over or under the projected figures. A line-item budget also makes it easy to project how much funding is needed for the coming year, based on inflation. *It does not indicate whether program objectives are being met.* Also, it is as easy to cut a line-item budget as it is to add to it. An administrator or library board can slash each item by 5 or 15 percent, and it is not easy to demonstrate how the reduction will affect overall operations—or even how it will affect a particular service.

If the personnel budget of a children's department were cut by 15 percent—perhaps by making one children's services librarian a part-time instead of full-time employee—it is unlikely that the department head would be able to tell the administrator exactly what the cut would mean in terms of the overall program.

Planning and Programming Budget

Various alternatives to the line-item budget have been developed, mostly by government agencies, as a way to link planning to budgeting. The goal of a planning budget is to analyze how much an agency's various programs should cost. A further refinement of this system is the Planning-Programming Budgeting System (PPBS) that was developed during the 1960s. This type of budget attempts to measure the output (the programs) through a systematic process. With this type of budget:

1. Broad goals and plans are developed and stated.
2. Short-term objectives are developed and stated in a measurable way.
3. Facts concerning needs are gathered.

4. Priorities are established.

5. Current programs are reviewed in terms of their necessity and effectiveness.

6. For new programs, alternatives are examined and the most effective chosen.

7. Once programs are started, they are periodically checked.

8. Programs are evaluated to see whether they fulfill objectives.

The difficulty in using this type of budget as an overall system is that specific programs are often difficult to identify and evaluate. This form of budget does not always work well in a public institution that deals in services rather than products. The need to measure the outcomes of programs sometimes leads to too much concentration on circulation and acquisition statistics, which are often not the best measurement of programs. Public library budgeting decisions cannot always be made on the basis of measured output and must be modified for political reasons. If a community feels strongly about a particular service, the library will probably maintain it, even though it is not as cost effective as other ways of delivering service.

Despite the difficulties, programming budgets provide a more analytic approach to budgeting than a simple line-item budget. They also have a built-in evaluation component that is useful in defending budgetary decisions to funders. Therefore, this method is a more effective way of planning and of using the budget as part of the overall library program.

Zero-Based Budget

In zero-based budgeting, allocations do not depend on what was done the previous year but grow out of the needs of programs for the current year. In other words, each year starts at a zero base. The budget is constructed through a series of tasks that examine every aspect of library service. The administrative team must identify and develop decision packages. This process involves describing each library activity and placing it in one or more decision packages. A decision package is "a request for allocation of funds budgeted to support a specific recommended level of services, activities, and programs" (Chen 1980, 32). Providing preschool storyhours or developing a collection of board books might be decision packages in a children's department.

After the decision packages are identified, they must be ranked. The assumption in zero-based budgeting is that any service can be provided at a minimal level, the current level, or an optimal level. Packages must be prioritized according to which are most central to the goals of the organization.

The next step is to allocate resources. All packages below a certain priority level are not funded. This means that if storyhours for preschoolers are ranked as a level one priority, while a homework hotline is ranked as a level three, the latter will not be funded if the overall budget covers only level one and two packages. One of the weaknesses of this type of budget is that it pits one department against another in vying for program funds.

The advantage of zero-based budgeting is that each program is scrutinized. Nothing is taken for granted. The minimum level of funding is generally lower than current levels. Traditional budgeting takes the current level for granted.

Trying to work out a zero-based budget is time consuming, but the process gives insight into the work of the library. Like programming budgets, zero-based budgets seem to work better for product-oriented organizations (in which it is often easier to evaluate results) than they do in libraries. Another problem with zero-based budgeting is that some choices are obvious given the nature of the library, and it wastes time to rejustify them every year. No library can consider abandoning collection development or basic reference services.

Zero-based budgets, which were popular during the 1980s, are no longer widely used as an overall budgeting system but can be useful as an internal planning tool for making decisions about programs or services.

Useful examples of library budgets of all three types are available in *Library Planning and Budgeting* (Ramsey and Ramsey 1986).

Scope of the Budget

Two levels of budgets apply to any department. The first is the overall departmental budget, which indicates how much is to be spent for categories such as personnel, materials, collection maintenance, programs, and supplies. The second level of budgeting concerns specific programs.

Departmental Budget

One method of developing a departmental budget from the ground up has been suggested by Arlene Bielefield (1978). Bielefield's methodology is a variation of the zero-based budget idea. The first step is to prepare an outline of department programs. To do this, each staff person lists all of the tasks he or she performs. If each task is entered into a database and tagged with index terms, they can be sorted and grouped under categories, such as public services, service maintenance, and administration. Each of these headings would have subheadings; for example, some subheadings under public service would include: information to individuals, information to groups, and community relations.

Bielefield suggests that once services have been established, the objectives of each service should be determined. Many authorities would argue that it would be better to develop the objectives first. Either way, comparing the tasks performed with the stated departmental objectives is an interactive process.

The next step is to determine how people spend their time—that is, how much of each person's time is spent on each task. Staff can keep track of their activities for four or five days, over a two- or three-week period. After the personnel's time on particular tasks is determined, the cost in dollars of each aspect of service can be easily calculated.

The department head can then create a program sheet listing each program, the objectives of each program, the manpower requirements, and other costs. For example, if one-quarter of a librarian's time is spent on service to groups, the cost of providing that individual's share of this service amounts to one-quarter of that librarian's annual salary. Add up the portions of other people's time spent on this service to find the total personnel cost. In allocating personnel costs to various programs, the total working time of each individual must be accounted for, with no more than 10 percent of the total time listed as miscellaneous.

There are no right or wrong allocations, but the results may prompt questions. If one of the department's objectives is to provide information services and only 10 percent of the personnel time is spent on information services, while 50 percent is spent on programming, the department may want to reexamine its objectives or priorities.

Knowing how the department's time and money are spent makes it easier for the department head to plan other programs and to see how they fit into the department's overall resources. Although the procedure takes considerable time, it does supply baseline data that can be used for years in planning the addition of or changes in programming. Adjustments must be made for changing salaries and other costs, but these changes are relatively easy to make. Changes in time allocation can be periodically monitored by asking each staff member to keep a time diary of daily tasks for a week or two. Changes in staff often lead to changes in the allocation of tasks, so it is important to keep the information up to date.

Program Budget

When considering the introduction of a new program or type of service, the first thing to determine is how it fits into the department's goals and objectives. Once it has been decided that the new program will help to meet the needs of the community and fall within the department's objectives, the department head must prepare a specific description of the program and a budget request.

To do this the manager must think through everything that will be involved in setting up the program, as well as each task that must be carried out by various levels of personnel. The department head must determine how much professional, clerical, page, or volunteer time will be involved. If volunteers are to be used, the time spent by staff members for recruitment and supervision should be included. Time requirements for resources outside of the department, such as the library's graphics or publicity departments, should also be included.

While it may be difficult to determine in advance exactly how much time each task will take, it should be possible to give a fairly accurate estimate based on the time involved in completing similar tasks for current programs. Because time estimates are usually low, about 10 percent should be added to the first figures suggested.

When all personnel needs have been accounted for, the need for materials should be assessed. The library's acquisition department can help the department head prepare estimates of material costs. The department head can augment these figures by investigating producers or suppliers of the required materials. The original figures should be increased by approximately 10 percent to account for the constantly increasing costs of materials.

After estimating the costs of personnel and materials, the total cost can be estimated. If the program is large and will require a major time commitment, it may be necessary to indicate what other program or service will be cut back. Or the department head may indicate the additional staffing that will be needed to provide the additional service. It is unwise to suggest that a large-scale new program can be offered without cutting back on other services, because this implies that the staff has spare time or time that is not used effectively.

The same principle is true of the materials budget. Requesting a new type of material, such as a selection of CD-ROMs, means either asking for additional money in addition to the annual increase necessary to keep up with inflation, or suggesting that another aspect of materials acquisition will be cut back. The costs of acquiring and processing the new materials should be described in specific detail.

In calculating the costs of a new program, be sure to include the cost of its evaluation. The evaluation will indicate whether the new program meets its objectives. Although the evaluation will require time—and, therefore, money—it is an important part of overall planning.

Preparing the Budget

The fundamental requirements for an effective budget are an accurate account of how the department's funds are currently spent and what changes are needed. Specific planning for the upcoming budget year usually begins five or six months before the end of the current fiscal year, but in reality budget planning continues throughout the year. A library manager should always know where the department stands in terms of the current budget year. The library's accounting office will maintain records that indicate where money is spent. Usually each department has access to the administrative database that contains the budget, or to the portion of it relevant to the department. The department head should take time to master the details of this record and see how closely spending matches the projections in each category. While overspending is the major threat to budgets, underspending in any category is an indication that something is wrong. Either the projected figures were not accurate, the need for the money was exaggerated, or the program is not being properly implemented.

Before proposing changes in the budget, obtain accurate cost estimates. Some estimates are most appropriately made by the library's accounting department, but estimates that relate specifically to children's materials and services often must be made by the children's librarian. While producers can provide the average cost of materials, the cost of programming and services are difficult to ascertain because it is hard to estimate the amount of time involved. Librarians who have instituted similar programs or services usually are good sources of cost estimates. Other knowledgeable people may include teachers, community workers, or other professionals. The key to obtaining accurate cost estimates is to allow plenty of time for gathering information.

Because most costs rise continually over time, an inflation factor should be built into estimates. In addition, it is important to allow a contingency fund of about 10 percent to cover the unexpected expenses of starting a new collection or service.

When preparing budgets for new services, it is useful to suggest alternatives. Thus, the cost of producing a new series of book lists could be given for two production alternatives: (1) in-house production, including buying a new laser printer, and (2) commercial production, including design, production, and printing.

Budgeting Tools

In large library systems, the software used for the budgeting system may be complex. Budgetary requests may be submitted on paper or electronic forms that go to centralized financial offices. Department heads may receive periodic reports of only the sections dealing with their department. This can sometimes make it difficult for a manager to keep track of the spending within the department. With a little effort, a manager can use a simple spreadsheet program on the departmental computer to keep track of the budget. Although it takes a few hours of work to become familiar with these programs, once the process is mastered, it will cut down on both time and effort in following budgets. Simple formulae can be designed to show the effect of a 10 percent across-the-board increase in funding or a five percent cut. Projections for the cost of materials over several years can be made based on different predictions for inflation. This allows a department head to make more sophisticated financial plans than were possible using traditional methods.

Accounting services are usually available within the library system and are invaluable in helping a department head understand and plan budgets. Sometimes it is tempting to hand the entire budgeting process over to an accountant, but a manager retains more authority if he or she remains informed of the accountant's plans and figures. This takes time, but it is the only way the librarian can control the budget.

12

Planning Facilities

A public library is a visible symbol of a community's commitment to provide educational and cultural services to all of its residents. Unlike schools, which offer structured educational opportunities, libraries are intended to provide to each individual the particular item required whenever it is requested. Buildings that effectively provide for the wide range of interests and tastes of users are not easy to design. "Librarians and other planners need to seek designs in their buildings that symbolize the offer of a convenient, attractive and varied opportunity for choice to each individual" (Lushington and Kusack 1991, 7). To do this librarians need to present materials in a way that enables users to locate and use the materials they want.

Although planning and building new libraries or making extensive renovations to existing structures are not done frequently, most librarians will find themselves involved in such planning at some time during their career. Decisions made at the crucial early stages of planning will affect the working conditions of current staff and of a future succession of librarians. Careful planning requires hard work over a period of time but the result can be a department that is both esthetically pleasing and provides a setting for efficiently organized services.

Because of the constraints on spending for public buildings, an increasing number of communities are converting buildings designed for other purposes into library facilities. These buildings include schools, churches, supermarkets, post offices, banks, and private houses. Some library advocates believe that the conversion of existing structures offers advantages over new buildings "in terms of donations, rent-to-own, lease backs, joint use, and neighborhood improvement and redevelopment incentives" (MacDonald 1996, 288). A reuse project, if approached in a positive spirit, can often generate more community support than a new building because taxpayers perceive it as offering tax savings while it results in a valued facility. Although conversion projects take less time than the construction of a new building, both require careful and time-consuming planning.

Background Information

Community Needs

Planning an effective facility requires that the planners know the community in which the library is being built and the community's uses for the building. Among the factors that affect planning are

- the number of people expected to use the building
- the demographics and growth pattern of the community
- the proportion of residential, business, and industrial use in the community
- the presence of other libraries and information services
- the availability of related institutions (e.g., museums, cultural institutions)
- the geographic location
- the community's social climate

The size of the community affects the size of the library, but the community's current population is not as important as the growth pattern. In a well-settled neighborhood where little space is available for new housing, the number of patrons may be stable. A new or expanding suburb, however, can be expected to grow over a period of years, and the clientele may strain the facility by the time it is opened. In a city where zoning regulations allow multiple housing to replace single-family homes, the population may dramatically increase. Most communities' planning offices can provide projected figures for the growth of specific neighborhoods. While these figures are not always accurate, they represent target growth and are likely to be the best data available. Librarians should become familiar not only with the overall number of new houses, but also with the expected size and style of housing units. These affect the size and composition of families moving into the area. High-rise apartments tend to attract single people or childless couples, while single-family homes generally indicate a higher proportion of children. Facilities designed for senior citizens yield yet another pattern of library clientele.

A community's zoning regulations indicate whether businesses are likely to locate in the area, offering another target group for the library. Existing schools or plans for new schools also affect how the library will be used, as do community colleges, universities, hospitals, and nursing homes.

The existence and accessibility of other libraries will affect the use of a new facility. The number and quality of school media centers affect use by students. Community college and university libraries have a greater or lesser impact on public library use depending on their collections, hours, levels of service, and policies toward community use.

In communities that do not have institutions, such as museums, art galleries, concert halls, or theaters, a public library building may incorporate these facilities. Planning a building to serve two or three different purposes is a challenging task, but the facilities can offer enrichment to a community. Designing a library as a community center requires an interdisciplinary approach and cooperation by a number of different institutions, but the librarian's job in this setting would remain the same.

The community environment affects the style of the building, as well as the requirements for heating, air conditioning, and lighting. The most obvious differences between libraries constructed in cold and warm climates is the building's shape and its use of outdoor space. Efficient heating in cold climates often dictates the use of square, compact buildings, while warm climates invite the use of rambling buildings and open courtyards to take advantage of fresh air and breezes. Libraries built in areas with harsh winter weather may need to provide shelter for staff members' cars and heated walkways. Those built in hot, sunny areas should be designed so that windows do not admit too much sunlight and heat. High humidity or excessive dryness can damage books and other materials, so the presence of these conditions influences some design decisions. Architects and planners are aware of these needs, but sometimes the desire to build a library in a particular style or as a complement to existing structures may result in an impractical building for a specific location. The library staff and the public have to live with the limitations imposed by planning decisions, so issues of practicality and comfort should be raised as early as possible.

The small-scale geographic differences of building sites include the presence of public transportation, sidewalks on adjacent streets, and the location of highways or major traffic arteries that may be barriers to pedestrian access. Adequate parking space is necessary, and access for bicyclists and pedestrians should be provided.

The proximity of other types of buildings affect library use patterns. A library in or near a shopping mall is likely to have a different pattern of use—more unattended children and shorter patron visits—than a library located in a residential area. Being situated in or near areas that parents think are unsafe, such as parks or industrial sites, may limit library use unless special efforts are made to provide appropriate lighting and security.

The social climate of the community, especially a small community, should also be taken into account in designing a library building. If families tend to engage in recreational activities together, the children's department will need more extensive adult/child reading areas than in a community where children tend to come alone to the library. Libraries in communities with extensive day care facilities will likely need more group activity space than those in communities where most preschool children are cared for at home. If many children in the community are homeschooled, provisions should be made for children's study areas. History also plays a role; a library that has traditionally hosted an end-of-school program for children will want to ensure that new facilities offer space to carry on the program.

During the early stages of planning, the library staff should make a conscious effort to list aspects of the community that might affect building plans. A file of suggestions from various staff members may give the planning committee insights it would not otherwise have.

Patterns of Use

The building planner must know how the library will be used by staff, patrons, and the community. Perhaps the most effective way to assess this use is to keep a record of the patterns of use over a period of weeks or months before formal planning starts.

Use of the children's department can be considered in terms of activities. Activities can be categorized as group activities and individual activities (see figure 12.1).

By looking at this pattern of activity, a librarian can make decisions about the space and furniture needed in the children's department. Library activities in figure 12.1 require space for 65 patrons at one time. Seating is needed for adults reading to children, groups of students working together, children doing school work, and children using audiovisual materials. Seating must be available in various sizes for ages toddler through adult. Programming space must allow for small toddler-adult programs and large audiences for film programs. Study tables and probably carrels are needed, as well as chairs or cushions for leisure reading. Terminals are necessary for using electronic resources, and a reference area is needed for print resources.

The personal activities listed at the end of figure 12.1—storing coats, boots, and hats and using washrooms and telephones—should be taken into account. In areas with severe winters, storing jackets and boots can pose a problem, especially during programs. The use of coat hangers or hooks and boot trays prevents damage to carpeting and furniture and frees up the chairs and tables that would otherwise be used to hold these items. It is a good idea to provide washrooms in a children's department as a convenience to staff and parents as well as children. Because many children are dropped off at the library and must call a parent or caregiver to arrange a ride home, providing a public telephone is useful. Otherwise, when a public phone is unavailable, patrons will frequently ask staff members for permission to use library phones.

Patron Activities in Children's Department

Group Activity	Age of Participants	Number of Participants
Storyhour	Preschool	20–25
Books for babies	Toddlers and adults	10 pairs
Showing films	8–12-year-olds	30–35
Group study	8–12-year-olds	4–6 each
Playing games	6–12-year-olds	2–4 each
Using computers	6–12-year-olds	2–3 each
Socializing	All ages	Small groups

Individual Activity	Age of Participants	Numbers
Choosing materials	Preschool	10–15 total
	School age	25–45 total
	Adults	4–5 total
	(Maximum total)	65 people
Reference	All ages	Individual
Reading	Preschool/adult	2 or 3 each
	School age	Individual
Using electronic resources	School age	Individual
Doing school work	School age	Individual
Storing outer garments	All ages	Individual
Washroom use	All ages	Boys and girls
Using telephone	School age	Individual

Fig. 12.1. Patron Activities in Children's Department.

The general needs assessment for the department facilities should be based on a careful evaluation of ongoing activities. Because the use of the library is likely to increase when a new building is opened, estimates should allow for a growth factor in addition to current use. If a branch is being built in a neighborhood that has never had a library, the patterns of use can be based on observation of other library branches in similar neighborhoods. Some common types of staff activity are shown in figure 12.2.

As in assessing patron needs, the needs of staff must be judged on the basis of systematic observation of their activities over a period of time. Librarians may know, in general, the amount of space and equipment they need to do their work, but correcting a lack of space or facilities for one task can lead to the creation of new problems. Noting staff activities and needs for several weeks will provide a more accurate record of what is necessary than asking staff members to estimate needs.

A common problem in new library buildings is a lack of work space for staff. When cutbacks have to be made, librarians are often reluctant to eliminate space for resources or programming. Although adequate and attractive public areas are important, it is also necessary to provide private working space for staff. Service is likely to suffer if public areas are used for mending or sorting books or if craft and publicity supplies have to be crammed into desk drawers. Work space for the staff to examine

Staff Activities in Children's Department

Activity	Number of Personnel at Any One Time	Facilities Needed
Administration	1	Private office Telephone/fax Computer
Reference	1 or 2	Desk visible to public Telephone Computer
Programming	1	Desk or table Storage for craft supplies and books
Selection	1 or 2	Desk, shelving Journals and computer
Circulation	1 or 2	Public counter Terminals Telephone
Mending	2 or 3	Work table Supplies
Shelving	2 or 3	Book trucks and shelving
Meetings	Entire staff	Access to meeting room
Personal	Entire staff	Access to lounge area and washrooms Personal lockers or storage space

Fig. 12.2. Staff Activities in Children's Department.

and discuss new materials is not a luxury but an important way to ensure knowledgeable staff assistance for patrons. In addition to providing adequate space for current needs, also allow room for some growth of both staff and services.

Community use of the library may affect availability of the public meeting rooms. Some children's departments provide space to community groups or schools for art shows or exhibitions of children's projects. Occasionally, small collections of art or natural objects are given to the library for display in the children's room. Providing display space serves a valuable public relations function. Community use of the children's facilities for public ceremonies, such as book awards, may be desirable, especially in a small community. Use of the library for these purposes is related to availability of other community facilities. When a new library building is being planned, library staff should investigate the possibility of such joint uses of the library.

Housing the Collection

The number of books in a collection is not the only factor to be considered in planning collection space for a children's department. Differences in format and in needs for access determine the type of shelving required.

Children's materials have traditionally been divided into preschool materials—primarily picture books—and materials for older children. Some libraries subdivide this further by having separate shelving for board books and for early reading books. Audiovisual materials are usually shelved separately from books. Although this arrangement may help the librarian to choose books for a child by going to the most appropriate shelf, it can make it more difficult for patrons to choose books on their own. Children and parents often do not know the difference between picture books, early reading books, and board books. A balance must be struck between segregating particular materials for the convenience of staff and following a simple order scheme that patrons can learn. The goal of most departments is to enable young patrons and their parents to select materials for themselves, rather than having to ask library staff for help. Unless a clear need for segregated collections is apparent, the simplest system is usually the best—picture books in one visible area, fiction in alphabetical order, and nonfiction in one sequence of Dewey decimal order. Audiovisual materials, such as videos, interfiled with nonfiction materials will be easier for most children to locate.

Special types of shelving are needed for picture books. Because most of these books are oversized and thin, with little information on the spine, the most effective shelving is face-outward. Slanting shelves, which allow browsers to see the front cover of the books and to open them easily, are highly desirable, but most collections are too large to allow all books to be displayed this way. One solution is to have most of the books shelved spine-outward on a set of low shelves and to have one row of slanted shelving above these to display a constantly changing selection of books. Some libraries have experimented with keeping picture books in large baskets, in bins, or on book trucks for easy browsing. Although these methods make it difficult to find a particular book, most children choose their books by browsing. Whatever shelving is used, estimate the number of picture books that are likely to be collected and house them separately from other materials.

Periodicals are similar in format to paperback books. Because most libraries do not bind children's periodicals, back issues soon become tattered and unsightly. The most frequently used system allows current issues to be shown face-outward and provides shelf space to stack back issues. Most periodicals are used in-house, so the shelving should be placed near comfortable seating for easy browsing.

Paperback materials are usually stored separately from hardcover books. Many libraries use spinners, revolving book racks, which allow books to be displayed face-outward. Spinners tend to attract several children at a time and may cause congestion if not allotted sufficient space. Because paperbacks are a growing part of children's collections, the plan for a new library should allow for an increase in their number.

The standard collection of children's fiction and nonfiction takes up more space than an adult collection of similar size because usually only low shelving is used. Children cannot reach high shelves, so books become inaccessible if adult shelving is used. Low shelving also makes it easier for the librarian to see what is happening in the department and to prevent discipline problems. The tops of such shelves can also be used for informal displays of new books or other items of seasonal or special interest. When predicting an increase in the size of the collection, the children's department's needs for easy access should be taken into account.

Nonprint materials require special types of storage: trays or spinners for cassettes and compact discs, shelving for games, cabinets for toys, and files for software. Equipment, such as compact discs or cassette players and video viewers, as well as computers, require space and electrical outlets.

In planning new facilities, make realistic predictions of both current and future needs. Electronic resources and Internet access are limited in many public libraries in the 1990s but are likely to be predominant means of delivering information in the early years of the twenty-first century. Sufficient space for CD-ROM towers, Internet access, and online searching should be allowed for both current and planned technologies. Provision should be made for extensive wiring so that computer terminals can be made available throughout the department. It is almost always less expensive to plan for these innovations during new building construction or renovations than to install them later. Children tend to make heavy use of electronic resources, and a shortage of terminals at busy times can be a deterrent to efficient library use.

Some libraries space terminals around the room so that they do not congest a single area, while other departments prefer to cluster them in one location. Consideration should be given to both of these options. Locating the computers in one area makes it easier to ensure appropriate lighting for computer use. Glare on computer screens is a problem, especially if computers are placed near windows. But, a central cluster of computers, as shown in figure 12.3, is likely to become a major attraction for children, leading to noise and crowding. Also, if the computers are isolated from the books, print resources may be neglected. Scattering terminals throughout the room so that they are used as complementary to print resources may encourage more balanced use of the collection.

Fig. 12.3. Computer Cluster in Children's Department.

When planning the table area for computers, allow space for two or three children or a child and an adult to use a terminal together. This saves staff time in training users in the use of OPAC and other online resources because children are willing and able to train one another.

Access to the collection is important not only for various age groups but also for patrons with disabilities. Government regulations, such as the Americans with Disabilities Act require that all new and reconstructed public facilities must be "readily accessible to and usable by individuals with disabilities" (Harrison and Gilbert 1992, 177). Whenever possible, a new building should go beyond the minimum requirements and make use by persons with disabilities as convenient and pleasant as possible. Children with disabilities especially should not be segregated from other children who are using the library.

In a new building, the shelves and spinners should be placed far enough apart to allow a person in a wheelchair to see all materials. Shelves should be neither too high nor too low to be reached by a person in a wheelchair. Most of the study tables and at least one table for computers should be designed to accommodate wheelchairs. (For guidelines, see Michaels and Michaels 1996.)

Signs in the library should be large enough to be easily read by individuals with limited vision, and their letters should be set in a simple, clear text with high contrast between the letters and the background. If the library has elevators, they should be equipped with Braille markings as well as a sound system to announce floors. Lighting should be sufficient in all sections of the library. Objects such as fire extinguishers and phone booths should not protrude into passageways or rooms. The traditional auditory alarm systems should be supplemented with visual alarms for hearing-impaired patrons (MacLachlan 1996).

Planning should include areas for displaying library materials or special exhibits. Changing displays can add visual excitement to a department, and displays will be more effective if appropriate space has been planned. Lockable glass-front cases make it possible for the department to display valuable borrowed materials as well as library materials. Display cases placed near the entrance to the department serve as an attractive introduction to the children's room.

Exploring the Possibilities

Knowing the way the library is likely to be used and the collections it will house are the first steps in planning facilities. After determining the needs, the planning committee should explore ways that these needs might be met. One way to do this is to visit other libraries, both locally and while attending conferences or workshops. Touring other facilities allows the planners to observe both successful and unsuccessful arrangements. It is useful not only to look at the library but also to talk to staff members to learn about unseen aspects of the design. Do certain colors tend to soil easily? Does the attractive soft sculpture pose any dangers to toddlers? Librarians who have experience with various approaches can offer invaluable advice about their efficiency and practicality.

Workshops and conference programs offer more formal advice on planning library facilities. At least one staff member should attend any program available during the planning period. Periodicals and books also offer helpful advice. *Library Journal* publishes an annual architectural issue that shows examples of new library buildings and gives specifications on their sizes and facilities. Some useful additional materials are included in the publication's reference list. New materials on planning are constantly appearing; a literature search of both print and electronic sources on the topic may locate new and helpful information.

Preparing Plans

Decision Points

One of the early decisions to be made in designing a children's department is its location within the building. This decision will be based on how much separation from the adult department is desired and on the practicalities of staffing and use.

In public libraries built during the first half of the twentieth century, the children's room was often placed at some distance from the adult sections because it was believed that the children's noise would distract adult patrons. Sometimes the children's department was on the second floor of the library above the adult department; and sometimes it was on a lower level. This was done because most school-age children can climb stairs more easily than adults, so the more convenient location was reserved for adults. Some libraries even provide separate entrances for children. This physical separation of the children's department from the rest of the library protected children from exposure to materials considered unsuitable for them and gave them a space planned for their comfort and convenience.

As public libraries began to reach out more to preschool children who would normally be accompanied by parents when using the library, the inconvenience of a department separated from the adult section became more noticeable. Adults wanted to browse for books for themselves and also keep an eye on younger children. Those with more than one preschool child found it difficult to maneuver infants or toddlers up and down stairs, a problem made more difficult by a separate entrance. Also, the library community began to feel that children should be able to move easily between the adult and children's collections, rather than having the "graduation" from children to adult status marked by the completion of a particular grade in school or reaching a specific age.

Most libraries built in recent years have had an open plan, with the children's section visible and accessible from the adult circulation department, but clearly indicated by decor and signage as a special area for children. The nature of the community can influence the desirable level of separation. If parents, children, and teenagers are the main users of a library branch, the traffic between adult and children's section is likely to be heavy, and noise from the children's department is unlikely to offend adult users. If, on the other hand, many adults are using the library for business or study, they may prefer to have the children's department out of sight and range of hearing. Usually, it is best to have the browsing shelves closest to the children's department and to place the adult reference and study areas at the furthest distance.

The placement of washrooms and other public facilities deserves careful thought. The best solution is to have children's washrooms within the department, with the entrance to them visible from the librarian's desk. This allows the library staff to monitor their use. If washrooms are available only in the adult department, children may disturb adults as they walk through the area, and the washrooms must be kept locked to protect children's safety. Washrooms in the entrance hall or on a corridor, out of sight of library staff, are particularly undesirable for children's use.

Lighting is a major factor in planning, as it can add to the comfort level of the library. Natural light is the best way to light a library, but direct sunlight can damage materials and make the building uncomfortably warm. Windows that bring light into the room without occupying too much wall space are ideal. Strip windows located across the top of wall shelving are practical, although they usually require drapes or blinds to prevent the sunlight from fading books and furnishings. Windows not only provide light but keep both staff and patrons aware of weather situations—snowstorms or rain—and may enhance the beauty of the room by providing a view of the sky, trees, or a cityscape.

Artificial lighting is necessary in a library, regardless of the number of windows. Most children's departments are busy in the evening because many parents and school-age children find this the most convenient time to visit the library. Since most library activities involve close viewing of print or nonprint materials, sufficient lighting should be available throughout the department. Some libraries find that lamps, placed on study tables or in carrels, add to the decor and are practical for students. Visually impaired children need special consideration. If they need additional light at study tables, high intensity lamps should be available at the circulation desk for temporary use. Standards of lighting have changed in recent years as scientists have come to understand that the glare of bright light on paper may make reading more difficult than a lower level of lighting. Glare can also make the use of computer terminals uncomfortable. If overhead lighting is used in a computer terminal area, it is better to install a glare-free louver instead of direct ceiling lighting. Consultation with lighting experts and vision specialists can help library planners choose the most effective lighting for a particular facility.

Sound control is important in children's departments because children tend to work and play together when they are using library resources. Ceiling materials, drapes, and wall hangings can deaden the sounds of library use and make the atmosphere more pleasant, especially when the library is crowded. The area to be used for programs should be designed so that a reasonable number of children can hear a storyteller's or reader's voice. If the area is clearly marked and has doors to close it off from the rest of the department, it is much easier for the library staff to present programs that include music or sound effects without disturbing other library users.

Spacing is another important consideration. The most practical shape for a room is generally a square, and space arrangements should be determined by traffic flow. The most heavily used resources are best located closest to the center of the room. Librarian's desks should be centrally located for easy access and to allow the librarian to keep an eye on all activities. Usually the librarian's desk is located near the reference section and computer terminals because children often need help with these items.

Some planners believe that wall space should be reserved for people and stacks should be placed in the center of the room. However, center stacks can prevent the librarian from visually monitoring the room. Wall shelving makes a small room look larger and can permit greater flexibility in the use of space. When working with the architect, the librarian should try to ensure that the space will allow flexibility in furnishing. Electrical outlets should be placed so that terminals and AV equipment can be used in any area of the room. Structural designs, such as a story pit, should be considered carefully because they are permanent and limit the use of space. Built-in features may determine the location of various sections for many years. It may be preferable to impose few structural limitations on the space allowed for the children's department.

Presenting Plans

As part of the planning process, each department will probably be asked to make suggestions about the department's needs and desires. This is the time when the initial work of observing and documenting library use will pay dividends. The department head who knows the average number of patrons in the department at various times, the activities of the patrons, and the needs of patrons and staff will be in a better position to present credible requirements than one who relies on intuition. The representative of the children's department who attends planning committee meetings should go prepared with written documentation of the department's concerns. Because all demands cannot be met, the department head should be flexible but make as strong a case as possible for planning an ideal facility. In addition to knowing the department's present uses and possible future trends, the department representative can provide examples of other children's departments that incorporate the requested features. Finally, the department should establish priorities for equipment or space that may be relinquished in case of cutbacks.

The planning committee usually includes members of the library board, but sometimes department representatives are expected to present their cases to the entire library board. Because the board members are less familiar with the day-to-day operations of the library than staff members are, the documentation given to board members should be complete and persuasive. At the same time, it is important not to waste board members' time with lengthy oral presentations. A clear, concise handout for each board member can provide the basic facts. The oral presentation should be brief and devoted primarily to answering questions about the plans.

The department head may speak with members of the public, usually represented by the parents of users or potential users. When planning new facilities, it is useful to ask the public for suggestions. The library website is a good forum for discussion of the facility's plans. E-mail messages from the public may be sent to the library staff, and popular suggestions can be posted on the site for further discussion and modifications. Many ideas suggested by the public will reinforce the staff's ideas about needs, such as space, seating, and room for programming. These suggestions validate the ideas proposed by the library staff. Other suggestions may be for facilities far beyond anything the library could hope to provide or for idiosyncratic items that would be inappropriate. When possible, the library staff should be ready to explain why certain facilities will not be provided or why an idea is not feasible. This is good public relations and can help to make the community feel a sense of ownership of the library. Children too can be drawn into the planning by being asked for suggestions or for pictures of their vision of the new library.

When the library board has decided on an architectural firm, the department head may meet with architects to discuss the plans. At these meetings, the librarian should make clear the requirements for maintaining an efficient department. The architects may have valuable and innovative suggestions for meeting these requirements, but it is the librarian's task to ensure that these requirements are met. Providing services takes precedence over constructing an eye-catching building. Every suggestion should be tested by asking such questions as the following:

- How will this suggestion help us provide better library services?
- Could this suggestion cause extra work for the staff?
- Could this suggestion cause a danger to children? (Attractive seating arrangements and sculptures, such as castles and dragons, have had to be dismantled in libraries because of their potential danger to young children.)
- Has this suggestion been tried in other libraries, and if so, how successful does the staff consider it to be?

Planning the Decor

Once the building plans have been finalized, attention will turn to the library's interior decor. Some architectural firms have design departments that work with clients in this type of planning. Or, the library may work with individual designers to coordinate color schemes, choose furniture and floor coverings, and add the finishing touches.

Setting Guidelines

Members of the library staff who will be working in the new or renovated building will want to have input into the decoration as well as the structure of the children's department. Their knowledge of the patterns of library use will help the decorator arrange it for maximum usability. The decorator, in turn, can guide the staff to a choice of colors and materials that will both result in the desired effect and be practical.

The goal of interior design for a children's department is to produce a space that is friendly, approachable, and welcoming for all users. The decor of children's departments in some libraries suggests that they have been designed primarily for preschool children. While space and facilities should be made available for young children, the entire department should not look like a nursery. Choosing colors and design elements geared to very young children can discourage school-age youngsters from patronizing what they see as "a baby room." The overall effect should be lively and appealing, with sections that visually indicate whether they are planned for toddlers playing with toys and board books or for school-age children using computers and reference materials for school projects.

Informal seating should allow for a variety of postures while reading or taking notes but should somewhat limit conversational groups. For children, carpeting and cushions can take the place of chairs or carrels. However, study carrels are good for children who have a difficult time concentrating. The ideal room provides a variety of types of seating and work areas. Children, as a rule, like to sit closer to one another than do adults. Furniture should be scaled for children but should also allow for adult use as adults frequently accompany children. Comfortable seating arrangements should be available for parents that read to their children.

Choosing Colors

Usually the colors used in the children's department are brighter than those in other sections of the library. The staff can gather ideas for effective color schemes by visiting other libraries. Some librarians are tempted to carry their personal color choices over into the library setting. This is unwise, because public spaces have different purposes than private spaces. It is better to look at public buildings—theaters, museums, and shopping malls, in addition to other libraries—for ideas about colors for walls, carpets, and furniture.

Signage is another important aspect of planning. Many new users, both young children and their parents, will be coming to a children's department, so signs should be large, clear, and well placed. Pictures that reinforce the meaning of the print help young readers. Signs that hang from the ceiling to indicate areas such as a reference desk, picture book area, or parents' corner, should be planned from the start. They are more obvious than wall signs and can be helpful, especially in a large room. The decorator can plan the colors, lettering, and style of the signs to fit in with the overall decorative plan.

Artwork adds color and interest to a department and should be incorporated in the department's design. Permanent works of art, such as murals, add color and interest to walls. However, they limit the amount of display space available for temporary exhibits and may lose their charm over time. Many libraries have found that changeable displays and exhibits are preferable to permanent, built-in art. Glass-front display cases in which pictures, art objects, and books can be placed offer flexibility. Space for hanging posters, children's drawings, and seasonal decorations is also useful. Areas of corkboard or other soft surface make it possible to hang pictures and other items easily and safely. The decorator can suggest practical ways to achieve flexibility in the display of artworks.

Moving into New Facilities

Changing Plans

Time lines are an important guide for planning, but they are seldom infallible. Both building and renovation are subject to delays caused by weather, labor problems, accidents, and unexpected difficulties in obtaining materials. Plans must be based on the expected date of completion, but contingency plans should always be in place for coping with delays. Announcements to the public about opening events should allow for such delays.

Cost estimates on buildings are subject to change because of rising prices. These cost increases may lead to cutbacks on sections of the proposed building. Establishing priorities in facility plans is important so that if cost overruns dictate the elimination of some features, the librarian will know which items can be given up with the least effect on library service. The elimination of decorative or comfort features, such as special seating, can be accepted more easily than the elimination of space. Many features can be added at a later date if cost permits, but space cannot easily be altered.

Moving the Department

A department head normally does not decide the procedure for the move to a new facility, but everyone on the planning committee should know the options and make suggestions. Although a professional moving company usually takes responsibility for transporting books and equipment to the new location, the library staff will need to plan every detail of the move. Public libraries often use volunteers to help in moving a collection, with the library staff supervising these volunteers.

To prepare for a move, the librarian must know the current collection, its space requirements, and its arrangement in the new facility. Computer programs are useful in planning the amount of space for housing a collection (Hamilton and Hindman 1987; Ellis 1988) and in determining the best layout for the collection in the new facility. Sufficient time (several months) must be spent in determining the exact requirements and how they can best be met.

Recruiting volunteer help for a move not only saves the library money but can also demonstrate to the public the range and size of the collection. If helping with the move is a positive experience, the volunteers may become lifelong supporters of the new library. Parents of children who use the library are often strong supporters of the service, and the children's department should make a particular effort to enlist them as volunteers. As taxpayers, most local residents understand the need to save public money and will respond to an appeal to substitute volunteer labor for tax dollars. Volunteers can be recruited through notices on the library's website; newspaper, radio, and television advertisements; posters in the library and community centers; and word-of-mouth by library staff. Careful scheduling, planning, and supervision will make the best use of the volunteer's services. Volunteers should receive an expression of appreciation, public recognition, and a small gift.

Settling In

Regardless of how efficient the move may be, some unexpected problems will occur in settling into a new facility. All of the equipment should be tested as quickly as possible so that any possible failures can be noted and corrected. Staff members may have some difficulty in adjusting to new conditions, so additional time may be required to handle routine tasks. However, this situation should rapidly improve.

Although the new facilities should be an improvement over the old building, it is wise to keep notes on any miscalculations or desired changes. Notes about disappointments and failings in the new building will make it easier to plan for the inevitable day when yet another change will be needed.

Post-Occupancy Evaluation

Although few new facilities are systematically evaluated after they have been built or renovated, a strong case can be made for including evaluation as part of the overall plan. As Lushington and Kusack (1991, 117) claim:

> No matter how excellent the architect or how diligent the planners are in evaluating the plans, the true test of the building comes when it is built, occupied, and used. Plan evaluation is abstract and primarily an intellectual exercise; post-occupancy evaluation is concrete and involves the natural complexity of real life. Both types of evaluation make important contributions to the improvement of library buildings.

Library staff is likely to be exhausted after a move to new facilities. The imposition of an evaluation exercise may be seen as a needless additional task. Nonetheless, evaluations are valuable in building a knowledge base of what does and does not work in libraries.

Evaluation should not begin until at least one year after the new building has been occupied. By that time, staff and patrons will have had time to become used to changes. Even if the entire library is not planning an evaluation, an individual department can carry out a small-scale study of how its particular service has been affected by a move.

The first step in an evaluation is to collect observations and evidence about visible problems. A notebook in which any staff member can record observations will facilitate the collection of information. A roof that leaks or a heating system that delivers uneven warmth are examples of obvious problems that should be recorded. Notable successes, such as a doubling of circulation or an increase in library card registration are also part of the record. Statistics of performance measures in the old building should be compared with those of the new facilities. These measures will indicate changes in service to the community. If time and resources are available, questionnaires may be administered to individuals using the children's department to determine their satisfaction with the facility. All of these efforts will result in a collection of useful data to indicate directions for planning future changes.

13

Community
Public Relations

Public libraries are dramatically changing and offering new materials and services to the community. Unfortunately, not all of the library's potential clientele are aware of what the library has to offer. When parents buy books at the supermarket or invest in a CD-ROM encyclopedia, because they are unaware of the library's resources, they are reacting to a lack of library public relations efforts. An effective library tries to ensure that all members of the community know about library resources and services through a carefully designed public relations program.

Many library activities involve a public relations component, but librarians should also give some thought to an overall, ongoing departmental public relations plan. The purpose of library public relations is, according to *Part-Time Public Relations with Full-Time Results: A Primer for Libraries*, "to develop ongoing programs of contact between the librarians and the population groups that they serve" (Karp 1995, ix).

Developing a Public Relations Program

A public relations program is not a one-shot effort to increase community awareness of the library, although such efforts may be a part of the program. The ongoing public relations program includes all of the contacts that librarians make with the community both inside and outside of the library and through websites, electronic or print announcements, displays, radio or television spots, and news stories. An effective public relations program provides an honest and persuasive account of what the library offers and its value to the community. Because the children's department is an important and highly visible part of library service, children's librarians should make an effort to publicize the department's services.

The first step in planning a public relations program is to choose the message to be delivered to the community about the library. The goals, objectives, and role of the department (discussed in Chapters 1 and 2) suggest ideas for the types of information given to library users and potential users. Many adults have the idea that a children's collection consists of picture books and literary classics and that services are limited to story programs for young children. Sometimes this image is perpetuated by newspaper or television stories that feature traditional library programs but do not mention parenting books, homework help, and electronic and print-based reference services. In recent years, the availability of computers in children's departments has caught media attention, but they are often presented as an alternative to traditional books, not as an integral part of an overall service program. Children's librarians should encourage the media to present a balanced picture of the department's services.

Just as many adults think of the children's department as primarily a story-telling room, they often think of children's librarians as women who love books and are more at home with *Peter Rabbit* than with science fair projects and databases. While children's librarians are knowledgeable about picture books and children's classics, they also know a great deal about other subjects. The objective of a public relations program is to ensure that librarians determine the message that will be conveyed to the public by consciously choosing factors to be publicized rather than relying on the media or others to decide what to share with the public.

Meeting the Public

A public relations program is often thought to be aimed at people outside of the library, but encounters within the library—the way patrons are treated by staff—affect the public's perception more than anything else. Every time a librarian helps a child or parent to find a book, explains the way the catalog works, or fails to locate information, he or she is affecting the way the patron thinks about the library. The first step for a department head in planning a public relations program is to make sure that everyone on the staff follows accepted standards for dealing with patrons. No amount of external publicity will make up for the rudeness or neglect of a staff member in the library. Publicizing library resources raises expectations, which the library staff must be prepared to meet. Otherwise, publicity will have a negative effect.

Staff Attitudes

A cheerful, knowledgeable, and willing staff is the greatest asset of any children's department. Any publicity efforts to bring more patrons into the library should be made in cooperation with staff members whose work will be affected by the additional traffic. If new services, such as Internet access or a homework hotline, are to be established, the librarians should ensure that staff members can efficiently handle these services. Premature publicity about services can give a bad impression about the ability of the library to help patrons.

Talking to Groups

The librarian is the public's chief source of information about library activities, and talks to community groups about this topic can be effective. Parent groups are a natural audience for librarians who can discuss the library's books and services for children. It is not necessary to wait for an invitation to speak to groups. A letter to a parents' group offering to speak at their next meeting about choosing books for toddlers, encouraging children to read, or another topic, can lead to invitations. A useful and effective talk may lead to future requests.

Most librarians are not practiced public speakers or entertainers, but almost anyone can learn to give a successful speech about a topic of interest. The keys are planning, enthusiasm, and clarity. Nothing is more discouraging than a rambling talk that attempts to cover the entire field of children's literature or mention all of the good picture books for children. Since most talks to community groups will be limited to about a half an hour, the librarian should try to make only two or three points, but make them effectively. Visual aids and handouts help focus attention during the talk and act later as a reminder to the listeners of a particular book or author. A blackboard or an overhead projector can be used for listing titles during the talk, but a handout that can be taken home is more convenient and permanent. The handout can also include information about library hours and service. Anecdotes about children's reactions to books bring life to a talk and emphasize the importance of books in children's lives. Showing books and having them available for browsing demonstrates their attractiveness. Lists of materials developed for a specific program can be mounted on the library website, where they create additional publicity and demonstrate the library's activities.

When giving a talk, the librarian should speak in a clear, enthusiastic, and informal manner; and rehearsal with a tape recorder can help to achieve these goals. The speaker may want to refer briefly to notes, but it is unwise to "read" to a group. In fact, it is better for the speaker to forget part of the talk than to read a prepared statement. Eye contact is important, but be sure to include the whole group, transferring attention from one person to another. This will help in gauging the listeners' reactions. If listeners appear puzzled, a point can be expanded or explained, and questions may be solicited. If the audience becomes restless, remarks should be cut short; at least some of the points will be made.

Time should be allowed for questions after a talk. This may lead one or two people to make statements or recall childhood experiences with books—an occupational hazard for children's librarians—but it does elicit feedback, which is important. Many people are reluctant to ask questions in an open forum, but may approach the speaker after the talk, so try not to rush away from the meeting. Stress that the library staff are available to answer questions in the library or on the telephone.

In addition to parents' groups, librarians should try to speak to business or service groups whenever possible. Discussions about the library's efforts to increase literacy or to help persons with disabilities may interest these groups and raise their awareness of the importance of children's services in libraries.

Participating in a Library Website

A website offers a public library the chance to give current information about its location, services, programs, and collections, as well as access to its catalog, community and regional information, and other electronic resources. Because many users of the Internet are young, the youth services department should make sure that it has a highly visible presence on the library's website.

The children's department should be listed on the home page of the library, not two or more mouse clicks away, through a "public services" heading. An attractive graphic next to the spot where children should click, will better entice the audience to go to the children's department page than a text-only entry. (For example, see the home page of the Detroit Public Library, figure 13.1.)

Designing the Children's Department's Home Page

The first step in designing a web page is to decide on the content. When planning a departmental home page, the staff should browse through a number of library websites to look at other departments' examples. The children's department page should not include a repetition of the basic library information that is shown on the main home page. Links to other information about the library can be included on the children's home page. Some types of information included by most children's departments are the following:

- location
- contact information
- library events
- programs
- reading lists
- homework help
- link to library catalog
- links to other sites

The information on the home page looks best if it is uncluttered and highlighted by graphics or varied text styles. Young people are attracted by graphics and are used to seeing them in the web pages that they visit. Large, complicated graphics slow the loading of the website, especially for patrons who do not have high-powered computers. If possible, a text-only version of the web page should be available for use with older computers. Background designs should be used sparingly. They can distract the reader from the information. Dark backgrounds with white lettering cannot be printed out on some printers, so when posting information that a patron might want to print out, the background should be light and the type dark enough to print out clearly, like the sample web page shown in figure 13.2.

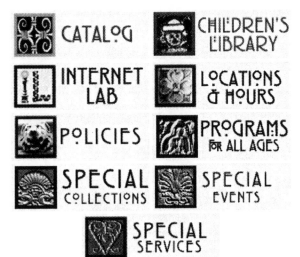

Catalog | Children's Library | Internet Lab | Locations & Hours | Policies | Programs for All Ages |
Special Collections | Special Events | Special Services

**Looking for information that we might have? Don't forget to look at our subject departments
for a quick overview of what you might find in the Main Library.**

MORE MENU ITEMS

Fig. 13.1. Detroit Public Library Home Page. Reprinted with permission.

Kid's Page I Internet Safety I Parents/Teachers I Teen Lounge I BPL Main Page I Help I

Explore the world through the Boston Public Library Kids' Page!

Homework Help I Boston Information for Kids

Fun and Games I Boston Public Library Information

Books and Magazines I About the Internet

Send your ideas and suggestions.

BPL Kids' Page: Just For Kids, August 29, 1997
URL: http://www.bpl.org/WWW/KIDS/KidsHome.html

Fig. 13.2. Boston Public Library's Kids' Page. Reprinted with permission.

A departmental home page creates an image of the department for the viewer. It reveals a great deal about the culture of the library. Some libraries include lively animated graphics or messages that crawl across the screen. The Multnomah County Public Library in Oregon features a "Joke of the Month." The Pasadena Public Library in California includes a link to a Spanish-language page for children (see figure 13.3).

Because the purpose of the web page is to inform people about local library services, these should usually be listed first on the home page. Links to outside sites can be listed below them or on a secondary menu. Often, a person who links to another site does not return to the original page, so the library loses the opportunity to provide information about programs or services.

The departmental home page should list the name and location of the library so that if a patron prints out only that page, the identification of the site will be clear. The full address, as well as the complete telephone and fax numbers and an e-mail address, should be supplied. Giving the name of a specific contact person encourages patrons to seek further information if they have questions.

For identification purposes, the URL should be a heading at the top of each page. Some browsers do not add the address of a document to the printed page. At the bottom of the departmental page, links back to the library's home page as well as to other pages of library information should be included. Also, each page should be dated so that users know the information is current.

Each link to the departmental home page should be clear, uncluttered and, if possible, include a graphic. Instead of crowding too much information on any one page, it is better to list the information about one program, or series of programs, on each page (as shown in figure 13.4) and provide links to other pages that contain more details.

When a link to a site outside of the library is provided, its status should be made clear to the user. Comments about the linked site help the user to decide whether to link to it. Some children's librarians include a disclaimer stating that the library is not responsible for material that may be found at links.

The links that are provided to sources outside of the library go beyond the realm of public relations. They are, in effect, an electronic collection of materials. The selection of these websites deserves the same kind of careful scrutiny that is devoted to selecting books and other materials. The number of Internet sources relevant to children's interests is expanding every day, so the selection of sites is time consuming and difficult. Many children's department's break the list down by subject and sometimes by age, in a manner similar to the way print sources are classified. Others list sites under broad headings, such as "Fun and Games," "Homework Help," and "Local History." Some library journals list appropriate Internet sources for children, but few overall selection aides exist. Until more adequate tools are developed, the best way to select sites to list is to look at other libraries' choices. The Multnomah County library website contains a detailed listing with inviting annotations (Multnomah 1997). Many other libraries also have useful listings that are worth studying.

P A S A D E N A   P U B L I C   L I B R A R Y

la página de los niños de la biblioteca

Any Time is Book Time
Children's Book Week Celebration

sponsored by the Friends of the Pasadena Library

Homework Helper
Got the homework blues? This list of helpful Internet sites might just be the cure!

Telling Tales
Four new professional storytelling programs in the Fall/Winter Series

Children's Storytimes
Come hear stories and have fun at one of our 15 storytimes each week.
There's one to fit into everyone's schedule!

Meet Max the Library Cat
Max was the "library cat" at the Hastings Branch Library. Here is his true story!

Pasadena Kids Page
(sponsored by Pasadena Online and E-ZNet)
This site includes a handy calendar of city-wide programs for children,
places to eat, a list of parks, and fun links for kids.

Pasadena Library Locations & Hours
There are 10 branches to serve you.
Find out where they are and when they are open.

Library Cards
This free card is the best deal in town.

Fig. 13.3. Pasadena Public Library Kids' Page. Reprinted with permission.

WEDNESDAY MORNING
PRESCHOOL STORYTIME SCHEDULE

OCTOBER 1997
    OCTOBER 8th -- FIRE SAFETY
    OCTOBER 22nd -- HALLOWEEN

NOVEMBER 1997
    NOVEMBER 12th -- FAIRY TALES
    NOVEMBER 26th -- THANKSGIVING

DECEMBER 1997
    DECEMBER 10th -- CHRISTMAS

JANUARY 1998
    JANUARY 14th -- WINNIE THE POOH
    JANUARY 28th -- DINOSAURS

FEBRUARY 1998
    FEBRUARY 11th -- VALENTINE'S DAY
    FEBRUARY 25th -- MONKEYS

MARCH 1998
    MARCH 11th -- ST. PATRICK'S DAY
    MARCH 25th -- BUTTERFLIES / HUMMINGBIRDS

APRIL 1998
    APRIL 8th -- EASTER
    APRIL 22nd -- ELEPHANTS

MAY 1998
    MAY 6th -- MOTHER'S DAY

All Storytimes begin at 10:00 a.m. Wednesday readings will be followed by a craft activity. Storytimes vary between a half-hour to an hour.

To volunteer to be a storyteller, or for further program information, contact us by e-mail or by calling

Fig. 13.4. Dixon Public Library Web Page. Web page designer, Ed Bartosh. Reprinted with permission of the Dixon Public Library.

Maintaining the Home Page

Errors can easily creep into web pages, so all work should be checked several times by different people. Spelling and usage should be checked not only on the screen but also from a printout of the pages. Often, mistakes are more easily found in hard copy text than on a screen.

Accessing the website should be tried with several different browsers. The aim is to develop a site that is accessible through many different browsers, including those that are text-only. All links should be checked several times to make sure that they work.

After the web pages are mounted, one person should be responsible to keep them current. Outdated information on a site reflects badly on a library. Notices about past events and programs should be promptly removed. Listings of awards, such as the Newbery or Caldecott Medals, should be updated as soon as the yearly announcement is made. Reading lists should be kept up-to-date by adding new titles regularly.

Maintaining useful and well-organized outside links takes considerable time. A portion of the department's materials selection time should be spent on monitoring the Internet for new sites to list. One of the advantages of electronic information is that it can be more current than print sources. When an important event occurs—an election, the Olympics, or a space flight—new websites will be set up to give immediate information. These sites can be valuable to young people, and every attempt should be made to provide links to them from the children's department's home page.

Periodically check links to outside sites. Sometimes a site is abandoned and ceases to provide relevant information. Other times the URLs are changed and the links no longer work. Each link should be checked every month or two, to make sure that the link works and that the site is still usable. Presence on the World Wide Web can be a powerful public relations tool for a library, but the impact depends on the care with which the site is maintained.

Dealing with the Media

Many people in a community do not visit the library regularly and depend on media sources for information about library services. The public services departments of the library can use the media to inform these residents about events and changes. The major forms for library coverage are news releases and public service announcements.

News Releases

Many local newspapers, television, and radio stations depend heavily on information sent to them by community groups as they are always looking for interesting local stories. The library should keep a file of contact information for local newspapers (including foreign-language papers) and radio and television stations, as well as the person at each source who is responsible for library coverage. News releases should be sent directly to that individual so that they are efficiently handled.

News releases should be sent for any special event or change of policy in the library. News releases can also:

Announce new programs or services at the library;

Report on the progress and success of a program or service offered at the library;

Provide new information about existing programs and services offered at the library;

Announce special events, seasonal programs, or meetings at the library;

Inform the public about positions or policies adopted by the library;

Communicate statements made by officers or directors of the library on topics of interest to the community;

Introduce new library staff to the community;

Describe materials that have been added to the library's collections (Banks 1995, 1).

Devising news connections for library events requires imagination. A successful summer reading program may warrant a story in the local paper if it can be tied in with a national issue, such as literacy. Media personnel may not think of the library as a source for stories, so it is up to the librarians to provide the connections. A community plan to encourage recycling might suggest a story about the library's books and films on environmental issues; a special exhibit at a local art or historical museum might lead to a story about the library's holdings in these areas.

News releases should be written clearly and concisely in newspaper style—that is, with the most important information presented in the first paragraph. The short paragraphs that follow give additional information that the newspaper may print or cut depending on the amount of space available. Releases for radio and television must be even more concise than those for newspapers; broadcast news releases should use short, easily understood words for broadcasting.

Make the connection between the library event and wider community interest explicit in the first paragraph of the release so that the journalist can see at once the reason for the release. Usually the story will be rewritten for presentation, so the library should concentrate on giving facts that will be useful in preparing the story. The name, telephone, and fax number of a contact person should be included with each release.

Photo Opportunities

A library event that warrants coverage by a newspaper photographer or a television station offers a department an opportunity to make a strong impact on the community. More people look at pictures in the newspaper than read the stories, and more people get their news from television than from newspapers. Some thought should be given to the impression of the department presented by pictorial coverage.

A picture of a person handing a check or a book to the librarian is not particularly interesting unless the individual is a recognizable celebrity. More engaging pictures will be taken if children are involved in an activity—reading the gift book, using the new computer, or thanking the benefactor. Pictures that show or imply action generally catch the viewer's attention better than static pictures.

Library staff generally dress up for special occasions and make sure that the library is tidy. However, it is a mistake to show the library as a sterile, dull place. Displays of brightly colored picture books, posters, or children's drawings make the department look appealing. They also provide a background against which people can be posed for still photographs.

The librarian should provide the photographer with a caption for each picture, including the names of the individuals shown. Names must be spelled correctly. If individual children are to be featured in a picture and their names given to a newspaper, obtain their parents' consent.

Just as with a news release, the photographer should be given the name of a contact person in the event that further information should be needed.

Public Service Announcements

Radio and television stations are required to carry public service announcements (PSAs), brief messages about nonprofit organizations. Some computer bulletin boards also carry them. Because the messages are short, they are most useful for giving general information about services rather than specific programs or events.

Messages to be broadcast on the radio are the easiest to prepare. They can be read live by the station announcer or prerecorded. Because they are designed to be heard, rather than read, the sentence structure must be simple and the message clear. The pronunciation for difficult words or names should be included.

Check with local radio stations to obtain the length of PSA that they require. Usual lengths are 10, 20, 30, or 60 seconds. If the radio station prefers a specific length, the PSA should not exceed that time. Only about 25 words can be said in 10 seconds. If a telephone number is included, each number counts as a word. A 10-second message might look like this:

> Have any questions?
> The Beaverton Public Library can send the answers to your home computer.
> Call three-four-two . . . one-four-six-eight for information.

PSAs are sent to radio stations in much the same format as news releases. The library should be clearly identified and a contact person's name included. Other items that should be included are an indication of the PSA's length and the dates for which the announcement is in effect. Radio PSAs should be triple-spaced and set in all capital letters (Banks 1995, 7).

Local cable television stations can be contacted for information about how much access they give to community groups. Some stations will give the use of a studio and perhaps some staff help to prepare PSA messages for television use. Professional help can make a library's message much more effective than an amateur effort. If the television station cannot provide expertise, volunteers may be found at a community college media program or among the Friends of the Library. Remember, however, that far fewer people watch community cable shows than listen to commercial radio stations. If resources are limited, the time and expense of preparing releases for television might not be worth the effort. More people can be reached by brief PSAs on radio at much less cost in time and money.

Media Interviews

Interviews with the media can be an important way to publicize the services of a department. Sometimes a journalist seeks an interview because of a sudden news development: a library patron has demanded the removal of a book from the library or someone has been charged with stealing library books. Most reporters will try to call the chief librarian, but sometimes one may contact someone at the department level. It is usually wise to suggest that questions be directed to the chief executive or to the library board as any information given to reporters may be made public. Such referrals are essential if a legal case is being brought against the library. If the issue is less formal—for example, someone has written to the local newspaper complaining about the availability of "immoral, sexually explicit" books in the children's department, and the reporter wants a department head or staff member's point of view—it is all right to speak for the department. Reporters may be friendly and imply that they understand the library's side of the story, but care should be taken in what is said. Casual or joking comments that sound innocuous in conversation may appear foolish or insulting in print. Reporters look for good stories. Drama and conflict are emphasized, and remarks may be quoted out of context, either through error or deliberate distortion. The interview should be handled carefully and nothing unnecessary should be stated. To avoid the risk of giving inaccurate information if questions are asked about dates, facts, or specific holdings, the interviewer should be told that time is needed to check these details. Most reporters try to present the news in a clear and unbiased way, but they do not have library backgrounds and often do not understand the problems of running a public institution or the reasons for many library regulations. Give the background of library practice whenever relevant, rather than dealing solely with the immediate conflict.

Most library interviews are not conducted in the rush of a news story but are planned as general-interest items for newspapers or for radio and television talk shows. If the library maintains contact with the media through news releases and publicity, it may be easy to suggest that an interview about children's books or reading might be of interest to readers and listeners. Sometimes the reporter or talk show host will suggest an interview on a library-related topic. Given time to prepare, a librarian should become familiar with the work of the journalist conducting the interview. What kinds of stories does this individual do? Do they prefer a folksy, neighborly tone or a more formal, professional one? The more that can be discovered about the interviewer's expectations, the more likely the interview will be successful.

In preparing for the interview, the librarians should think of one or two points to be made. These points can be worked into the interview and, if repeated several times, will usually be reported in the written story. Questions that the interviewer is likely to ask should be considered, and answers prepared for them. Specific facts and statistics can be written down to be given to the interviewer or consulted when questions are raised. A librarian who is not accustomed to being interviewed may stage a mock interview with a friend or colleague to practice responding to questions.

Most interviewers are skilled in making their subjects feel at ease, so the nervousness that comes with a public appearance is likely to be lessened when the talk actually starts. Interviewers like subjects to respond completely to questions, neither answering briefly with a "yes" or "no" nor being long winded. While most of the direction comes from the interviewer, the subject may take the opportunity to lead the questions into useful areas. When asked, for example, whether *Alice in Wonderland* is an appropriate gift for an eight-year-old, the answer can include suggestions of suitable choices for children's gifts. The librarian is being interviewed because of expertise in the area, and this expertise should be used to make the interview valuable to the public.

Librarians should remain on good terms with the media. Keeping the media informed about library news, being available for interviews, and being courteous to reporters, no matter how difficult the occasion, help to ensure the library good coverage in newspapers and on radio and television. This link with the public is invaluable for maintaining visibility in the community.

14

Fund-Raising Activities

Libraries, like other public institutions, have recently become more dependent on outside funding. "Even a casual reading of the library press reveals the increased pressure to raise private dollars for library activities that were once thought to be either the responsibility of direct tax dollars, as in the case of public libraries, or indirect tax dollars, as in the case of public institutions of higher education" (Burlingame 1995, v). Many communities have cut back on library funding at the same time that the demand for library services is increasing.

Although the major burden of raising funds for the library rests with the chief executive officer, each department has a role to play in fund-raising activities. The services provided by the children's department are highly valued in most communities. This means that children's department projects should have a broad appeal for potential funders. Children's librarians owe it to their patrons to try to raise money that will enhance services. "When library budgets do not stretch far enough to meet all of the priority information needs, there are really only three options: you can choose not to deliver the services, you can reduce other services, or you can seek alternative funding sources" (Des Enfants 1995, 22).

Fund-raising initiatives can be focused on private individuals, government and philanthropic foundation grants, or corporate sponsors. Some funding efforts may be aimed at providing ongoing annual support, some may be designed to fund capital expenditures (a new building or a computer lab), and others may be for a specific departmental project.

Funding from Private Individuals

Many individuals, even those who frequently use the library, have never thought of giving money to a public library. They assume that the funding provided by tax moneys is adequate. One of the first steps for a librarian who want to raise money from local benefactors is to identify potential library supporters and educate them about the needs of the library.

165

Many public libraries have a Friends of the Library group. Friends of the Library groups are nonprofit organizations formed to promote a better understanding of the library's facilities, needs, and services. Often the Friends group plans and sponsors events, such as book sales, art exhibits, or performances, for the benefit of the library. Some Friends groups operate a library cafe or a store offering writing supplies to library patrons. The group may organize volunteers to read to children or to help with special events. They also encourage gifts, endowments, and other donations.

When a Friends of the Library group is large, their contribution to the library can be financially substantial. The Friends of the Seattle Public Library has 3,000 members and an annual budget of more than $90,000 (Seattle Public Library Friends of the Library 1997). Friends groups may purchase computers and software for libraries, provide Internet access or purchase a special collection or art works for the library.

Although Friends groups in most communities do not include individuals who are able to make large gifts to the library, the members provide varied talents and resources that help in fund-raising. Individuals with expertise in public relations and fund-raising or with knowledge of foundations and how to approach them may be found in Friends groups. They provide links to other institutions and community groups that may collaborate with the library in fund-raising projects.

The organization Friends of Libraries USA has a website (www.folusa.com) that contains a sampling of ideas about Friends groups and how they can help libraries. The site includes fact sheets, news about other groups, and links to related sites. By joining this organization, a Friends group can learn about the activities of other groups across the country.

Friends groups are independent of the library and set their own agenda, but most groups appreciate receiving suggestions about what other similar groups are doing. Many Friends groups have their own websites. A librarian, especially one who has not worked with Friends groups in the past, will find these sites useful sources of information about group projects. Library journals and conferences also frequently offer information about projects initiated by Friends groups.

Grant Support

Grants from private foundations and government agencies are an important source of money for specific projects. The "Money Matters" column in *American Libraries* regularly announces the receipt of an important grant by a public or academic library. One writer comments, "If there are services or materials which your library should offer to children in your community but can't afford, it may be time to consider writing a grant" (Des Enfants 1995, 22). Grants can pay for the provision of computers in the children's department, the establishment of a literacy program, or the development of a collection of multicultural materials. Grants are targeted funds; they cannot usually be obtained to pay ongoing library costs. Grant money allows the library to initiate a new program or service. After the project has been established, the library is responsible for its maintenance. In applying for grant money, choose projects that are central to the library's mission so that they can be continued after the grant funding is ended.

Locating Grant Opportunities

The first steps in obtaining a grant are to identify an unmet need and to learn about available grant sources. These two are intertwined. A librarian might recognize the need for Internet access beyond what the library budget can provide, for example, and search for an agency that might provide grant funding. Another librarian might learn that a large foundation is interested in funding literacy projects and recognize that the children's department could organize such a project in his or her community. Whether the impetus comes from the library's need or from the foundation's funding interests is not as important as how well the two aspects match.

Many resources are available for locating funding agencies. The first are individuals within the library system or region who have been successful in obtaining grants. State and provincial library agencies and associations usually have listings of agencies that have given grants to libraries. Members of the library board and individuals from other community agencies are also good sources of information.

The source of funding for many youth services in libraries is the Library Services and Construction Act (LSCA) Title I grants. These funds come from the United States Department of Education and are administered through state library agencies. The ALA Washington Office (http://www.ala.org/washoff/) provides information about these grants and other federal government grant programs.

The Foundation Center, a clearinghouse for information about foundation funding, has an informative website (http://fdncenter.org) that provides a wide range of resources, including information on individual foundations, lists of the largest foundations, reports on trends in grants, articles on how to write a grant proposal, and individuals to contact for further information. In addition to the website, the Foundation Center maintains libraries in five U.S. locations, offers workshops, and publishes books to help nonprofit organizations to apply for grants.

Another important Internet location is the Support Centers of America website (www.supportcenter.org). This organization provides management support services for nonprofit organizations. Its support includes general management training and information, as well as fund-raising information. Its website often features articles written by foundation representatives that describe how granting agencies look at proposals and how they decide which ones to fund. The Support Centers also maintain regional offices in 12 cities across the United States.

The librarian who has an idea for a fundable project but does not know which foundation to approach can search for a foundation through a subject approach, a geographical approach, or by using individual contacts. If a project falls within a specific subject area—developing an AIDS information collection for teenagers, for example—locating agencies that have a mandate to give to AIDS research or, more generally, to health research is a good starting point. A more general project, especially one that involves collaboration with other institutions, such as a literacy program for new immigrant families, might call for a geographic approach. The librarian could look for foundations that focus on promoting the development of a particular community or region. Several books listing foundations and their patterns of giving grants can be found in any large library. The newer, online listings are more up-to-date and are a better source of current information. Most large foundations have their own websites with descriptions of the kinds of projects they seek and guidelines for proposals. The online resources (most of which are available on the Foundation Center's website or its CD-ROM) can be searched by name, by subject, or by geographic location.

Personal contacts with a funding agency are always useful, so if someone in the library, on the board of trustees, or in the community has a link to a foundation, this can be a great benefit. A grant will not be given on the basis of personal friendship, but an individual who knows the foundation from the inside can give valuable advice about the approach to take, the kind of proposal to write, and the amount of money likely to be forthcoming.

Planning the Grant Proposal

The first step in preparing a grant proposal is to think through the project for which funding is being requested. Specific questions, such as the following, may be asked:

- Does the project fill an unmet need?
- What group of people will benefit from the project?
- What will be the result of the successful project (e.g., more children prepared for school; better integration of an immigrant group into the community)
- Do the children's librarians have the expertise to carry out the project?
- Does the project duplicate or complement other social projects in the community?
- How will you know whether the project is successful? How will it be evaluated?
- How much will the project cost?
- How will the project activities continue in the future?
- Is there a specific time period during which the proposal must be undertaken?

Answering these questions will usually involve meeting with other staff members and perhaps outside experts in a planning session. Granting agencies want to see documentation for claims that a project is worthwhile. Locate facts concerning the number of individuals into the target group, related activities of other social agencies, and realistic cost estimates for equipment and personnel time. Careful planning makes a grant proposal more effective.

The planning process will help in deciding which funding agency to approach. The required size of the budget is one important indicator. Many large foundations are not interested in funding small projects, and they may define these as "projects of $10,000 or less." Other grants, such as the LSCA Title 1 grants, can be obtained for projects costing less than $1,000. Projects that seek to take advantage of a specific opportunity and need to be funded fairly quickly are not appropriate for large funding agencies, which usually require several months or more to make decisions. As the requirements of the project become clear, it will be easier to target the appropriate agency from which to request support.

Writing Proposals

Grant proposals normally follow a standard format. Librarians should always obtain information on guidelines from the specific foundation or grant that has been identified, but most guidelines are similar. The standard format includes the following parts:

- Executive summary
- Statement of need
- Project description
- Budget
- Information about the organization applying
- Conclusion

The length of a proposal rarely exceeds 10 pages. Some agencies prefer to have small grant proposals, which are no longer than one or two pages. No matter what the length, each proposal should include all of the basic elements.

Executive Summary

Although placed first in the final report, the executive summary is usually written after the rest of the proposal has been completed. "A well-written summary will help the reviewer understand the need for the project and the results expected" (Carlson 1995, 55). In a short proposal, the summary may be only a paragraph or two. A proposal of five pages or longer requires a one-page summary. Some funding agencies make this a requirement in the submission of the proposal.

Ideally, the summary should express, in brief, the most compelling aspects of the proposal. Key items from each section should be used in the summary. These should include a statement of the need for the project, an outline of the project itself, the amount of funding requested, and a statement about the department's ability to carry out the project.

Statement of Need

The statement of need is usually the first section written. This statement enables the reader to understand the background issues. "It presents the facts and evidence that support the need for the project and establishes that your nonprofit understands the problems and therefore can reasonably address them" (Geever and McNeill 1993, 27). The facts about the situation should be framed in terms of the local conditions and needs, not general statistics about national problems. Be sure that the need is stated in terms of client need, rather than library need: *Only 12 percent of school-age children in our community have access to a home computer,* **not** *The Pine Grove library does not have a single public access computer in the children's department.* Explain that the problem could be helped or alleviated by some change in circumstances. Show that the program to be funded presents a better or different approach to the problem than those now available. If other community agencies are addressing the same problem, describe how the project complements their work or that collaboration with them may be possible.

Project Description

The project description usually starts with a statement of objectives—the measurable outcomes of the project (see Chapter 2). For example, the objective of a parenting program might be *Each parent will learn five finger plays and will become familiar with the library's collection of books for toddlers.* The objectives must be realistic. It is unwise to promise more than can be delivered because the funder will expect a final report documenting the achievement of the project's objectives. A proposal for a small grant might have only one or two limited objectives; a larger grant request might have several objectives, perhaps extending over a period of time.

The methods by which the project will achieve its objectives must be clearly stated. The funder expects to see a list of the specific activities to be undertaken. The method of recruiting participants, what activities will be offered and by whom, and the time lines for the project should be spelled out. For example, a proposal to institute a series of storyhours for children speaking English as a second language would need to describe how the children are to be identified and recruited, how the materials for the storyhours will be collected, those to present the storyhours, and the duration of the program.

The way in which the project is to be evaluated should be planned as the project is developed. An evaluation of the project is usually required in the final report to the funding agency. Some projects have obvious evaluation criteria. For example, if the objective of the project is to obtain computers for the children's department, a report of the number of computers installed can be one evaluation measure. In this example the librarians would also want to keep a record of the number of children who use the computers. Other projects—for example, providing a program to help toddlers develop language skills—are more difficult to evaluate. The number of participants is one measure of success. The librarian may want to solicit anecdotes from the participating parents about their children's growing use of language. Most funding agencies like to see quantitative evaluation measures of a project's success, but qualitative, anecdotal evidence can also be impressive.

Budget

Before preparing the budget, review the project description and make notes of the costs of each aspect of the project. The budget should include the cost of staff time, additional personnel, materials, supplies, publicity, and equipment. The library's accounting department can provide information about these costs, although outside estimates on some costs may be necessary. If a small grant is being requested for a specific purpose, such as buying materials for a special collection, including the costs of staff time might not be necessary. For large grant applications, staff time to administer the grant, evaluate it, and prepare a final report should be part of the budget request. The time period for the budget request should be determined. Money should be available for preparation before the actual project begins and will be needed for the report after the project ends. The time frame of the budget should be long enough to meet these needs. Budget requests must be realistic. Asking for too little money may result in having to return to the agency for additional funding while the project is in progress. This is embarrassing and does not create a good impression with the funder. On the other hand, overestimating costs may lead to a rejection of the grant; or, if the money is given, having the unspent portion refunded to the agency at the end of the project. This, too, gives a bad impression of the library's ability to handle grants. A carefully planned and clearly stated budget makes the proposal look professional and, therefore, more likely to be funded.

Information About the Organization

Because libraries are well-established institutions in the community, not much additional information will be needed by the funding agency. Many agencies require that specific information be attached to a proposal—a listing of the library board, the staff, and financial data. If the library has received grants in the past, these should be noted. In making awards, funding agencies also look for a successful track record in handling grants projects.

Conclusion

Only a short paragraph or two is needed for the conclusion of the proposal. This conclusion briefly states the importance of the project and its expected accomplishments. Possible future activities that will grow out of the successful project might also be mentioned.

Letter proposals

Proposals for small projects, those for less than $1,000, often require only a two or three page letter rather than a formal proposal. This is especially true if the agency has previously funded library projects. No matter how brief the letter, it should include the elements of a proposal as outlined in the previous sections.

Value of Writing Grants

Although preparing proposals for grants is time consuming and difficult, the process reaps rewards beyond the value of the grants themselves. Even if the grant proposal does not receive funding, the process of writing it forces library staff to think about their objectives and the way they may be attained. Often, an unsuccessful grant application can be sent to another agency and eventually find funding. Occasionally, community officials may recognize the value of the project and authorize its funding from regular tax sources.

Being awarded a grant by a government agency or respected foundation is a tribute to the strength and value of the library. Even though the monetary value of the grant may not be large, the award means that an objective agency has analyzed the proposal and acknowledged that the library is doing important work.

Corporate Support

In addition to individuals and funding agencies, local businesses and industry are important sources of support and possible funding. Companies that sell products aimed primarily at children can be approached to support library activities through donations of materials or publicity. Toys or books for awards in summer reading programs may be obtained from booksellers, publishers, or distributors. Restaurants that want to attract families may provide publicity on napkins, place mats, or containers. Many large corporations encourage their local branches to support community activities of this kind. Members of the library board are often good contacts to reach local businesspersons.

In arranging for publicity backed by business interests, there is some danger that the library could be seen as endorsing a particular product or company. This is not permissible for a public institution, and the library must be sure that sponsorship is free of commercialism. Businesses and industries can donate to public service organizations, such as libraries, but they should view these dona-tions as ways of promoting name recognition and good will, rather than using them to advertise their products or services. The library must maintain control over any material prepared, printed, or distributed by companies on its behalf.

In ensuring that requests are coordinated, a children's librarian who wants to approach a firm would usually begin by suggesting the idea to his or her immediate supervisor—the branch head or chief administrative officer. The children's librar-ian should state clearly but briefly the project that needs funding, the choice of the sponsor, and the rationale that will be given to the sponsor. If the supervisor approves the plan, the children's librarian should prepare a more formal proposal for approval by the library board. The proposal may be made to the company by the chief librarian, a member of the library board, or the head of children's services, depending on the political climate and relationships within the community.

One special form of support that some children's libraries have obtained is celebrity tie-ins for programs. Having a well-known sports or music figure give his or her endorsement and picture to a summer reading program, for example, can create exciting publicity for the library. When an arrangement is made with a celebrity for endorsement, the individual ordinarily does not contribute money but gives time for an appearance at a library event, as well as the value in the use of his or her name. Arrangements for this kind of endorsement can be made through the celebrity's agent or publicist. A librarian would usually approach someone who has displayed some interest in similar projects or who is a native of, or closely identified with, the community. Many celebrities welcome the opportunity to be identified with a valued institution because of the good will it engenders for them.

Cyber-Fund-Raising

Public libraries develop a presence on the Internet primarily as a service to the community. A by-product of that service is that the library becomes more visible to its patrons and to individuals who surf the Internet. Many nonprofit organizations find this visibility is useful for informing the public about their programs and for reaching potential members and donors who discover them on the World Wide Web. Fund-raisers find that the Internet offers a way to reach individuals who pay little attention to traditional fund-raising techniques. "The public awareness element of maintaining a presence on the Internet grows in value as general access to the Internet expands. Without a doubt, public awareness and fundraising go hand-in-hand" (Zeff 1996, 91).

Although most public librarians would not want to use their websites to aggressively pursue funding, these sites can open the door to donors in a number of ways. Inviting visitors to the website to join a Friends of the Library group is one way to attract individuals. A membership form can be mounted on the website so that an individual can immediately send the information to be added to the Friend's group mailing list. Newsletters can be mounted on the website and messages sent to e-mail addresses to supplement the printed information that the Friends group distributes. Distribution of information to an e-mail list is much less expensive than sending it by regular mail. Even cancellations due to storms or other emergencies can be easily distributed to members of the group who have e-mail addresses.

Several nonprofit organizations include a donor solicitation page on their website. Raising money for a specific project, such as enabling the library to purchase CD-ROMs useful for homework help or to develop a toy collection, might be particularly appealing to World Wide Web browsers. Donors are more apt to give money for a particular purpose than to give to general library funds. Because the transmittal of funds over the Internet can still be a problem for the average person, the library will probably want to list a telephone number for the donor to call to complete the transaction.

Library fund-raising products can be advertised and sold over the Internet. The ALA displays a variety of library-related products on its website, including posters, tote bags, and paperweights. One of the advantages of showing products on the Internet is that attractive full-color graphics may be provided much less expensively than could be done in a brochure.

The funding structure of most public libraries does not allow for the direct sale of products. The financial arrangements for such a project would usually be made through a Friends group. Some public libraries have set up foundations to raise money for the library. The Atlanta-Fulton public library system, for example, was able to create "a private, nonprofit foundation whose sole function would be to seek, receive, and administer private gifts on behalf of the library system" (Guy 1995, 39). Lawyers in the community may donate their time to help in establishing such a foundation.

Because saving money is just as useful as raising additional funds, every attempt should be made to cut costs by utilizing electronic services. New programs can be announced on the library website and provision can be made for individuals to register online, thus eliminating the costs of a mailing or of staff taking telephone registrations. Until online access becomes universally available, of course, the library will also want to use other methods to inform the public about programs. No one should be uninformed of a new program simply because they lack access to the library through a personal computer.

Attitudinal Change

Public libraries have not been aggressive fund-raisers in the past and many librarians find it difficult to ask for money. They are not alone. Many professionals working in hospitals, universities, museums, and the arts also dislike fund-raising. Nonetheless, the majority of taxpayers in the United States have decided to cut back tax funding to nonprofit groups. The only way to maintain services is to obtain money from the private sector. Because most librarians believe strongly that the services they provide are valuable to the community, they should be willing to take on the burden of asking for money. The discomfort of asking disappears when the funding arrives and the project has been achieved. The satisfaction of seeing the library live up to its potential makes the drudgery of fund-raising worthwhile.

Relating to School Media Centers

The two major community institutions designed to provide information to children are the school media center and the public library. Although in most jurisdictions they are administered by different departments, the children and adults who use their resources generally see them as serving the same basic needs. The proliferation of homework help centers in many public libraries is an acknowledgment that school assignments dictate the use of the library by many students. A symposium in *Public Libraries* (Sager 1997) brought together librarians from all parts of the country to discuss the ways in which libraries are trying to help young people with their schoolwork. The computer technology to integrate school media centers and public libraries, providing access to collections and services in both facilities, already exists, but current reality is far short of what is technically feasible. As Sager (1997, 23) writes, "Most schools do not have a sufficient number of computers, and students' access to state-of-the-art hardware and software is limited. The public library can play an important role in improving access to these resources, and this opportunity merits both local and national initiatives." In addition to providing access to electronic resources, school media centers and public libraries can cooperate in a number of other ways.

Sharing Information

A perennial complaint of public libraries has been the difficulty of coping with large numbers of students seeking information for school assignments. Typically, one or two students appear in a library asking for information on a particular topic. With or without help from the library staff, they locate and borrow materials. Hours or days later, other students appear seeking the same information. When they are unable to find material on the shelves, they approach the library staff who join the search. Whatever circulating material the library owns has been borrowed, and little can be found for these unlucky students. Internet access in most public libraries is too limited to allow a large number of students to seek information in a short time. As a result, students are unhappy, library staff are frustrated, and teachers and parents may be given a false impression that library resources are inadequate.

A homework help link on the library's website provides access to many online sources for young people who have computers at home. Often, however, these sources provide limited resources sometimes at a reading level too difficult for the younger children. The large number of young people who do not have home computers must sign up for limited time on the library's computers to search for their information.

Several solutions have been proposed for this problem. Because some assignments recur year after year, librarians can record the assignment that caused the problem one year and be alert for its future appearance another year. Many children's departments keep files of assignments that have caused heavy demand on particular materials. When a question about one of these topics arises, the librarian questions the student about whether an assignment has been given. If it has, material on the subject can be put on special reserve so that each student is allowed to borrow only one or two items; periodical material or short sections of books can be photocopied; and alternative sources from the adult collection or encyclopedias can be gathered together. In this way, a greater number of students can be served.

Another suggested remedy involves letting teachers know why the library cannot supply the requested material. Librarians must exercise patience and persistence when informing teachers of the problems caused by unanticipated assignments. Instead of merely complaining about the difficulties caused by students seeking information for assignments, librarians can focus on the advantages of working with schools to ensure better service.

School media personnel should be a first line of communication for public librarians. Regular meetings with personnel from the schools served by a branch library may help avoid problems associated with heavy school-oriented use. The public library should take the initiative in contacting school personnel. A coffee hour or other informal annual meeting may be scheduled at the beginning of the school year or some other convenient time. At this meeting, mutual concerns can be discussed before they become problems. The meeting should focus on finding solutions. Many school media centers have the same problem as public libraries with unexpected assignments. When the school media specialists find that all of the information on a topic has been taken, they may suggest that students go to the public library. The more that each institution knows about the resources of the other, the more likely it is that appropriate referrals will be made.

Continuing contact maintains strong relations between the school media center and the public library. A newsletter or information sheet informing the school media specialist about relevant new acquisitions or services can be a helpful supplement to the annual meetings. E-mail connections between the public library and the schools can also provide an excellent format for efficient communication. Certainly, school media personnel should receive any press releases or information sent out by the department.

Contact with Teachers

In addition to the school media staff, librarians will want to keep local teachers informed about the library's collections and services, as well as any problems with students. Letting teachers know why the public library cannot provide some materials for school assignments is one form of communication, but negative feedback should not be the only type of communication. The library should send information about library services to schools at the beginning of each school year. This information is particularly useful for new teachers but can also remind all of the teachers about the hours, services, and limitations of the public library. Brief, clear information presented with a touch of humor is most effective. In the mailing, teachers can also be invited to schedule class visits to the library. Also, information about school assignments, science fair projects, and other activities that may affect the public library should be requested.

Not all teachers will respond to the invitations and requests. Teachers tend to be overwhelmed with paperwork, in addition to their teaching duties, and a request from the public library adds to their burden. To make responses easier for the teacher's, include a prepared form asking for subjects of upcoming assignments and their approximate dates. Include an envelope addressed to the library. No method will garner a 100 percent response, but teachers who take the time to let the library know about their assignments should be rewarded by extra service. Teachers who realize that the library can make their jobs easier are likely to make their satisfaction known to other teachers. Gradually, the library may build up a solid core of teachers who keep the library informed about assignments and projects that require materials beyond the resources of the school media centers. While no public library can hope to have enough materials and staff to supply the needs of all students for all assignments, cooperation with the schools can help both agencies provide the best service possible with their limited resources.

Learning About Curricula

Public librarians should become familiar with the general curriculum as well as with specific assignments. Although the public library does not usually build its collection around curricular needs, subjects covered in the school will undoubtedly be reflected in requests for materials. Publications about the public school curricula are usually available from boards of education. Librarians should be alert to major shifts in topics covered or the introduction of new subjects. If the schools in a community begin instruction in a new language, for example, the public library is likely to want to strengthen its collection in this language. Similarly, a new health education curriculum stressing the importance of AIDS education will surely lead to heavy demand for this type of material in the public library. Information about extracurricular school activities—theatrical productions, sports, extended trips—are often reported in local newspapers. Public librarians can capitalize on this information by displaying materials related to, for example, a school trip to Hawaii or a school production of *Anne of Green Gables*. Anything that enhances communication between schools and public libraries is likely to increase the services of both.

Private Schools

While public schools outnumber private schools in most communities, librarians should make a special effort to communicate with private schools. Some independent and parochial schools have fewer resources than the public schools and will be especially receptive to overtures from the public library. All of the suggestions made for public schools apply to private schools as well. The public library's services should be made available to all of the schools in the community.

Sharing Services

Class Visits

In many communities, class visits to the public library are the principal form of interaction between schools and libraries. Sometimes these visits are formalized so that all the children in a certain grade visit the library once during the year. In other communities, individual teachers or schools arrange for class visits, which may involve any grade level. Either the public librarian or the schools can make the initial contact. Once a routine is established, the practice may continue without much further input.

The purposes of class visits may include

- a general introduction to the library;
- library registration;
- a lesson in how to use the library;
- a demonstration of Internet resources;
- introduction of materials for a specific school project;
- encouragement of recreational reading;
- a recreational program of story reading, films, etc.; and
- introduction of a summer reading program.

The teacher and the librarian should understand and agree on the purpose of a particular visit. If a teacher expects the librarian to teach the Dewey Decimal System, while the librarian plans to read the latest Caldecott Medal-winning book, both may be disappointed, and the relationship between the school and the library strained. To avoid this problem, the librarian should always ask the teacher what he or she expects from the visit and tell the teacher about the library's plans. If the library plans to give the children library cards, the librarian should inform the teacher in writing about any necessary documentation. If the teacher wants the children to be introduced to materials on a particular topic, the librarian should try to obtain a copy of the assignment or lesson plan for that topic. This makes it easier to gather and present appropriate material. Librarians should also ask about any special needs. Children with disabilities, non-English speaking children, and those with behavioral problems may require particular care.

Purposes of Class Visits

Librarians who are organizing a program of school visits to the library will want to consider overall department goals in deciding the objectives of these visits. If schools in the area have adequate school media centers, public library visits will probably not involve library instruction or an introduction to materials for class assignments. In such situations, visits are more likely to focus on the public library as a source of recreational reading, programs, and other services. In rural areas, where most children are bused to school, and even in urban areas, where children's parents do not use the library, many children may be unaware of the public library, unless they are introduced to it during school visits. In these situations, the library should use the class visit to introduce a range of materials and services that the child and other family members may wish to use. Storytelling, puppet shows, film programs, and crafts are appropriate ways to introduce the library as a pleasant place to visit. The emphasis on recreational activities clearly differentiates the public library from the school media center, with its mandate to support the curricular needs of the school.

Time spent preparing for a class visit will make it go well. Librarians often ask the teacher to send a class list so that name tags can be made for the children. This is particularly useful for kindergarten and primary grade children, who like to feel that the librarian is interested in knowing them as individuals. Book lists or bookmarks (personalized with the child's name) make good souvenirs and will remind the children and their parents of the services and materials available. Brochures and newsletters aimed at parents and older siblings make useful handouts because they encourage the use of the library as a family resource. Depending on the season, information about holiday or summer programs should be available as well.

Although class visits to libraries can further cooperation between schools and public libraries, the practice should always be viewed in the light of overall departmental goals. Other types of services, such as preschool programs and service to day care centers, should not be downgraded to provide service to school-age children unless that conforms to library goals. Because many library branches serve areas with six or more schools, encouraging all teachers to bring their classes may overwhelm the library. Many librarians find it difficult to limit service to any group, but it is unfair to other patrons to allow school visits to drain library resources. Setting parameters, such as having odd-numbered grades visit one semester and even-numbered grades the next, or limiting class visits to one per school year can help to ensure that adequate service will be provided to everyone. Local conditions are the most important factor in setting parameters for services to schools. If a school district relies upon a public library to provide library instruction and resources, it makes sense to request funding to cover the additional staff time and materials to meet this need. In the final analysis, it is better for everyone if services to children are seen in the context of the entire community, rather than just one agency.

Librarian Visits to Schools

As an alternative to class visits to the library, a public librarian may visit schools. Having one person travel to a school to visit three or four classes is more economical than having dozens of children and several teachers traveling to the library. The disadvantage is that children do not have an opportunity to see the library building and the range of materials available. If children have never been inside the library, the librarian's visit does not encourage them to visit to the same extent as does a trip to the library.

Despite these drawbacks, visits to the schools can publicize library services and introduce programs. Some librarians schedule visits to the schools at the end of the school year to encourage children to register for summer programs at the library. Most teachers enthusiastically support summer reading programs and welcome the opportunity to inform children about the opportunity to continue their reading during the summer.

Visits at the beginning of the school year can focus on the public library as a source of recreational reading and information for school projects. And visits during the year can be tied to holiday programs, science fairs, or other seasonal activities.

Preparation for school visits includes obtaining as much information as possible about the class—the names of the students, current curricular projects, interests, and individuals or groups with special needs. During the class visit, most librarians give a booktalk on materials chosen to match the grade level and interests of the group. Use attractive and appealing materials and present them in an enticing way. (For suggestions about booktalks and other ways to introduce children to books, see Bauer 1993; Bodart 1992; Kimmel and Segel 1983.) Children in a classroom are a captive audience and can be difficult unless the librarian quickly establishes a rapport with them. Primary-grade children are usually receptive to a visitor talking about books and reading, but those in the junior or intermediate grades may require skillful handling. An honest, informal presentation usually makes a better impression than one that strains at humor or relevance. The best approach is to emphasize how the library can help the students without gushing or overselling library resources.

While a school visit may sound like an intimidating experience, most librarians meet with enthusiastic and pleasant receptions in classrooms. Attractive handouts help to make the librarian's visit memorable. If each child can be given a personalized packet of materials to take home, the library's public image may be enhanced throughout the community. Sometimes the librarian can leave books as a long-term loan for the classroom. This allows the children to read the materials that they are interested in and may increase their desire to visit the public library.

The teacher should not be forgotten during a classroom visit. The librarian should give the teacher a packet of materials about the library and its services, as well as a list of all the titles mentioned during the booktalk. The librarian should take the opportunity to discuss the teacher's perceptions of the library and to ask about possible future needs for library services. If any problems have surfaced in regard to unannounced assignments, this can be an unthreatening time to raise the issue.

Sharing Resources

Perhaps the most difficult aspect of school-public library cooperation is sharing resources. Because materials for the schools and those for the library are usually funded from different budgets and from somewhat different tax bases, each institution may feel the need to protect its resources from damage or loss. In many communities, almost no sharing of resources takes place, but budgetary constraints on public spending is forcing many institutions to rethink this position.

Sharing Catalog Information

The least threatening type of sharing is the sharing of catalog information. The introduction of computerized catalogs linked to library and education systems makes the sharing of catalog information relatively easy. Many public libraries have mounted their catalogs on the Internet, where they are easily accessible by school media specialists. Fewer school systems have made their catalogs accessible by modem, but these numbers will undoubtedly grow.

When each institution has access to the other's catalog, teachers (with the help of school media personnel) can make more realistic assessments of the kind and amount of materials students can be expected to obtain from the public library. Public librarians can more easily evaluate the extent to which school media centers can be expected to provide curricular support for students. When weeding collections, each institution can check to see whether they might be discarding materials that would be useful to the other or that are unique in the community.

In addition to sharing information about collections, school and public libraries may develop complementary collection development policies. School media centers are obliged to maintain collections that support the curriculum, while public libraries often feel pressure to buy materials that do the same. If an agreement can be reached whereby the public library acquires materials in particular areas (those that can be used by both adults and children or that serve both recreational and information needs), while the school purchases other curricular-support materials, both agencies will have more money available for other resources. Divisions based on content area, format, and age level allow for the best overall development of both libraries' resources. Municipal authorities are usually pleased to support collection development plans that make the best use of tax money.

Sharing Materials

Sharing materials has been difficult to put into practice. Some communities have attempted to maximize the use of school media center materials by making them available to the public library during the summer. School authorities may object to this practice because of the possibility of damage and loss of materials. Many schools practice a higher level of inventory control than public libraries, and they find the loss rate of public libraries unacceptably high. Both institutions must be determined and patient to work out acceptable ways to deal with these differences. An informal account of losses could be recorded to see whether the two libraries balance out. Compensation in the form of materials or payment could help ensure that an unacceptable loss does not occur on either side.

Expensive materials, such as reference books, films, and audiovisual and computer equipment, are probably the best candidates for sharing. In most communities, however, these materials are made more widely available through sharing among several schools or public libraries, rather than by cutting across type of agency on a community basis. The reasons for this are political and based on financial accounting, rather than on convenience or geographical location. The pattern is difficult to break; however, it can be worthwhile to overcome this difficulty. In small, isolated communities, in particular, some form of materials sharing between schools and public libraries seems a desirable goal. A successful plan in one community can be used as a model in other communities. In the long run everyone benefits by such cooperation.

Sharing Space

The final type of sharing of resources is the sharing of space. Many communities have considered the desirability of having the public library located in a school building so that one facility could serve the needs of the school and the public more efficiently. The appeal of this solution lies in the apparent logic of spreading underutilized resources throughout the community as widely as possible. Communities that have tried the system have met with varied success. In part, this seems to result from the different purposes of the parent institution.

Schools are generally located away from major transportation routes to ensure the safety of children walking to and from school. This means that a public library in a school is less accessible to the public than one located in a high-traffic area. The most effective location for a school media center is at the heart of the school, easily accessible from classrooms and labs. If a public library shares this space, the entire school building must be kept open, and security must be provided during after-school hours. The expense is often prohibitive.

Many members of the public do not consider schools to be welcoming institutions, and adult use of the public library often drops when it is housed in a school. Some adults believe that only materials suitable for children will be chosen for the collection.

Service to preschool children is particularly difficult in a school-housed public library, because the noise and activities of young children in the media center and in hallways can distract students. Elderly people also may find it difficult or distracting to use a library that is dominated by schoolchildren.

Finding acceptable standards for the collection may be difficult because schools traditionally choose materials that are aimed at children. A school-housed library may be constrained from including adult materials that may be considered offensive.

In spite of these problems, some communities have found that school-housed public libraries are a desirable alternative to the provision of two separate collections aimed at the same clientele. This trend toward joint-use facilities has grown during the 1990s (Goldberg 1996). The pressure on local governments to reduce spending levels has influenced this trend, and this pressure is likely to continue. The role that public librarians can play is to document how joint-use facilities have worked elsewhere, to work with schools to clarify the goals of each institution, and to develop clear guidelines for continuing the public library's programs and services if a joint-use facility is developed.

Whatever pattern of cooperation evolves between schools and public libraries, attempts to create closer cooperation will undoubtedly continue. Information technology has made it easier for services to be provided, regardless of their physical location. As this technology becomes available to everyone in the community, schools and libraries will have to work together to ensure that every member of the community has access to the widest possible range of information.

Serving Children Outside of Schools

Most children learn about the public library through visits to the library with their parents or school classes. However, these contact points do not work for all children. To serve the greatest number of children in a community, public librarians should also try to reach children who do not attend formal schools but are educated at home. In addition, some children, especially those who are homeless or who move frequently between various relatives or foster homes, have a closer relationship with a community agency than with the school system. Librarians should establish cooperative relationships with other community agencies that are interested in these children's welfare.

Homeschooling Families

Although most children attend school from the age of about six, a significant minority are educated at home. The number of homeschooled children appears to be growing, so they have become an important client-group for library services. Parents who decide to homeschool do so for different reasons. Four of the most important include: 1) religious parents who feel that schools do not teach their children certain ideas; 2) parents who want to shield their children from the bad experiences they had in schools; 3) parents whose political beliefs lead them to avoid institutions of all kinds; and 4) parents who like to have their children close at home (Falbel 1997).

Some home educators follow a formal curriculum, several of which are available from correspondence schools and publishing companies and on the World Wide Web. Other parents, especially those who call themselves "unschoolers," do not follow formal lesson plans. Topics of the child's interest are covered, and often, no specific daily time is scheduled for lessons. Children learn through their everyday activities. Some of these parents also do not believe in testing or setting standards but prefer an individualized learning experience. Homeschooling families are a diverse group, and librarians should be ready to serve the needs of both parents and children.

Services for Parents

Parents who homeschool their children need a number of specific resources in addition to general education materials. The state or provincial regulations governing homeschooling are a necessary reference for parents. These vary widely from one jurisdiction to another and are frequently modified by new laws or regulations. These materials may be kept in the adult department, but, for referral purposes, children's librarians must be aware of their location and how to access them.

A number of books cover the topic of homeschooling (Bell 1997; Brostrom 1995; Gutterson 1992; Pitman and Van Galen 1991). Some of these would be appropriate to include in a parenting section in the children's department as well as in the adult collection. Several magazines are devoted to homeschooling. While some of these may be deemed too closely related to a religious denomination to be appropriate in a public library, others are more general and would be of interest to many parents. Internet sites on homeschooling are a growing resource (Homeschooling 1997), and many of them provide links to other sites. Librarians may want to bookmark some of these on the library computers so that parents can find them easily. Homeschooling resources might also be posted on the library's website so that parents can access them from home.

Librarians can reach homeschoolers through self-help groups and newsletters published in many communities. A library may wish to make meeting space available to such groups. This is often convenient for homeschooling parents because they can meet while the children use library resources.

Services for Children

Children who are being homeschooled often rely heavily on the public library for books and other resources. Most of the resources they use are the same as those used by children in school, but they may use them more intensively because they lack access to a school media center. Libraries can provide study space for the use of reference materials and electronic resources. Occasionally, the library might be able to arrange longer loans for homeschooling families, especially those in rural areas.

Bookmobile service is especially helpful to homeschooled children in rural areas (Lockwood 1996). Children and their parents can request particular books or materials on a specific subject to be brought on the bookmobile. The librarians serving bookmobile clients are able to become familiar with and tailor their materials selection to patrons' needs. They can recommend new titles and even order books that fill a need for several homeschooling families. Homeschoolers can use bookmobile service both for subject-specific materials and for recreational reading.

Homeschooled children who have access to computers and modems at home are heavy users of the library's homework helper services. Several websites are designed especially for homeschoolers, while other, more general sites are also useful for them. A number of homeschoolers have mounted home pages, which show their work, offer reviews of books or media, and provide interaction with other students. In developing links for the library's website, librarians should consider the needs of homeschoolers and try to find sites of interest to them.

Although homeschooling families are a minority in any community, they are a group that needs special attention from public libraries. As a central information link, the library can help foster cooperative efforts from the schools and other agencies to enable homeschooling families to succeed in their educational efforts.

Community Agencies Dealing with Children

In every community, a number of agencies work with children or are concerned about community services to children. Many of these groups have little knowledge of the public library and often fail to think of it as an agency with parallel concerns. A library with an active public relations program will want to build bridges between the library and these agencies. The librarian usually initiates these efforts because professionals in other agencies are often unaware of the library's resources.

Children's librarians should focus on agencies that serve children. Rather than working in isolation, many libraries have found that collaborating with other social agencies ensures a wider distribution of services and heightened publicity for the library. As one writer states, "It is clear that in terms of time saved, audiences reached, resources information shared, and sometimes joint funding obtained, collaboration between the library and other community agencies is advantageous" (White 1997, 218).

Government Agencies

Most communities have at least one social agency that is primarily responsible for caring for children. This agency often operates children's shelters and administers the foster parent program. Libraries can provide services, such as collections of materials for temporary residences or shelters, programs for group homes, and book lists and information about library services for foster parents and childcare workers. Publicity information may be routinely distributed to the agency, but the most effective way to publicize library services is for the librarian to make personal contact with individuals at the relevant agencies. This can be done on a one-to-one basis by telephone or visits or through an open house or coffee hour for the childcare workers.

Hospitals are another agency through which libraries can publicize their resources. Some large libraries maintain deposit collections for hospitalized children. This requires that staff members periodically visit hospitals. Volunteers can administer the program, but the library will be responsible for their training. Unless the children's department has sufficient resources and personnel, it is probably better to start with a less ambitious program than deposit collections. Services might include book lists for parents and hospitalized children; special monthly, annual, or semiannual programming; and a packet of library information for the parents of newborn babies.

The health department may maintain well-baby clinics that will accept library publicity, book lists, and possibly a deposit collection. A library staff member could maintain and update the collection if the clinic staff would supervise its use. Many people first become interested in library services when they become parents, so it is useful for librarians to reach parents of young children. Both the parents and children can benefit from the library's resources, and the library may gain a new family of patrons.

Children gather at municipal recreational centers, such as day camps, swimming pools, hockey rinks, and community centers. These locations offer an opportunity for the library to publicize its services. Lists of books and other materials tailored to the interests of the specific group—books about swimming for the neighborhood pool, videos on tennis for the sports camp, and instructions for nature crafts for the day camp—will be of help to the adult leaders and will publicize the library. Recreational facilities are useful places for deposit collections if the library has enough staff for their maintenance. Teenagers who work in recreational programs at these facilities are often enthusiastic recipients of information about activities and services they can use with campers.

Religious and Social Agencies

Many nongovernmental social agencies and community groups that work with children will welcome information about library materials and services. Boy Scouts, Girl Scouts, 4-H Clubs, and their associated groups are active in most communities. These groups have traditionally had close relations with libraries. Most scout leaders encourage scouts to use library materials in working for badges and preparing for activities. The Association for Library Service to Children, a division of the ALA, maintains a formal liaison with the Boy Scouts and the Girl Scouts on a national level. Distributing special book lists or publicity to these groups will help ensure continuing cooperation. Local groups connected with other national organizations, such as Camp Fire Inc., Boys Clubs and Girls Clubs of America, or other groups may also welcome information about library services.

Day care facilities, whether private, religion-related, or public, continue to be a major area of interest to children's librarians. Many libraries find it difficult to build and maintain relationships with these facilities because of their numbers and scattered locations throughout the community. Most communities maintain lists of approved day care facilities. These lists can serve as the basis for an outreach attempt. Personal contact might be made with the largest and the closest facilities. A quarterly or semiannual newsletter to providers could publicize library events of interest to preschool children and child-care workers. The key is to maintain contact rather than making a one-time attempt to arouse interest. Although the attempt may not result in an influx of day care groups for library programs, the message will be received. It is difficult to identify library use by day care workers, so the results of the publicity are difficult to track. Sometimes a special offer, such as long-term loans to day care centers, will help to identify the facilities that use library services.

Agencies Concerned About Children

Some groups within the community are concerned about services to children, although work with children is not a function of the group. The library may be able to obtain publicity and support from these groups if they are convinced of the value of library services.

Business Groups

Fraternal and business organizations, such as the Rotary Club, Lions Club, Chamber of Commerce, and similar groups, are one source of support. Several methods are used to make these groups aware of the library.

News releases should be sent out to the group's public relations officer or newsletter editor when an interesting project or program is under way. Any library activity that ties in with programs sponsored by the group should be noted in a newsletter or mentioned at a meeting. Speaking at a meeting is the most effective way to let the group know about the library's work. Most often, the chief librarian rather than the children's librarian is asked to speak, but as long as the speaker knows about the relevant children's programs, the identity of the individual does not matter.

Members of the library board offer the easiest access to community groups because they are usually active in community affairs. Library board members should be aware that the library staff is available to attend civic group meetings and discuss possible joint projects.

Corporations that offer day care facilities for employees may be receptive to offers of library service. The same procedure would be followed as with any other community group: The library could offer special lending privileges to the day care group, book lists and other materials for parents, and perhaps a deposit collection. In some cases, it might be possible to offer library programs at the business site. The offer is generally made directly to the person in charge of the day care facility. Arrangements to provide services to business-sponsored day care children could result in a close, supportive relationship between the library and the business community. If the cooperation is considered successful by both groups, the industry might support the library's services to other groups in the community.

Community Groups

Most parents' organizations have an interest in library services to children. The library may circulate materials to parent-teacher associations to encourage parents to bring their children to the public library. Many communities have a variety of other parent groups, from small informal groups in neighborhoods or housing complexes to local affiliates of national groups serving special groups of children. While it is difficult for a library to find small groups, a list should be made of those that are known. These groups can be added to the mailing list for children's services publicity.

Local affiliates of national groups can usually be found in the telephone directory's yellow pages under social service organizations. Many of these groups focus on specific groups of children—those who are gifted or those with disabilities, learning difficulties, allergies, or chronic illnesses. The focus of these groups suggests the type of materials and services that would be appropriate. Librarians can provide lists of appropriate reading or other materials for parents, offer meeting rooms, or organize programs for the parents of children with special needs. Not every group will respond to these offers, but forging ties with even one or two of these groups is worthwhile.

Ideas about other groups that might be interested in library services can be gained from the list of associations with which the Association for Library Services to Children maintains liaisons, such as the following:

- Association for Children and Adults with Learning Disabilities
- Association for the Care of Children's Health
- Big Brothers and Big Sisters of America
- Boys and Girls Clubs of America
- The Child Welfare League of America
- Council for Exceptional Children
- Head Start
- National Committee for the Prevention of Child Abuse
- Salvation Army

Ethnic organizations that sponsor heritage language classes or social events may be interested in library services. Children's departments that have collections in several languages have the most to offer these groups. Staff members who speak the appropriate language will be helpful in approaching ethnic groups.

Cultural groups, such as music schools, museums, and children's theater groups, exist in many communities. Libraries can offer these groups services tailored to their needs. Most libraries have a wide range of materials of value to these groups, but unless the librarian makes the effort to inform the group, the materials may go unused. Because the public library is a cultural institution, it is a natural ally of other cultural groups. A close relationship between the two will benefit both agencies.

Maintaining Contact with Community Groups

Maintaining contact with a number of groups in the community is time-consuming. Librarians should start out slowly, targeting one or two groups for an initial approach and gradually broadening the base. The basic task is keeping each agency informed about library materials, programs, and services that will be of interest to the group. A standard newsletter about library activities may be too general to appeal to a specific group. However, one of the advantages of producing a newsletter electronically is that it becomes fairly easy to individualize various versions of the same news. After a format has been established, information can be tailored to each group. The day camp groups can therefore receive a list of new craft and sports books, the Chinese cultural association receives a list of new Chinese-language books, and the art museum's education director receives a list of new art books.

A database of acquisitions can be tagged by subject, age level, language, and interest to special groups, allowing the librarian to produce targeted book lists quickly and effectively. This information is useful for more than preparing newsletters. The lists, themselves, can be one of the most effective marketing tools the department provides. Creative librarians will find many uses for a database of children's materials from which varied individual and group listings can be prepared.

Maintaining contact with a number of organizations can place the library at the center of the community. Approaches should be carefully planned to realize the greatest mutual benefits.

Tips for Organizing Contact with Groups

- Try to maintain contact with a specific individual, rather than sending information to the group in general.

- Tailor information to specific groups, rather than blanketing the community with generic news releases. Information that is directly relevant to the needs of the group is much more likely to be read than general information.

- Systematically update address lists so that personnel or address changes are noted. Assign one clerical staff member the responsibility for maintaining a list of community contacts and for noting changes that are announced in publicity or the media. Once a year, the clerk should check with each agency to make sure that the library information is correct.

- Use as many channels as possible to deliver information: personal visits, group meetings, or coffee hours at the library; news releases and announcements in the media; and informal contacts in the library.

- Spread the responsibility for maintaining contact with community groups among staff members, with each person taking responsibility for a limited number of groups.

Taking the initiative in setting up collaboration is not easy, but the rewards are great. "If we reach one teacher, one parent, or one child we would have otherwise never reached, our success is manyfold" (White 1997, 218). By reaching beyond the library to other individuals and community agencies, children's librarians broaden and strengthen services to all young people in the community.

17

Networking with Other Children's Librarians

Most librarians work in groups and are most frequently in contact with coworkers. However, many other children's librarians can share professional viewpoints and potential solutions to problems. Technology has made it possible to maintain contact with colleagues far beyond the individual library.

Electronic Links

The Internet provides an easy way for individuals with similar interests to communicate with one another. Because libraries were among the first institutions to establish links to the Internet, many electronic discussion groups, or listservs, are devoted to librarians' concerns. When librarians join these groups, they receive messages by e-mail from other group members. Electronic links provide access to a group of experts who can answer questions, suggest solutions to problems, or recommend materials.

To join such a listserv, a librarian should identify one that is targeted to his or her interests. The ALA's website (http://www.ala.org) contains the Association's various lists and directions for subscribing to them. Another good source for learning about listservs is *The Public Service Librarian's Professional Guide to Internet Resources* (http://k12.oit.umass.edu.libguide.html). ALA's Association for Library Services to Children's *Journal of Youth Services in Libraries* periodically lists sites of interest to children's librarians, as do several other professional journals. Other children's librarians are also good sources for such discussion lists. Figure 17.1 contains a list of some listservs of interest to children's librarians.

To subscribe to a listserv, the librarian sends a message to the list's server telling it which list he or she want to join. The address to which this message is sent is usually *Listserv@ . . .* or *Majordomo@. . . .* The convention for many listservs is to leave the subject line blank and simply write as the message: "subscribe PUBYAC

193

(or another name)". The librarian will receive a confirmation of the request as well as information about the procedure for sending messages to the list and how to unsubscribe. This message should be saved for future reference.

Selective List of Youth Services Listservs

Lists Sponsored by the American Library Association

alsc-l@ala.org	Association for Library Service to Children
homepage@ala.org	Developing Content for Your Home Page
issues@ala.org	K12 Internet Issues
slms21st@ala.org	School Library Media Specialists in the 21st Century
yalsa-l@ala.org	Young Adult Library Services Association List

To subscribe to any of these lists, send an email to LISTPROC@ALA.ORG. Leave the subject line blank. In the message area write:

subscribe [listname] [your first name] [your last name]

Other Listservs

CHILDLIT	Children's Literature Discussion Send mail to majordomo@email.rutgers.edu
KIDLIT-L	Discussion of Children's Books Send mail to listserv@bingvmb.cc.binghamton.edu
LM_NET	Library Media Network Send mail to LISTSERV@SUVM.SYR.EDU
PUBYAC	Public Library Youth and Children Send mail to majordomo@nysernet.org
STORYTELL	Storytelling Discussion Group Send mail to storytell-request@venus.twu.edu

Note: Discussion groups change frequently. Some of those listed may cease operation or change their addresses. Current addresses can be found by checking World Wide Web resources.

Fig. 17.1. Selective List of Youth Services Listservs.

Most listserv groups are active, containing a dozen or more messages each day. Some of them offer a digest format so that the messages are consolidated and sent once daily. Some lists are moderated, meaning that an individual reviews each message to make sure it is relevant to the list and is not offensive. On other lists, the messages are sent automatically. Most library-related lists are free from the acrimonious messages that occur on some Internet discussion groups.

On any discussion list, most members read the messages but do not post any themselves. Individuals who receive, but do not send, messages are sometimes called "lurkers" by more active group members. Many librarians prefer to lurk when they first subscribe to a list. Later, when they understand the tone and content of the discussion, they will answer or post messages of their own.

Messages can be sent to the entire list by pressing the *reply* indicator on the browser. A message sent this way will go to everyone rather than just to the person who posted the original message. To respond privately to the individual who posted a message, send the message to the individual's e-mail address. Inadvertently posting private message to a listserv is one of the hazards of using this form of communication. Many people develop professional friendships by starting a private e-mail correspondence with colleagues first encountered through a discussion group.

Networking Within a System or Region

In developing face-to-face professional networks, a children's librarian should begin with librarians working in other branches throughout the library system. The size of the library system usually determines the formality of this group's organization. Large systems often have an association of children's librarians that holds regular meetings for materials selection, workshops, or other topics. The coordinator of children's services generally plans and chairs these meetings. In smaller systems, children's librarians may maintain contact through periodic meetings at the main library or at one of the branches. The head of the main library's children's department often takes responsibility for arranging these meetings, but sometimes each librarian takes a turn in their planning. In some jurisdictions, a number of libraries form a regional system that has many of the characteristics of a large library system.

Regardless of the specifics, these meetings will be enhanced if each individual works to make them useful. Part of the value of these meetings is purely social—to get together with coworkers and to share news. The larger professional aim is to improve children's services throughout the system or region. Each individual has a responsibility to bring to the meetings information and ideas that will help others in the group. If one branch has particular problems, discussing them with other librarians may help resolve them. If particular programs or specific materials have proved notably successful, this information should be shared so that others can benefit from it. A willing, cooperative spirit that stems from these meetings generally leads to better service for the entire community or region.

Visiting other local children's departments enables librarians to see the value of different room arrangements, decorations, or materials. Some systems and regions hold rotating meetings so that librarians eventually see most of the departments, but other jurisdictions hold all meetings at one central location. If the latter is the case, an attempt to visit other departments is well worth the effort. Such visits need not be long; many ideas can be gathered in about 20 minutes.

Meetings with local librarians need not be limited to professional staff. These meetings can become opportunities to recruit other staff members into the profession. Many people become librarians after some years of work in libraries. The decision to enter the field may result from the interest and encouragement of the librarians with whom they work. When employees in the library show an aptitude for the work and appear to be capable of undertaking graduate education, it is worth discussing the possibilities with them. Library assistants who might be interested in becoming professionals should be encouraged to attend conferences and workshops so that they can learn more about the range of options in the field. Recruiting effective new librarians is one of the major obligations of library professionals.

Moving Beyond the System

Although the librarians within one system or region form the first level of professional association, most librarians also belong to larger groups. The geographic range of regional groups depends largely on the population density of the area. Some places have county or area groups; others have state or provincial organizations. Interactions between librarians working in different systems in the same geographic area allow the sharing of information and experience. Such groups can offer workshops or host programs that might be too costly for an individual system. The first professional association that a new librarian usually joins is the state association. For many librarians, this continues to be the major focus of their professional life.

Beyond the region, national and international associations of children's librarians exist, where librarians can meet their counterparts in various locations and situations. Most contacts with these groups result from membership in professional associations and attendance at conferences.

Benefiting from Professional Associations

Choosing an Association

Because membership in many professional associations is expensive, new librarians often decide to limit the number they join. Those who belonged to various organizations through inexpensive student memberships while in library school have the advantage of knowing something about different groups. Once on the job, a librarian's decision whether to join a group is based, in part, on the extent to which a library will support professional association work. Some library systems encourage their employees to attend state and local groups, rather than national ones, while others take the opposite position. Almost all library systems regard membership and participation in professional associations as a sign of commitment to librarianship. They may reward this work with commendations on annual reviews and merit pay increases.

Encouragement from the library is an important factor, but individuals must choose for themselves which associations will be most helpful in their professional development. Many librarians join the state or provincial library association early in their career. Most of these organizations have sections for children's librarians, and many of them publish journals or newsletters and provide workshops, professional development, and children's services activities at conferences.

National associations offer exposure to a more diverse group of librarians who work under a wide variety of conditions. One reason to join these associations is to receive the association's journals and other publications. Having a larger number of people from which to draw, the national associations can present specialized programs and publications dealing with particular groups, such as children with hearing disabilities, new immigrants, or Native American children. The large conferences sponsored by national associations attract many exhibitors and may alert librarians to obscure materials and equipment.

International associations, such as the International Federation of Library Associations and Institutions or the International Board on Books for Youth, hold conferences throughout the world and publish journals of interest to children's librarians, but few library systems encourage or support participation in their work. The costs of attending international conferences are high. A decision to participate in international organizations is usually made by an individual librarian who has a personal interest in widening the horizons of his or her professional life.

In addition to library associations, other groups exist in allied fields. The Children's Literature Association focuses on children's literature rather than library services for children. Educational associations, such as the International Reading Association and the National Council of Teachers of English, publish journals that include articles about children's books. Their conferences have sessions of interest to librarians, in addition to teachers and often feature talks by noted children's authors.

Professional library associations not only provide professional development opportunities for members, they also lobby to enhance the status of the profession. The groups also work to alert the public to the importance of libraries in the community, the state, and the country. Participation in association work may bring enhanced career performance and professional visibility (which can lead to increased job opportunities), as well as offer professional contacts that often develop into long and rewarding friendships.

Attending Conferences

Professional conferences are costly, in terms of both time and money, yet many librarians find them worth the expense. They offer professional programs, well-known speakers, social contacts, exhibits, and professional tours. Unless an individual is already active in the association, a decision whether to attend a conference is usually based on its professional programs. Programs tend to focus on topics of concern and to feature speakers with experience in the area. A typical format is to have one speaker give an overview of the topic—serving latchkey children or selecting children's videos, for example—and then to have a panel of four or five librarians respond. The program's value depends upon how well the speakers prepare and present their talks. No one program will make the entire conference worthwhile. Librarians should look for a number of topics of interest and plan to attend at least half a dozen sessions.

Talks by authors of children's books are featured at most professional conferences and tend to be popular. Authors are generally fluent and entertaining speakers, and many of them have experience in public speaking. Their talks deepen a librarian's appreciation of the author's books, but in a broader professional sense, they do not serve to improve library services. They are cultural rather than professional events, and despite their inherent interest, they should not dominate a librarian's conference schedule.

Contacts made at conferences can help to solve professional problems, gather new information, and enlarge the view of the profession. The most important contacts are usually made through committee work.

Exhibits are a valuable part of most conferences and one of the major reasons that librarians attend conferences year after year. For librarians in small systems, conferences may be their best opportunity to see new materials and equipment. Children's publishers have booths at many large conferences, and librarians can browse through the new books to make ordering decisions. Conferences also offer opportunities to examine the newest technology and see demonstrations of new software. Librarians can compare brands and ask questions of the salespeople at each booth. A large conference, such as the ALA's Annual Conference, will have more than 1,000 exhibitors offering an overwhelming variety of products. Any conference attendee should allow several sessions of two or three hours each to look at the exhibits. Trying to view them all in one day guarantees total exhaustion. In addition, most children's publishers and many other exhibitors give away attractive posters that can be used to decorate the children's department. Exhibitors also distribute catalogs, which alert librarians to new materials that are available. However, being added to the publisher's mailing list is generally more efficient than trying to carry catalogs home.

Tours of libraries and other sites of interest, such as processing centers or media production units, can be valuable. Children's librarians can gather many ideas about how children's rooms are designed and operated in other communities. Most local librarians are eager to show conference visitors their operations and explain their programs and services. Special collections of children's materials may offer insight into the types of collections that can be developed.

The value of conferences can be gauged by the fact that attendance at most of them grows each year. Libraries support conferences because they increase knowledge about the profession and heighten commitment to it. A good conference lifts an individual out of a particular job and offers them a glimpse of the wider world of librarianship.

Serving on Committees

Most of the work of a professional association is carried out by volunteer committees. Serving on a committee is the best way to find out how an organization works and to meet other members. Some libraries will send individuals to conferences only if they are members of a committee. Library associations seem large and impersonal to newcomers, who may feel that it would be difficult to get to know people and to be invited to join a committee. In most library associations, however, it is actually easy to become a committee member. Before becoming involved, however, a new librarian should realize that while being a committee member is the best way to benefit from association membership, it requires regular meeting attendance. Unless a person can commit to attending conferences for two or three years, it is unwise to seek committee membership.

The first step in becoming a committee member is to decide which committees to join. Obviously, it is not sensible to choose the largest and most prestigious committees as a first step. In many children's librarians' organizations, the media evaluation committees are considered the most desirable; their membership is often reserved for people who have served well on other committees. The committees that form the backbone of any organization are the local arrangements committee, the membership committee, the organization and bylaws committee, and other hardworking groups. A newcomer can get a sense of the committee's work by attending committee meetings as a visitor. Although visitors do not participate in meetings, they are often given a copy of the agenda. The committee chair usually records the names of visitors. This list may be used as a source of nominations. Another way to indicate interest in joining a committee is to write to the person in charge of committee appointments (often the vice-president/president-elect) and offer to serve, either on a specific committee or wherever a children's librarian's services might be helpful. Associations are always looking for active new members for committees.

Once on a committee, the time and effort necessary to complete committee work should become a priority. Although the demands of a job naturally take precedence over organizational activities, time must be allowed to complete committee tasks. Most libraries allow some organizational work to be done during the work day, but most people do a great deal of committee work on their own time. Libraries also differ in the amount of association work they will support financially. Committee work often involves photocopying, long-distance telephone charges, and postage. Associations often have committee budgets for these items, but they also rely on members' libraries to support some expenses. Before incurring any expenses, the librarian should check on his or her library's policy.

Immediately after returning from a conference, committee obligations should be scheduled on the calendar and should be attended to as dutifully as any other professional task. Ample time should be given to checking facts, corresponding with members, writing reports, and doing other assigned tasks. The committee chair should be kept informed about committee activities. Most associations have guidelines on sending copies of correspondence and minutes of meetings to particular individuals. Such procedures keep the association running in a business-like manner, which is important to accomplish its objectives.

Contributing to the Professional Dialogue

Reviewing

Children's librarians buy a wide range of materials. They are constantly looking for evaluations of books, periodicals, records, films, and other possible purchases. Professional journals carry such reviews. Many library systems arrange for local reviews so that new materials can be judged on the basis of community standards. Some librarians work for systems that do in-house reviewing, and this is excellent professional training because it forces the reviewer to articulate a reaction to the item and to choose specific examples to back up judgments. Because many in-house reviews are presented orally at staff meetings, differing points of view can be raised and questions about the assessments can be asked. Beginning librarians benefit from listening to the evaluations of more experienced colleagues, while those who have been in the field for some time can also learn from the fresh approach of newer staff members.

After some experience reviewing for the local library system, many librarians find it challenging to review for a larger audience. Some of the professional journals that review children's materials rely on a corps of volunteer reviewers. A librarian who wants to become a reviewer is usually given some materials and asked to write sample reviews. If the work is satisfactory, the new reviewer can expect to be added to the journal's list of reviewers. Although the pay is usually only a copy of the book being reviewed, reviewing can be a satisfying professional opportunity. It offers a chance to read and judge new books, and the opportunity of having work published. Most libraries encourage staff members to review in their fields, so a successful record of reviewing is an asset on a résumé.

Journals that commission reviews want well-written, competent reviews, and they want them on time. The best way to be a successful reviewer is to take the job seriously and treat it as a professional obligation (England and Fasick 1987). Most reviewing has to be done outside of normal working hours. Reviewing draws on the background knowledge and skills developed in the library.

Writing for Journals

Reviewing is one of the most common ways of breaking into publication, but other types of writing are also important. Professional journals exist to maintain communication among various people in the field. Children's library work is not as well represented in the journals as some other specializations. One reason for this may be that most children's librarians are relatively busy with their day-to-day work and do not have time to write about their activities. Many librarians throughout North America are struggling with the same problems. If one finds a solution and writes about it, others can benefit. In order for the profession to grow and to share a common base of knowledge, the work must be recorded and published.

Library journals are generally receptive to articles that deal with realistic problems and solutions or that offer helpful insights. A librarian who reads professional literature becomes aware of the kind of articles published by various journals. Many journals offer guidelines for the type, length, and style of articles wanted. An author should be sure to follow the editor's suggestions as articles that follow the guidelines will be considered more seriously.

The articles in many professional journals are not chosen by one editor but are sent to a panel of reviewers (often called referees) for assessment. This long selection procedure can make the author feel that the manuscript is lying unnoticed on someone's desk. Eventually, however, the editor and referees will make a decision, and the author will be notified that the article is accepted, that revisions are suggested, or that it is rejected. Occasionally, when an article is rejected, the editor will suggest that it be sent to another journal.

It is usually sensible to agree to make all suggested revisions unless they change the focus of the article. Revisions are usually designed to make the article clearer and more useful to potential readers. Paying attention to the type of revisions suggested can help a writer learn how to write more effective articles. Needless to say, revisions should be made quickly, and the article returned to the editor so that publication will not be delayed.

Organizing Workshops

Another way to join the professional dialogue is to organize lectures and workshops for children's librarians. Many large libraries and regional systems run a number of workshops and other continuing education programs for librarians. Other programs are developed by library associations, and occasionally, by groups of libraries.

The most important decision in planning a workshop is selecting the topic. A number of perennial themes are available, including storytelling, programming, services to various groups of users, and audiovisual services. Other themes are more topical and are suggested by changing conditions. These might include service to latchkey children, dealing with difficult patrons, legal aspects of library work, and the like. The key to mounting a successful workshop is to choose a theme that is relevant to a number of librarians but that has not been overused. Talking to librarians with different interests and levels of experience is helpful in gathering suggestions.

The choice of topic will depend on both the interests of the potential participants and the availability of appropriate speakers. The usual pattern is to find one or more outside speakers whose reputations will attract participants and then to ask a few local librarians to serve as a response panel or discussion leaders. The outside speaker is generally expected to discuss the issues in general or theoretical terms, and the reaction panel to relate the issues to the local library situation and experience. This format works well because it allows for interaction between the speaker and participants and ensures that aspects of particular interest to the group will be raised.

After the topic and speakers have been chosen, the organizer's task is to arrange appropriate publicity. A memorable title and an attractive brochure help to attract attention. Time the publicity to give people time to make arrangements for attending the workshop, but material sent out too early can be put aside and forgotten. Many organizations find that publicity sent out about two months before a one-day workshop tends to be most effective.

Many of the suggestions in Chapter 8 apply to professional workshops as well as library events. Careful planning and attention to detail help to make the event useful for all involved. One point that organizers should keep in mind is that much of the value of a workshop comes from the informal interaction between participants. Coffee breaks and lunch can be as valuable as the formal sessions, so allow sufficient time and space for them.

Evaluating the Professional Dialogue

Although preparing reviews, writing articles, and organizing workshops may not seem central to the work of children's librarian, they are all part of what makes librarianship a profession rather than just another job. A librarian is called upon to make decisions almost every day and often has little time to consider their long-term impact. Yet, unless the decisions are based on a coherent philosophy of service, they may not fulfill the library's mandate. It is through the literature and professional associations and activities that librarians develop their attitude toward and judgment of library services. Like members of all professions, librarians need to take time to consider the basis of their daily work. The thoughtful analysis of ideas and trends is the foundation upon which meaningful library service is built. Every professional librarian should try to become a participant in the professional dialogue that helps library service grow to meet the needs of all children.

References and Further Reading

ALA. 1997. *Access for Children and Young People to Videotapes and Other Nonprint Formats: An Interpretation of the Library Bill of Rights.* Available: http://www.ala.org/ICONN/ICONN-website/video.html. (Accessed July 27, 1997).

———. 1996a. *Access to Electronic Information Services, and Networks: An Interpretation of the LIBRARY BILL OF RIGHTS.* Chicago: American Library Association.

———. 1996b. *Intellectual Freedom Manual/Compiled by the Office for Intellectual Freedom of the American Library Association.* 5th ed. Chicago: American Library Association.

Allen County Public Library Website. 1996. Available: http://fuji.acpl.lib.in.us:80/About_the_ACPL/unattended_children.html. (Accessed July 27, 1997).

Arterburn, Tom R. 1996. Librarians: Caretakers or Crimefighters? *American Libraries* 27 (August): 32–34.

Baltimore County Public Library. 1987. *STEPS: Staff Training for Emergency Procedures at the Baltimore County Public Library.* 2d ed. Baltimore, MD: Baltimore County Public Library.

Banks, Lynne Reid. 1981. *The Indian in the Cupboard.* Garden City, NY: Doubleday.

Banks, Paula. 1995. News Releases, Photo Releases, Public Service Announcements. In *Part-Time Public Relations with Full-Time Results.* Edited by Rashelle Karp. Chicago: American Library Association. 1–9.

Bauer, Caroline. 1993. *Caroline Feller Bauer's New Handbook for Storytellers.* Chicago: American Library Association.

Bell, Debra. 1997. *The Ultimate Guide to Homeschooling.* Dallas, TX: Word.

Benne, Mae. 1991. *Principles of Children's Services in Public Libraries.* Chicago: American Library Association.

Bertot, John Carlo, Charles R. McClure, and Douglas L. Zweizig. 1996. *Public Libraries and the Internet: Survey Results and Key Issues.* Washington, DC: National Commission on Libraries and Information Science.

Bielefield, Arlene. 1978. Time-and-Money Management Plan. In *Reader in Children's Librarianship*. Edited by Joan Foster. Englewood, CO: Libraries Unlimited. 341–52.

Bodart, Joni Richards. 1992. *The New Booktalker*. Vol. 1. Englewood, CO: Libraries Unlimited.

Brophy, Peter, and Kate Coulling. 1996. *Quality Management for Information and Library Managers*. Brookfield, VT: Aslib Gower.

Brostrom, David C. 1995. *A Guide to Homeschooling for Librarians*. Highsmith Press Handbook Series. Fort Atkinson, WI: Highsmith Press.

Burlingame, Dwight F., ed. 1995. *Library Fundraising: Models for Success*. Chicago: American Library Association.

Carlson, Mim. 1995. *Winning Grants Step by Step: Support Centers of America's Complete Workbook for Planning, Developing, and Writing Successful Proposals*. Jossey-Bass Nonprofit Sector Series. San Francisco: Jossey-Bass.

Carson, Paula Phillips, Kerry David Carson, and Joyce Shouest Phillips. 1995. *The Library Manager's Deskbook: 102 Expert Solutions to 101 Common Dilemmas*. Chicago: American Library Association.

Champelli, L. 1996. *Understand Software that Blocks Internet Sites*. Available: http://www.monroe.lib.in.us/~lchampel/netadv4.html. (Accessed July 27, 1997).

Chen, Ching-chih. 1980. *Zero-Base Budgeting in Library Management: A Manual for Librarians*. Phoenix, AZ: Oryx Press.

Chicago Public Library Website. 1997. Available: http://cpl.lib.uic.edu. (Accessed July 27, 1997).

Cirillo, Susan E., and Robert E. Danford, eds. 1996. *Library Buildings, Equipment, and the ADA: Compliance Issues and Solutions*. Preconference sponsored by LAMA Buildings and Equipment Section, New Orleans, LA, June 24–25, 1993. Chicago: American Library Association.

Cleveland Public Library Website. 1997. Available: http://www.cpl.org. (Accessed July 27, 1997).

Curry, Ann. 1996. Managing the Problem Patron. *Public Libraries* 35 (May/June): 181–88.

Curzon, Susan C. 1989. *Managing Change: A How-to-Do-It Manual for Planning, Implementing and Evaluating Change in Libraries*. New York: Neal-Schuman.

Dalrymple, Prudence W. 1997. The State of the Schools. *American Libraries* 27 (January): 31–34.

Deerr, Kathleen. 1995. Budgeting. In *Youth Services Librarians as Managers: A How-to Guide from Budgeting to Personnel*. Edited by Kathleen Staerkel, Mary Fellows, and Sue McCleaf Nespeca. Chicago: American Library Association. 11–21.

Des Enfants, Sherry. 1995. Seeking Alternative Funding: Grantsmanship. In *Youth Services Librarians as Managers: A How-To Guide from Budgeting to Personnel*. Edited by Kathleen Staerkel, Mary Fellows, and Sue McCleaf Nespeca. Chicago: American Library Association. 22–40.

Dolnick, Sandy, ed. 1996. *Friends of Libraries Sourcebook*. 3d ed. Chicago: American Library Association.

Dowd, Frances Smardo. 1996. Homeless Children in Public Libraries: A National Survey of Large Systems. *Journal of Youth Services in Libraries* 9 (2 Winter): 155–65.

———. 1991. *Latchkey Children in the Library and Community: Issues, Strategies, and Programs*. Phoenix, AZ: Oryx Press.

———. 1989. Serving Latchkey Children: Recommendations from Librarians. *Public Libraries* (March/April): 101–6.

East, Kathy. 1995. *Inviting Children's Authors and Illustrators: A How-to-Do-It Manual for School and Public Librarians*. New York: Neal-Schuman.

Ellis, Judith Compton. 1988. Planning and Executing a Major Bookshift/Move Using an Electronic Spreadsheet. *College and Research Libraries News* 49 (May): 282–87.

England, Claire, and Adele M. Fasick. 1987. *ChildView: Evaluating and Reviewing Materials for Children*. Englewood, CO: Libraries Unlimited.

Falbel, Aaron. Homeschooling FAQ. Available: http://www.hsnp.com/gok/faq.html. (Accessed November 1997).

Farmer, Lesley. 1993. *When Your Library Budget Is Almost Zero*. Englewood, CO: Libraries Unlimited.

Fine, Sarah. 1996. How the Mind of a Censor Works: The Psychology of Censorship. *School Library Journal* 42 (1 January): 23–27.

Fitzgibbons, Shirley, and Verna Pungitore. 1989. Educational Roles and Services for Public and School Libraries. *Indiana Libraries* 8: 3–56.

Flint Public Library Website. 1997. Available: http://www.flint.lib.mi.us. (Accessed July 27, 1997).

Garlock, Kristen L., and Sherry Piontek. 1996. *Building the Service-Based Library Web Site: A Step-by-Step Guide to Design and Options*. Chicago: American Library Association.

Geever, Jane C., and Patricia McNeill. 1993. *The Foundation Center's Guide to Proposal Writing*. New York: Foundation Center.

Giesecke, Joan, ed. 1997. *Practical Help for New Supervisors*. 3d ed. Chicago: American Library Association.

Goldberg, Beverly. 1996. Public Libraries Go Back to School. *American Libraries* 27 (December): 54–55.

Greene, Ellin. 1991. *Books, Babies, and Libraries: Serving Infants, Toddlers, Their Parents and Caregivers*. Chicago: American Library Association.

Gutterson, David. 1992. *Family Matters: Why Homeschooling Makes Sense*. New York: Harcourt Brace Jovanovich.

Guy, Jennye E. 1995. Establishing a Library Foundation and a Fundraising Campaign. In *Library Fundraising: Models for Success*. Edited by Dwight F. Burlingame. Chicago: American Library Association.

Hagloch, Susan B. 1994. *Library Building Projects: Tips for Survival*. Englewood, CO: Libraries Unlimited.

Hamilton, Patricia, and Pam Hindman. 1987. Moving a Public Library Collection. *Public Libraries* 26 (Spring): 4–7.

Harrison, Maureen, and Steve Gilbert, eds. 1992. *The Americans with Disabilities Act Handbook*. Landmark Laws Series. Beverly Hills, CA: Excellent Books.

Hauptman, Robert. 1988. *Ethical Challenges in Librarianship*. Phoenix, AZ: Oryx.

Homeschool Resources on the Web. 1997. Available: http://www.mint.net/~caronfam/links.htm. (Accessed July 27, 1997).

Homeschooling Information and Homeschooling Resource Pages. 1997. Available: http://home-ed-press.com. (Accessed July 27, 1997).

Immroth, Barbara Frohling, and Keith Curry Lance. 1996. Output Measures for Children's Services in Public Libraries: A Status Report. *Public Libraries* 35 (July/August): 240–45.

Jenkinson, David. 1986. Censorship Iceberg: Results of a Survey of Challenges in Public and School Libraries. *Canadian Library Journal* (February): 7–15.

Jones, Patrick. 1992. *Connecting Young Adults and Libraries: A How-to-Do-It Manual*. New York: Neal-Schuman.

Karp, Rashelle S., ed. 1995. *Part-Time Public Relations with Full-Time Results: A PR Primer for Libraries*. Chicago: American Library Association.

Kay, Alan. 1994. *Observations About Children and Computers*. Prepared for Apple Computer, Inc. Cupertino, CA: Advanced Technology Group. Learning Concepts Group Note #15.

Kimmel, Margaret Mary, and Elizabeth Segel. 1983. *For Reading Out Loud! A Guide to Sharing Books with Children*. New York: Delacorte Press.

Kratz, Abby, and Melinda Flannery. 1997. Communication Skills. In *Practical Help for New Supervisors*, 3d ed. Edited by Joan Giesecke. Chicago: American Library Association. 43–57.

Leigh, Robert. 1950. *The Public Library in the United States*. New York: Columbia University Press.

Lincoln, Alan Jay. 1984. *Crime in the Library: A Study of Patterns, Impact, and Security*. New York: Bowker.

Lindsey, Jonathan A., and Ann B. Prentice. 1985. *Professional Ethics and Librarians*. Phoenix, AZ: Oryx.

Lockwood, Annette. 1996. Bookmobile Provides Home-Schoolers with Regular Library Period. *American Libraries* 27 (November): 32–33.

Lushington, Nolan, and James M. Kusack. 1991. *The Design and Evaluation of Public Library Buildings*. Hamden, CT: Library Professional Publication.

MacDonald, Gregory. 1996. Building ReUse: Right for the Times. *Public Libraries* 35 (September/October): 288–91.

MacLachlan, Rachel. 1996. Safety and Security Considerations. In *Library Buildings, Equipment, and the ADA: Compliance Issues and Solutions*. Edited by Susan E. Cirillo and Robert E. Danford. Chicago: American Library Association. 53–58.

Magid, Lawrence J. 1996. *Child Safety on the Information Highway*. Produced by the National Center for Missing and Exploited Children and Interactive Services Association. Available: http://www.missingkids.org/childsafety.html. (Accessed July 27, 1997).

Mathews, Virginia H., ed. 1994. *Library Services for Children and Youth: Dollars and Sense*. New York: Neal-Schuman.

McCallister, Myrna J., and Thomas H. Patterson. 1997. Conducting Effective Meetings. In *Practical Help for New Supervisors*. 3d ed. Edited by Joan Giesecke. Chicago: American Library Association. 58–74.

McClure, Charles R., Amy Owen, Douglas L. Zweizig, Mary Jo Lynch, and Nancy Van House. 1987. *Planning and Role Setting for Public Libraries: A Manual of Options and Procedures*. Chicago: American Library Association.

Merriam, Eve. 1987. *Halloween ABC*. New York: Macmillan.

Michaels, Andrea, and David Michaels. 1996. People, Assistive Devices, ADAptive Furnishings, and Their Environment in Your Library. In *Library Buildings, Equipment, and the ADA: Compliance Issues and Solutions*. Edited by Susan E. Cirillo and Robert E. Danford. Chicago: American Library Association. 40–47.

Michigan Library Association. 1995. *Youth Access to the Internet Through Libraries*. Available: http://statelib.ut.us/intacc.txt. (Accessed July 27, 1997).

Mississauga Library System. 1996. *The Little Library That Grew....* Mississauga Library System 1996 Annual Report. Mississauga, Ontario, Canada.

Multnomah County (Oregon) Public Library Website. 1997. Available: http://www.multnomah.lib.or.us/lib/kids. (Accessed July 27, 1997).

National Guide to Funding for Libraries and Information Services. 1993. 2d ed. New York: Foundation Center.

National Survey of Public Libraries and the Internet: Final Report. 1996. Syracuse, NY: Syracuse University.

Negroponte, Nicholas. 1996. The Future of the Book. *Wired* (February): 188.

Padilla, Irene M., and Thomas H. Patterson. 1997. Rewarding Employees Non-monetarily. In *Practical Help for New Supervisors*. 3d ed. Edited by Joan Giesecke. Chicago: American Library Association. 35–44.

Parent Education Services Committee Public Library Association, ed. 1993. *Homeschoolers and the Public Library: A Resource Guide for Libraries Serving Homeschoolers*. Chicago: Public Library Association.

Pistolis, Donna. 1996. *Hit List: Frequently Challenged Books for Children*. Chicago: American Library Association.

Pitman, Mary Anne, and Jane Van Galen, eds. 1991. *Home Schooling: Political, Historical, and Pedagogical Perspectives*. Norwood, NJ: Ablex.

Pomeroy, Wardell B. 1981. *Girls and Sex*. New York: Delacorte Press.

Prentice, Ann. 1996. *Financial Planning for Libraries*. 2d ed. Library Administration Series. Edited by Lowell A. Martin. Lanham, MD: Scarecrow Press.

Ramsey, Inez L., and Jackson B. Ramsey. 1986. *Library Planning and Budgeting*. New York: Franklin Watts.

Razzano, Barbara Will. 1986a. *Public Library Services to Children and Young Adults in New Jersey*. Trenton, NJ: New Jersey State Library.

———. 1986b. Young Adult Services in New Jersey Public Libraries: A Status Report. *New Jersey Libraries* 19 (2): 5–7.

Reichman, Henry. 1988. *Censorship and Selection: Issues and Answers for Schools*. Chicago: American Library Association.

Roberts, Anne F., and Susan Griswold Blandy. 1989. *Public Relations for Librarians*. Englewood, CO: Libraries Unlimited.

Rollock, Barbara. 1988. *Public Library Services for Children*. Hamden, CT: Library Professional Publications.

Rovenger, Judith, and Ristiina Wigg, eds. 1987. *Libraries Serving Youth: Directions for Service in the 1990s*. Sponsored by New York State, April 16–18, 1986. New York: New York Library Association.

Rubin, Richard. 1992. The Future of Public Library Support Staff. *Public Library Quarterly* 12 (1): 17–29.

Russell, Thyra K. 1997. Interviewing. In *Practical Help for New Supervisors*. 3d ed. Edited by Joan Giesecke. Chicago: American Library Association. 6–14.

Sager, Don. 1997. Perspectives: Beating the Homework Blues. *Public Libraries* 36 (January/February): 19–23.

Salazar, Ramiro. 1994. The Bottom Line: Saving Youth Means Saving Our Future. In *Library Services for Children and Youth: Dollars and Sense*. Edited by Virginia H. Mathews. New York: Neal-Schuman.

Salter, Charles A., and Jeffrey L. Salter. 1988. *On the Frontlines: Coping with the Library's Problem Patrons*. Englewood, CO: Libraries Unlimited.

Salvadore, Maria B. 1995. Recruiting and Retaining Youth Services Librarians. In *Youth Services Librarians as Managers: A How-to Guide from Budgeting to Personnel.* Edited by Kathleen Staerkel, Mary Fellows, and Sue McCleaf Nespeca. Chicago: American Library Association. 74–82.

Schexnaydre, Linda, and Nancy Burns. 1984. *Censorship: A Guide for Successful Workshop Planning.* Phoenix, AZ: Oryx Press.

Seattle Public Library. Friends of the Library. 1997. Available: http://www.spl.lib.wa.us/friends/friends.html. (Accessed July 27, 1997).

Services and Resources for Young Adults in Public Libraries. 1988. Prepared for Office of Educational Research and Improvement, U.S. Department of Education. Washington, DC: National Center for Education Statistics.

Staerkel, Kathleen, Mary Fellows, and Sue McCleaf Nespeca, eds. 1995. *Youth Services Librarians as Managers: A How-to Guide from Budgeting to Personnel.* Chicago: American Library Association.

Symons, Ann K., and Charles Harmon. *Protecting the Right to Read: A How-to-Do-It Manual for School and Public Librarians.* New York: Neal-Schuman.

Tannen, Deborah. 1994. *Talking from 9 to 5: How Women's and Men's Conversational Styles Affect Who Gets Heard, Who Gets Credit, and What Gets Done at Work.* New York: William Morrow.

Toronto Public Library. 1913. *Annual Report.* Toronto, Ontario, Canada: Toronto Public Library.

UNESCO. 1994. *Public Library Manifesto.* The Hague: International Federation of Library Associations and Institutions.

Valauskas, Edward J., and Nancy R. John, eds. 1995. *The Internet Initiative: Libraries Providing Internet Services and How They Plan, Pay, and Manage.* Chicago: American Library Association.

Van Orden, Phyllis. 1988. *The Collection Program in Schools: Concepts, Practices and Information Sources.* Englewood, CO: Libraries Unlimited.

———. 1992. *Library Service to Children: A Guide to the Research, Planning, and Policy Literature.* Chicago: American Library Association.

Wagner, Mary M., and Gretchen Wronka. 1995. Youth Services Policies and Procedures. In *Youth Services Librarians as Managers,* Edited by Staerkel et al. Chicago: American Library Association. 41–50.

Walling, Linda Lucas, and Marilyn H. Karrenbrock. 1993. *Disabilities, Children, and Libraries: Mainstreaming Services in Public Libraries and School Library Media Centers.* Englewood, CO: Libraries Unlimited.

Walster, Dian. 1993. *Managing Time: A How-to-Do-It Manual for Librarians.* New York: Neal-Schuman.

Walter, Virginia. 1992. *Output Measures for Public Library Service to Children: A Manual of Standardized Procedures.* Chicago: American Library Association.

Weingand, Darlene E. 1997. *Customer Service Excellence: A Complete Guide for Librarians*. Chicago: American Library Association.

———. 1987. *Marketing/Planning Library and Information Services*. Englewood, CO: Libraries Unlimited.

White, Barb. 1997. Connections: Building Coalitions to Serve Our Youngest Patrons. *Youth Services in Libraries* 10 (Winter): 215–18.

Willett, Holly. 1995. *Public Library Youth Services: A Public Policy Approach*. Norwood, NJ: Ablex.

Willhoite, Michael. 1990. *Daddy's Roommate*. Boston: Alyson Publications.

Willits, Robert L. 1997. When Violence Threatens the Workplace: Personnel Issues. *Library Administration & Management* 11 No. 3 (Spring): 166–71.

Wirth, Eileen. 1996. The State of Censorship. *American Libraries* (September): 44–48.

Zeff, Robbin. 1996. *The Nonprofit Guide to the Internet*. Nonprofit Law, Finance, and Management Series. New York: John Wiley.

Index

DATE DUE

MAY 1 5 1998			
MAR 1 8 1999			
GAYLORD			PRINTED IN U.S.A.